How Not to Die (Too Soon)

How Not to Die (Too Soon)

The Lies We've Been Sold and the Policies That Can Save Us

DEVI SRIDHAR

PENGUIN
VIKING

VIKING

UK | USA | Canada | Ireland | Australia
India | New Zealand | South Africa

Viking is part of the Penguin Random House group of companies
whose addresses can be found at global.penguinrandomhouse.com

Penguin Random House UK,
One Embassy Gardens, 8 Viaduct Gardens, London SW11 7BW

penguin.co.uk

First published 2025
002

Copyright © Devi Sridhar, 2025

The moral right of the author has been asserted

Penguin Random House values and supports copyright. Copyright
fuels creativity, encourages diverse voices, promotes freedom
of expression and supports a vibrant culture. Thank you for purchasing
an authorized edition of this book and for respecting intellectual property
laws by not reproducing, scanning or distributing any part of it by any
means without permission. You are supporting authors and enabling
Penguin Random House to continue to publish books for everyone.
No part of this book may be used or reproduced in any manner for the
purpose of training artificial intelligence technologies or systems. In accordance
with Article 4(3) of the DSM Directive 2019/790, Penguin Random House
expressly reserves this work from the text and data mining exception

Set in 12/14.75pt Bembo Book MT Pro
Typeset by Jouve (UK), Milton Keynes
Printed and bound in Great Britain by Clays Ltd, Elcograf S.p.A.

The authorized representative in the EEA is Penguin Random House Ireland,
Morrison Chambers, 32 Nassau Street, Dublin D02 YH68

A CIP catalogue record for this book is available from the British Library

ISBN: 978–0–241–74284–6

Penguin Random House is committed to a sustainable future
for our business, our readers and our planet. This book is made from
Forest Stewardship Council® certified paper.

For L & K, for making me smile every day

Contents

Prologue: Bad News on the Bus	1
1. Eternal Life	5
Turning Down Harvard	6
Where Are You From? No, Where Are You Really From?	7
Life Expectancy Is Going Down	8
But, We All Want to Live Longer	10
Getting to 100 as a Collective Endeavour	11
2. Exercise: Just Do It	15
Yes, I'm a Personal Trainer	20
Why Is Physical Activity So Good for Health?	25
We Know We Should Move but We Don't	28
Going Dutch	31
Why Are the Dutch So Fit?	32
Building the 'Fifteen-Minute City'	34
#Dubai30×30	38
YouTube Fitness Campaigns	40
When Being Sedentary Is a Sign of Wealth	41
Overcoming the Laziness Gene	42
3. What's a Balanced Diet?	45
It's Common to Live to 100 in Japan	46
From Fad Diets to Simple Advice	48

Why Is Being Obese Bad for Health?	52
Diabetes as a 'Lifestyle Disease'	54
Boris Johnson's Efforts to Lose Weight	55
How I (Try to) Eat	56
Make Fruit and Vegetables Accessible	60
Make It Easier to Eat Well and Harder to Eat Badly	63
Prevent Childhood Obesity	66
The (Second) Fattest Country	68
650 Per Cent Increase in Obesity: Guess Where?	71
The Maharaja Mac	74
Taking on the Ultra-Processed Food Industry	81

4. Don't Smoke — 84

How Does Smoking Affect Our Body?	85
Playing Trumpet in Smoky Jazz Clubs	87
Making It Expensive and Difficult to Smoke	88
Cigarettes Are Eating You Alive	92
Regulation Only Works If It's Enforced	94
Where Even Doctors Smoke	97
Taking on the Tobacco Industry	100
Vaping: How Bad Is It Really?	101

5. Struggling to Cope — 106

I Struggle Too	107
Poor Mental Health Makes Us Die Sooner	112
It's Hard to Get Depression Taken Seriously	115
We Know What Works with Depression	117
What Causes Poor Mental Health?	120

Provide Trained Local People to Listen	122
Make It Harder to Buy Stuff That Kills People	124
Provide Universal Access to Therapy	125
'Be Happy' Campaigns	126
Japan's Suicide Struggle	127
Making People Feel Cared For	129

6. Guns, Guns, Guns — 131

Andy Murray	134
Are Guns More Dangerous Than Cricket Bats and Tennis Rackets?	136
Over 90 Per Cent of Gun Homicides Are in Stable Countries	138
What's the Point of Being in Office If You Can't Make Life Safer?	140
When Never Again Means Never Again	142
When People Are Sick of Violence and Want Peace	144
From Widespread Gun Ownership to Mass Disarmament	146
The Land Where Guns Are the Leading Cause of Death in Children	148
How to Stop People Killing Themselves and Others	153

7. Vision Zero — 156

Road Deaths Are Going Up	159
Accidents Are Unavoidable, but Fatal Accidents Are Preventable	163
Provide Cheaper, Faster Alternatives to Cars	165
Improving Roads When 30 Per Cent of People Live in Poverty	168

Children: The Most Vulnerable Road Users	169
Where Fatal Road Accidents Cause a Third of All Deaths	172
If We Know What Works, Why Isn't It Being Done?	174

8. The Water Fountain — 177

What Would You Like to Be When You Grow Up? Alive	180
John Snow: The King of ~~the North~~ Public Health	182
How to Build a Water System	184
The Lucrative Market of Bottled Water	186
When No Water System Exists	188
Broken, Neglected Systems	191
'Profit Over Human Health' Systems	193
Clean Water Shortages	196
'Água': Cristiano Ronaldo's Message to the World	197

9. Just Breathe — 200

Vomiting Cricket Players	202
The 'Pay to Breathe' Industry	204
Dirty Air Kills	205
Why Is Air Pollution Bad for Our Health?	208
The Lucrative Industry of 'Bottled Air'	209
We Know What Causes Dirty Air	211
Does Any Major City Have Clean Air?	212
Creating Ultra-Low Emission Zones	214
Those Who Create Pollution Should Clean It Up	217
When Breath Becomes Poisonous	219

10. I Need a Doctor	222
Going Broke Paying for Medical Care	223
Insanely High Medical Costs: United States	224
Going Blind on a Waitlist: Britain	226
Imprisonment Until Payment: Nigeria	228
Be Born a Boy, or You're on Your Own: India	229
How Can Governments Provide Health Care?	231
The Poster Child of Health Care	234
Making Universal Health Care a Key Election Promise	236
Framing Health Care as a Social Right Instead of a Commodity	238
Medical Care: Whether You Live or Die	242
11. How to Live	245
Wearing Flip-Flops to Buckingham Palace	247
The Happiest Place on Earth	250
How Much Money Is Enough Money?	254
More Action, Fewer Excuses	257
Who Wants to Be a Politician?	262
What We Can Control	264
Epilogue	267
Five Asks of Your Government	267
Don't Accept Lazy Excuses	271
Acknowledgements	273
Bibliography	275
Index	305

Prologue: Bad News on the Bus

The conversation passes in a blur with phrases such as 'results took longer than usual', 'abnormal cells', 'possibly cancer'. The nurse is vague when I ask what happens next. 'Well, you'll get a letter, probably in the next few weeks, that you're on the waitlist, and then a letter with your appointment a few weeks after that sometime. It might take a couple months to get you in, possibly six months, I don't know. We have a large backlog. But keep calling in asking about cancellations and maybe you'll get it sooner. Sorry.' She hangs up the phone.

I sit there paralysed by the call. The woman behind me pats my shoulder. I wonder what she must think, overhearing someone getting potentially life-changing bad news on a bus. A bus to work on a freezing Scottish winter's morning.

In my routine smear test with the National Health Service (NHS) three months earlier, high-risk human papillomavirus was found, and this has caused changes to my cervix. I know there's a vaccine highly effective at preventing HPV, but I'm too old to be covered by the NHS vaccination programme which targets teenagers. It was only approved in 2006, when I was already twenty-two. If you're vaccinated before being exposed to HPV, it's 97 per cent effective at preventing cell changes that could lead to cervical cancer. But that doesn't help me right now.

When I am lecturing my students about public health, I tell them that more than 95 per cent of cervical cancers are caused by high-risk HPV. Thousands of women are diagnosed each year and more than a quarter die. Famously, TV personality Jade Goody died of cervical cancer at just twenty-seven, and it's a cancer most frequently diagnosed in women between thirty-five and forty-four. It's survivable if precancerous cells are treated at an early stage, but my lab results are from months back, and I know the long NHS waiting lists mean it might be months before I see a doctor for further examination and treatment.

I also tell my students that the UK has one of the worst survival outcomes for cancer in Europe and North America because of late diagnosis, delayed treatment, and an overstretched health service. When cervical cancer is diagnosed at an early stage, I tell them, the five-year survival rate is 92 per cent. If it's diagnosed, and treated, after it has spread throughout nearby tissue and organs, this drops to 59 per cent. Luckily, I've been identified by routine screening, but I'm dependent on the overstretched NHS for rapid investigation and, if necessary, treatment.

As I sit on the bus, my mind wanders. What if my dream to move back to the Florida coast never happens? What if I can't go see my mother again, and I end up dying before her? What if it's nothing and I'm freaking out for no reason . . . but also what if it *is* something?

The word cancer feels like a death sentence. The tough paths of chemotherapy, radiation, surgery. I've seen it all closely when my dad was sick to the point where you wonder whether living with this kind of pain and treatment is worth it. Could it even be worse than just living and dying with cancer?

My father, who himself was an oncologist, was diagnosed with lymphoma in his early forties. I was twelve. There were two possible conversations at each blood check or screening: a crossroads of good news or bad news, with whatever the doctor said leading you down very different paths.

I remember one of my father's colleagues saying, 'Cancer will get you in the end, whether it's now, or a bit later or a lot later. Treatment can push back the outcome, but it lingers and never really goes away. Even when you're in remission.' This is not entirely true, but it was true enough – or scary enough – to stick in my mind.

Before each of my father's doctor's appointments, my high school friends would comfort me. 'Of course it's going to be good news. Statistics show he'll be fine.' And that's exactly what I am hearing now: the nurse trying to reassure me with statistics about survival rates and treatment.

I am told what I already know. More than 80 per cent of women have HPV at some time in their lives and most HPV resolves on its own. In 95 per cent of cases, the HPV virus causes no symptoms or health problems, and in the roughly one in twenty women who have abnormal smear results (like me), only about one in 2,000 will have cancer. Pre-cancerous cells can be detected and killed early. Most women go back to living their life, perhaps slightly more conscious about their mortality and the other path their life might have taken.

But statistics didn't work for my dad. They didn't work for twenty-seven-year-old Jade Goody. Statistics help at a population level, but how relevant are they to me? Will I die too soon?

This could have been a book about how I have accepted the possibility of death. Since my father's diagnosis when I was a teenager, I have thought a lot about life's deeper meaning: what is it all about? How do we live a meaningful life and find happiness? What ultimately makes people feel fulfilled, and how do we balance daily stress and distractions with the many chapters of our lives? Is there a way to accept our mortality – even when it comes at a time when we don't expect it?

But no. I don't want to write about being at peace with dying, because I am not. I like my life. This is not a book about how to die. This is a book about how to live longer. Because while there's a randomness in life – like the thunderbolts of bad news that strike on your morning commute – we know from scientific studies and decades of public health research not only how to increase life expectancy but also how to maintain quality of life.

My story isn't unusual – we all have our brushes with death. We tend to take our health for granted until faced with death, or even chronic pain. Fortunately, mine has a happier ending (so far). Taking the nurse's advice, I kept calling the NHS hotline in case there was an appointment cancellation and managed to have my colposcopy within a few months of my lab results. I was treated at a local hospital by an experienced physician, with a one-year follow-up. My scare wasn't fatal.

From working in global health, I know quite well that if I lived in Tanzania or Zambia, or even India or Brazil, my story might have had a different ending. Avoiding an early death to cancer had less to do with any individual choices I made during my life, and more to do with living in a country, in this case Britain, that has free high-quality health care with a cervical cancer screening programme. My thanks to the government in 1948 who created the NHS and the people who voted for these visionary leaders.

I am living longer because of political choices made more than half a century ago. And in this book I will show that, despite a thriving individualistic, self-help economy, your life expectancy is much less about your own choices and is instead tightly linked to where you live and the political choices made by your government.

1. Eternal Life

While searching for the fountain of youth and eternal life in 1513, Spanish explorer Juan Ponce de León discovered Florida. I grew up near a street in Miami that bears his name. More recently, you might have seen headlines about American tech multimillionaire Bryan Johnson who spends £1.6 million a year on an intensive regime designed to reduce his biological age from that of a man in his forties to that of an eighteen-year-old. Part of this plan involves injecting himself with his teenage son's blood, after studies in mice indicated that younger plasma rejuvenated ageing tissue.

In laboratory experiments, two mice (one old and one young) were stitched together to share a circulatory system. Within five weeks, the blood from the younger mouse had restored muscle and liver cells, and enhanced growth of brain cells, in the older one. On the other hand, young mice who were exposed to older blood suffered reduced growth. The experiments were not without risk, with several mice dying due to tissue rejection.

Bryan, currently forty-six, claims to have reversed his ageing by 5.1 years, with biological tests estimating he has the heart of a thirty-seven-year-old and the lung capacity of an eighteen-year-old. The madcap things he is doing seem to be working for him, but we don't all have the luxury of that kind of money – or time – to invest in our longevity. Never mind the mass appeal of familial blood transfusions. But while Bryan's money might help him live longer, he cannot buy immortality – he'll be lucky to live beyond 120.

Humans haven't (yet) figured out how not to die. Most people are just trying to figure out how to keep on top of their bills, stay pain-free and get by each day. Even so, it's become a fixation of the rich, such as billionaire Jeff Bezos who has invested in start-up companies looking at cellular rejuvenation, and Google founders Sergey Brin and Larry Page who have launched Calico, a business venture which tracks mice from birth to death in the hope of understanding markers for ageing-related diseases.

I'm not interested in being immortal, or even being the oldest person alive. My ambitions are more universally achievable. I'd like to live to 100 with – importantly – good health, and I'd like to help others do the same. Research into reversing the biological effects of ageing, including (let's say creative) studies about mice-blood transfusions, will continue to be well funded and make advances, but bold claims of banishing disease are far-fetched, not to say (at the moment at least) ridiculously expensive. It's unlikely to affect our own lives or the lives of most people on this planet. It's caught in a billionaire bubble.

If we all want to live longer, most answers can be found in public health research. You might be surprised to know that we in the field of public health already have the knowledge to prevent the majority of premature deaths around the world. This is true of deaths from infectious diseases like cholera, and chronic diseases like heart disease and stroke, as well as from injuries whether violent or unintentional, such as on the roads. In total, it's estimated that 20–40 per cent of all premature deaths (depending on where you live) are preventable and could be delayed.

Turning Down Harvard

In my day job as a public health professor at the University of Edinburgh, my colleagues and I try to figure out what makes people die too soon and then advise governments on how to implement policies to support people living long and healthy lives.

When my dad became sick, I saw intimately how ill health affects daily life, and learned the important lesson that health is true wealth. We don't think about pain or our body much when we're healthy and going about our routine. But once we get sick or injured, it consumes our entire life. I remember thinking at sixteen: 'We can put men on the Moon, we can talk to people instantly across the world, why can't we solve something as basic as keeping people healthier longer? Why aren't more people working on this problem?'

My personal interest in health and wellbeing transformed into a professional career, including an offer of a full scholarship to Harvard Law School. When I was about to confirm my dorm in Boston, I decided that I wasn't yet done with research and academic life in Oxford. I wanted to understand public health first-hand, starting with infectious disease and malnutrition in the villages of Tamil Nadu and the slums of New Delhi.

My friends and family were in shock when I told them this decision: 'You're turning down Harvard to collect data in rural India? Your parents left India to bring you to America and give you a better life, and now you're going back to study poverty? What kind of career and security will you have going for a PhD?'

Twenty years later and I stand by this decision: it opened the world of research, data analysis and collection, and academia to me. The Japanese would refer to this as *ikigai*, or life purpose and meaning: find something you love, that you're good at, and that the world needs. You'll be the only person to know what your ikigai is, and it might be a totally different path to your peers or family. But it's your life to make the most of and to find happiness within.

Where Are You From? No, Where Are You Really From?

I'm now a dual British-American citizen of Indian heritage. All three countries are fascinating in their own way, and in how they've attempted to address (or ignore) major health challenges. Britain and America are countries with a similar language and a completely different culture. Americans are enthusiastic, optimistic, with a 'can do' attitude. The British are more realistic, with a 'but you can't' attitude.

If you say you're okay at something and you're American, you've probably done it once or twice. If you say the same and you're British, you've probably been to the Olympics or won the Nobel Prize. If an American person says your idea is interesting, it means they want to hear more. If a British person says the same, it means they think it's bonkers and are trying to change the topic.

The US and UK are both highly unequal countries with an

ever-growing political divide between the left (dismissed by the right as 'woke' and 'elitist') and the right (labelled by the left as 'fascist' and 'establishment'). Over the past two decades, the rich have become richer and the poor have become poorer. America has the world's largest number of billionaires, up from 607 in 2019 to 735 in 2023. At the same time, the child poverty rate has stayed around 16 per cent across the country – around 11.6 million kids.

The same story could be told about Britain, where the poorest quintile (bottom 20 per cent) of households have seen their income reduced, while the richest fifth's income increased. During the pandemic, a record number of billionaires were created in the UK (171 in total). Meanwhile, child poverty hovers around 30 per cent. These are children living in unheated homes in households struggling with food bills, and who miss out on play, activities and growing up with security.

India is one of the most unequal countries on the planet: the bottom 50 per cent in India own only 6 per cent of the total wealth, while the top 1 per cent own 33 per cent. I found it astonishing to visit Delhi and compare the glistening supermalls full of luxury brands and eyewatering price-tags (often higher than in London or Miami) with the slums sprawling out across the road. On one side opulence and showy wealth, on the other malnourished children playing half-dressed on the street.

I try to share this knowledge with younger generations in my university lectures. I'm competing for students' attention with the person sitting next to them, with their phone, with their urge to make up for sleep lost to a night partying, so the lecture has to be engaging. I guess I'm doing the same thing with you: you could be watching the latest Netflix series instead of reading this book.

Life Expectancy Is Going Down

In my role as an expert in global public health, government officials often come to me and ask, 'How should we prepare for the next pandemic?' My response is that the top lesson for all countries must be that preparing for pandemics means investing in broader health and wellbeing. Not during a crisis, or in hospitals, but right now in communities, schools and homes.

Take Japan, which has one of the healthiest populations in the world. Its life expectancy is the highest of high-income countries at 84.4 years. Its 'preventable' mortality, at 130 per 100,000, is far below the high-income average of 199 per 100,000. This is with over a quarter of its population over the age of sixty-five. Only 27 per cent of its population has a body mass index (BMI) over 25 (seen as a metric for being overweight/obese), making it the lowest of the high-income countries. Perhaps it's not surprising, then, that Japan had one of the world's lowest COVID-19 death rates (246 per million people) without implementing lockdowns or government mandates.

A similar story can be told about Denmark if we compare the country to its European neighbours. Life expectancy is high at 81.6, and 70 per cent of Danes say that they're in good health. Obesity rates are around 16 per cent of adults, with physical activity levels around the European average.

Just contrast this with Scotland, where life expectancy is 76.6 years for men and 80.8 for women. This is the lowest life expectancy at birth of any Western European country. Scotland also has high inequality, with those in deprived areas such as Inverclyde and North Ayrshire dying younger and spending more than a third of life in poor health.

Obesity is a major problem, with roughly 70 per cent of men and 64 per cent of women categorized as being an unhealthy weight. This has led to media articles under headlines such as 'How Scotland became Europe's unhealthiest country', which focus not only on the poor diet, but also binge drinking, drug overdoses and wider deprivation.

Unsurprisingly, the COVID-19 death rate in Scotland was eye-wateringly high (2,315 deaths per million people), even with a cautious pandemic approach focused on containment. In a comparison of England and Scotland, Scotland had higher per capita deaths recorded in January 2023, despite lower estimated overall infections. Basically, the likelihood of someone dying was higher if they got COVID-19 in Scotland.

In contrast, Denmark experienced 3.5 times fewer COVID-19 deaths relative to its population size than the European average at 440 per million. Policy responses were central to this, including strong containment and early access to widespread testing, but the government implemented these in a healthy and compliant population.

The take-away is that if your population was healthier going into the pandemic, as in Japan or Denmark, you could manage a wave of infections better than if you had poor underlying health such as in Scotland. Countries with healthier populations (defined as a lower burden of disability and deaths given their population size) had fewer hospitalizations per capita and fewer deaths per infection. This of course leads to the question: why are Japan and Denmark healthier than Scotland? More on that soon.

Unfortunately, general population health is not improving in most countries, certainly not the United Kingdom or the United States. Quite the contrary. Key measures of progress in public health are going backwards. Since 2020, most countries, including Spain, England, Italy, Belgium and the Netherlands, have seen reductions in life expectancy and reversals in progress on reducing mortality. Oxford researchers have highlighted that most life expectancy reductions were attributable to direct and indirect COVID-19 deaths. For example, in Britain the pandemic reduced life expectancy by half a year, and in the United States by 2.33 years.

But, We All Want to Live Longer

While life expectancy stagnates, or even goes backwards at a population level, our individual desire to live longer is stronger than ever. We can talk all we want about 'accepting death' and 'being at peace with mortality', but like me, when most people are faced with their own mortality, or the death of somebody they love, above all they want everything to be done to live longer. This is a key trait of being human.

It is one of the reasons why such a huge amount of money is spent on end-of-life care, where we try to prolong someone's life by a month, a week, even a day. In the US in one year (2019), $365 billion, or 10 per cent of all health care spending, was spent in the last six months of someone's life. Greg Eastwood, a leading expert in this area and a professor at Upstate Medical University, has confirmed what we all might expect to be true: money is often a secondary consideration for a family dealing with the potential death of a loved one. Whatever their financial situation, families will spend anything for more time together.

Having been in this position, I can understand it. More than anything, I wanted my father to live. I wanted him to see me graduate high school and university. To meet his future grandchildren. I wanted to watch him get older and enjoy his retirement. I wanted him to be there to give advice when life gets rocky. To make sure my mother wasn't lonely and help her raise me and my four siblings.

Getting to 100 as a Collective Endeavour

Getting to 100, or past 100, has largely been seen as an individual enterprise. Beyond the strange methods of billionaires, walk into any bookshop and you'll find a huge body of literature telling you all the things you can do to improve your life expectancy, from the superfoods to eat, to how much sleep you should be getting, to the optimal amount of exercise at each age, as well as the ideal level of hydration.

Tied to this, the concept of 'blue zones' went global in 2008: that is, places in the world where people live longer than anywhere else and have lower rates of chronic disease. Dan Buettner and Michel Poulain, who coined the term, looked at the behaviours of people living within these zones (such as the Italian island of Sardinia and Ikaria in Greece), examining their diet, exercise routine, sleep patterns and religious or spiritual community links. Based on this, they suggest changes we could all be making at an individual level to live longer, such as moving to a largely plant-based diet and sleeping seven to nine hours per night.

If you want to live longer, yes, you need to make healthy choices throughout your life, and this book will cover those choices in the chapters around diet and physical activity. But the society in which you live also plays a huge role. Notably, these so-called blue zones are not areas where individuals each optimize their lives to live longer, but instead these are places where healthy lives are normalized by government and culture. I suspect that hardly anyone in these areas has read a self-help book.

I find the rampant individualism regarding health frustrating and the advice over healthy habits devoid of context. If we want to live longer, we've got to push beyond the superficial layer of individual advice to tackle the deeper issues of public health policy and government action that affect us on a societal level. The UK isn't fatter than Japan because it is a country filled with people who choose to be overweight – that kind of logic is not only naive, but it stigmatizes overweight people when, as we will see later, the finger might better be pointed elsewhere.

In search of longevity, you could expose yourself to sunlight first thing every morning or take an ice bath, but if the air you are breathing is not clean, the water you are drinking is dirty, the roads you walk or drive on are unsafe, or many people you meet in the street carry military-grade weapons . . . well, your gratitude journal isn't going to do much. We have been focusing on the wrong thing: namely, we have been focusing on ourselves.

This book, rooted in public health, is about living to 100, but I'm more interested in making this a collective enterprise as a society. This means looking at government policies that promote long lives. I will take you through nine of the most important risk factors affecting healthy life expectancy in all countries, and as you will see, most of them are dependent on the government in charge and the policies they adopt. The nine risk factors I've chosen are: physical activity, diet, smoking, mental health, gun violence, safe roads and transport, clean water, clean air, and access to quality health care.

No country has it all figured out, but on every single one of the nine health challenges I cover, there are positive examples of policy impact. On every single issue, one place or another has worked out a solution. This book will spin from one part of the world to another, to illustrate that we can learn across governments and cultures. Policy experiments are happening all the time, and instead of reinventing the wheel, countries can borrow ideas and see how best to adapt them to their own national context.

You might wonder why you should read this book if it's about our limited individual agency. You might think that it sounds disempowering. Perhaps you just want simple tips to be a bit healthier. I will provide these tips on health issues like smoking or physical activity, where you can indeed affect your life in a big way by things you do individually.

But on other issues such as clean air and water or access to quality medical care, you do still have the power to affect your life. In these cases, we must demand that our governments implement better policies. We must elect leaders who propose and enact concrete action. You have the power through your vote. My aim with this book is to show you that we know what works in solving the major health challenges, to give you the 'key asks' of leaders and to show how these have worked, not in theory but in practice, somewhere in the world. We know how to prevent millions of unnecessary early deaths around the world, both in developing countries and closer to home.

The growing literature on 'how to be healthy' puts such heavy responsibility for a healthy life on each of us that when someone becomes ill, often there is stigma attached. But there should be no blame involved. I know from experience the questions that come from others when sharing bad health news. 'Did you smoke?' 'Have you been too stressed?'

While this correlation is useful at a population level – we call these risk factors – this approach can unfairly allocate blame at an individual level for circumstances outside our individual control. Is it someone's fault that they're born into a city with high levels of air pollution, live somewhere with limited green space, or grow up in a neighbourhood with high levels of gun violence?

There are plenty of examples of blame making matters worse. For instance, in many countries of the world, an HIV diagnosis comes with stigma and exclusion through its (incorrect) depiction as a 'gay disease', and its link to sexual relations that are often taboo in many cultures. This came to the forefront also during COVID, when people hid their positive test results because the next question was, 'What did you do to get infected?'

It's not just infectious disease. Even with cancer there's a psychological human need to link something bad happening with a cause. 'Why? What did you do?' Getting my own health news sent me down this spiral too. I've tried very hard to do what I can to live longer based on what I've learned, including exercising regularly, eating a balanced diet, not smoking, and managing chronic stress. Bad health news wasn't supposed to happen to people like me. Hadn't I done everything 'right'? In the end, it wasn't my personal choices that mattered, it was that I was fortunate to live in a country with free access to quality medical care.

Of course, there's a randomness to life that we have to accept in terms of who lives and who dies: the 'shit happens' perspective. Sometimes we're just in the wrong place at the wrong time. We can't all live to be 100. But we can all be *more likely* to live to 100 if we take a public health approach instead of an individualistic one. Here's how.

2. Exercise: Just Do It

I exercise whenever I can. It's my default 'non-work' activity. Partly because I enjoy it, and partly because I think that exercise is the most effective intervention to stay disease- and pain-free. I often find myself hiding from friends how much time I spend in the gym each week, out of fear of judgement. People talk about Netflix binges without much shame. What about fitness binges? Some people go to cafes or bars when they want to get away from the walls of their home. The gym for me always had that attraction: a place to see other people without directly engaging with anyone. A place to escape the outside world, especially the Scottish winter.

In late 2020 when gyms were shut due to the pandemic, but outdoor exercise was permitted, I attended a daily boot camp in the park. One evening, the instructor didn't show, so I called the boot camp owner and offered to run the class. I had been attending religiously for weeks and knew the drill. While appreciative of my enthusiasm, she declined, saying I didn't have professional personal training certification and wouldn't be covered by the company's insurance.

Two years later, I qualified as a personal trainer, a way to combine my lifelong interest in staying fit and healthy with my professional career in global public health. Most of the others studying alongside me were in their late teens or early twenties. I was probably the oldest person on the course.

Often my colleagues in public health combine their research work with a clinical career: three days a week in research, and two days working in a GP clinic or in a hospital. This means they see patients coming in with various medical conditions, while also doing research about what is making their patients sick, the diseases and their risk factors.

But my interest (and why I went into public health) is in how we can prevent someone becoming sick in the first place. It feels almost too late by the time they show up in a medical clinic because they're already ill, often from conditions that could have been prevented with earlier intervention.

My interest in fitness goes back to my dad's childhood in India. He loved sports and played tennis, cricket and basketball while in school and college. His free time back then in Chennai, and as a young dad in Miami, was spent doing some form of sport. My earliest memories are watching him play doubles tennis in our local park, while I bounced a ball back and forth with my older sister, Divya, at the side of the court. We then got into our beat-up silver Toyota van and went for a special meal at Hardee's, a fast-food takeaway of American hashbrowns, donuts and coffee (for the adults). These childhood experiences made exercise seem fun and social. What else would you do on a Sunday morning?

My parents didn't want my siblings or me to fall into traditional gender roles, or to think of ourselves as foreign or different. I was never stuck at home having to cook or clean. I didn't have to conform to traditional Indian 'girl' roles. They wanted us out of the house being active, whether it was on sports teams, wearing whatever we were comfortable in (even if that meant exposing our arms and legs), or studying hard at school and becoming women who would be equal to and just as strong as any man. They didn't talk about gender equality, but they imprinted it in each of us in the way we were raised.

I never felt any less or different being an immigrant child or being a girl. I still feel that way: I don't think about my skin colour or gender actively. It's only when it's raised by others that I notice it. Skin colour is probably the least interesting aspect of someone. We're all the same species who started in Africa before migrating to various parts of the world. Our skin colour evolved to fit the UV light wherever we ended up: pigmentation is a balance of the skin absorbing enough vitamin D without becoming damaged from the sun. With this logic and my darker skin, it makes no evolutionary sense that I've ended up in Scotland.

My dad was unique for an Indian father. In general, for cultural reasons, brown women don't engage in enough physical activity. Not only in Britain, but globally, South Asian women are the group that exercises the least. If you're told from childhood that exercise is for boys, that muscles look manly, and that being outside could be dangerous, then of course you avoid it. You're not encouraged to be in sport, and there are few role models. I've lost track of the number of times that I've been asked at the gym in Oxford or Edinburgh which tanning studio I used because my colour was so uniform. It was easier to believe that I'd spent hours on sunbeds, than that a brown woman would be dead-lifting weights or doing heavy squats.

When I've done literary festival events, the chair will often ask how I've merged two such opposing careers as a professor and a personal trainer. Frank Skinner, during a Sky Arts recording at the Hay Festival, pointed out that personal trainers are people who wear tight Lycra, have fake tans and go to Ibiza. Social media hasn't helped this view of personal fitness trainers. Instagram and TikTok posts often link exercise to the already-fit who wear branded spandex (sponsored by expensive clothes companies) with Jennifer Lopez curves and men with six-packs who look like they could be in a Marvel movie.

The rise of fitness social media accounts that focus on what a 'beach body' looks like – whether that's visible abdominal muscles or a thigh gap – can put people off exercise completely. The bar is so high that it simply feels unattainable to most. It's also questionable that aesthetic goals relate to optimal health.

For most women, achieving visible abs requires an extremely low body fat percentage (less than 17 per cent, below the 20–23 per cent healthy range), which is often linked to irregular menstruation, brittle nails, feeling faint and disrupted hormone production. The only time I had visible abs was when I was running cross-country as a teen in Miami and not eating enough calories to cover my training and races. My body was literally starving and at an unhealthily low weight. My period stopped for several months, and during the school day I felt faint and had to sit down often. I felt much stronger after changing my diet and exercise schedule to increase my body fat (which meant covering up that previously visible muscle).

Over a decade later, in 2012, the Victoria's Secret fashion show aired with several models walking in lingerie showing off thigh gaps. This became a social media trend, with young women posting photos of themselves with their feet together and indicating if they had a gap between their thighs. The goal was to show that your thighs were so thin that they didn't visibly touch in a short skirt or dress, part of the 'thinspiration' online community. Those whose thighs touched labelled themselves as 'fat' and charted their journey to lose weight and achieve the gap.

That same year, 2012, a major study from Denmark was published which had tracked the body measurements and health outcomes of 2,816 men and women over 12.5 years. They found that people with big thighs had a lower risk of heart disease and early death compared to those with thin thighs. Progressively thinner thighs were linked to progressively higher health risks.

Why is this the case? The researchers suggested that thinner thighs lack muscle, and leg muscle is linked to regular exercise, lifting weights and an active lifestyle. Aside from genetic factors which give people a certain body type, the only way to achieve thin thighs is to reduce not only body fat to an unhealthily low level, but muscle too.

In addition to the rampant misinformation on social media, there's also constant product promotion, often sponsored by clothes or supplement companies. It's typical advertising: an influencer is paid to share posts showing you something that if only you had, you might be happier, such as a trendy new sports bra, a protein supplement or a laxative drink. The influencer, usually projecting the image of a certain body or lifestyle across their feed, and building their follower base on this narrative, makes you think you'd be just as happy as they look in their posts if you had this product. It's commercialized FOMO.

The main difference now from previous advertising is that it's 24/7, fed directly through mobile phones to teens without parental oversight and built on algorithms that target specific interests or demographics. For example, if you look at a few posts around 'thigh gap', the algorithm will continue to feed you more and more of this content in an addictive way. Or if the phones around you are looking at 'thigh gap' (such as in your school classroom), then the algorithm will assume you're in the same social setting and feed you that content, hoping it will trigger your interest too.

It's smart advertising for companies (and influencers) looking to make money, but it can often have detrimental physical and mental health consequences for those consuming these posts. For example, Khloé Kardashian used her Instagram account with 309 million followers to promote Flat Tummy shakes, claiming they help with weight loss and getting a flat stomach before beach holiday season. The company Flat Tummy Co. claims, without evidence or research, that drinking their product is three times more effective than diet and exercise alone.

How do they work? Each shake contains roughly 140 calories and is supposed to replace one to two meals per day. One of the ingredients, magnesium oxide, is often used as a laxative for those struggling with constipation, while others like inulin (a plant-based fibre) don't digest completely and sit in the colon where they ferment and produce gas. Basically they make you flatulent and give you the runs. If anyone does lose weight on them, it's likely because of the laxative effect (which isn't great for overall health) or because of the replacement of proper meals with a lower-calorie option, creating a calorie deficit.

These shakes aren't approved by the US Food and Drug Administration and have side effects such as cramping, stomach pains, diarrhoea and even liver damage. After experts pointed out that her posts were false advertising and even dangerous to health, Khloé deleted them. But by that point, her millions of followers had been exposed to them.

The focus on aesthetics (do I have a 'beach body'?) distracts from the real purpose of our body and the functionality of fitness, exercise and nutrition: do I feel strong and healthy within my body, and can I do what I want to do with it? Just being a certain size or shape doesn't mean someone is 'healthy'. It can be intimidating for those who might just want to move more, and get a bit fitter, without wanting to conform to a certain ideal of what 'fitness' is on social media. My motto is 'form follows function': if your body does what you want it to do and you feel strong, then the way you look will follow that.

Social media posts and photos are also misleading: images are largely filtered and photoshopped. I've seen this myself. *Grazia*

Pakistan asked me to do a cover shoot, and I showed up in baggy jeans, a hoodie and messy hair in a bun. The *Grazia* team did my makeup, hair and outfits. The final photos are beautiful art, but they don't look like me, even on my best day. I intentionally posted the *Grazia* photos next to makeup-free selfies to show how much work goes into making someone appear Instagrammable. It's not real, and it can be off-putting to those who just want to exist in the world as a normal human being with flaws, bumps and wrinkles.

Yes, I'm a Personal Trainer

Here are some things I've learned both from my career as a professor and from working individually with those wanting to become fitter. The reality is that despite the proliferation of new fitness fads and endless columns dedicated to new tricks and tips, my advice sounds much more like what you'd hear from your doctor.

First, basic physical measurements are a quick way to assess health status (and no, thigh gap is not one of them). For example, BMI or body mass index (a measurement of weight for height squared) is a crude measure of whether someone is overweight, underweight, or within a healthy weight range.

Internationally, overweight is classified as a BMI between 25 and 30, and obese is 30–40. But BMI is a flawed measure and not great at assessing someone's health status, as I'll talk about more in the next chapter. If someone comes to me wanting to know how 'healthy' they are, BMI is one of the measurements but there are other key things to look for too.

I always take physical measurements of body fat percentage (given the links between body fat and metabolic disease), of waist circumference (given the links between abdominal fat deposits and metabolic disease), and of blood pressure (given the links between high blood pressure and chronic disease).

Body fat percentage is the amount of your total body weight that's made up of fat, and it should be between 20 and 30 per cent for women and 14 and 24 per cent for men. Waist circumference is taken by running a fabric tape measure around the waist from the top of the hip bone, across the belly button and around the body. It should be less than 80 cm (31.5 inches) for women and 94 cm (37 inches) for men.

Blood pressure is usually taken using a monitor, and a healthy range is between 90/60 mmHG and 120/80 mmHG. The top number (systolic) is the pressure when the heart muscle contracts and pumps blood around the body. The bottom number (diastolic) is the pressure on the blood vessels when the heart relaxes. High blood pressure (or hypertension) causes damage to blood vessels and body organs. People can live with this condition and have no symptoms until they have a heart attack or stroke, which is why it's often referred to as a silent killer.

Next are fitness assessments such as of strength (how many push-ups someone can do in a minute: more than twenty-five is good for men and more than fifteen for women); of endurance (how long it takes to walk or run a mile: less than fifteen minutes is average); and of flexibility (can someone touch their toes?). I would say that all three components are equally important, and will explain why soon.

This kind of holistic screening sets a baseline to understand where someone is physically (their so-called 'real age' versus biological age) as well as to detect any early signs of disease. I should note that each of the ranges above varies based on the age and gender of the person completing the test, as well as their body type. But the numbers are rough guides.

The second thing I've learned is that something is better than nothing. There is no 'perfect' fitness plan or approach to becoming stronger and healthier. If you cannot manage an hour-long HIIT workout every day (which is probably too much anyway) and all you can do is a daily fifteen-minute walk, then great: that's better than a ten-minute walk which is better than a five-minute walk, and it's a whole lot better than doing nothing. Same with a shorter gym session, or doing a boot camp once a week in the park. Goals don't always have to be lofty like finishing a marathon or having visible muscles. Your goal could just be to do something each day and to aim for a reasonable amount like thirty minutes of activity.

If you're looking to go further and fully develop your health in a holistic way, I tend to follow a weekly plan that involves cardio exercises (which increase heart rate), resistance training (which builds muscle) and flexibility and core strength training (to avoid injury and chronic pain). There are plenty of ways to build this triangle of cardio, strength and flexibility within the body.

Cardio training is simply any activity that increases your heart rate and breathing rate. This could be jogging, cycling, walking, rowing or swimming, and it can be done over longer stretches at a slower pace or in tiny sprints at a very fast pace. These exercises increase the oxygen needs of our muscles, which means the heart needs to pump faster to carry oxygenated blood across the body.

A 2009 meta-analysis looking at studies in over 100,000 people found that better levels of cardio fitness were strongly associated with lower all-cause mortality and reduced risk of having a heart attack, blood clots, a stroke, and coronary artery disease.

How does cardio fitness do this? The need to pump more blood around the body strengthens the heart muscle. In addition, cardio exercise lowers blood pressure and reduces triglycerides (a type of fat in the blood linked to heart disease and stroke), while increasing high-density lipoproteins (which absorb cholesterol in the blood and carry it back to the liver to be flushed from the body).

I'll usually start my workout with ten minutes on the treadmill (walking or with a slow jog), on the rowing machine, or cycling. If I'm feeling energetic, I try the Stairmaster, which is basically a hamster wheel for humans. This is to get the body warmed up through blood flowing to the muscles, stretching out the connective tissue, and getting the lungs to take in oxygen at a faster rate.

Resistance (strength) training involves exerting and strengthening our muscles using an opposing force, which could be dumbbells, weighted bags or even our own body weight. As we get older, we naturally lose muscle as part of the process of ageing. If muscles atrophy too much, we lose the ability to get up from the toilet, to get out of bed, to go grocery shopping, and to do all the things that allow us to live independent lives. Staying out of a care home requires a certain level of strength in old age, and that process of building muscle needs to start much earlier on.

The simplest way to build muscle is to lift weights. Lifting weights overloads our muscle, causing damage to the tissue. This is why you might feel sore after a hard workout. The damage triggers an inflammatory response over the next twenty-four to forty-eight hours, which activates the repair of these muscle fibres to form new, thicker muscle strands or myofibrils (called hypertrophy). Growing muscle, and becoming stronger, is a relatively slow process in most people and becomes harder to do as we get older. This makes regular strength training more important as we age. A set of exercises such as squats, deadlifts, push-ups and pull-ups can work most of our muscles in a short period of time.

Strength training complements cardio training: strength training is about muscle and bone maintenance, while cardio is about muscular endurance. This doesn't have to mean bulking up or being muscly. It's hard to put on visible muscle, especially for women, without a tailored diet and workout plan.

I usually orientate my gym workout around three lower body exercises such as lunges, squats and dead-lifts; then three upper body exercises such as chest presses, bicep curls and tricep dips; and then three 'core' exercises which use the back and abdominal muscles, such as plank, sit-ups and dead bugs.

Flexibility – and I'd add in here core strength around the central muscles such as abdominals, hip flexors and back – helps stabilize the body and avoid injury and chronic pain. Reduced flexibility is linked to joint pain (shortened muscles and reduced blood supply can compress nerves), increased injury risk (stiffer connective tissue is more likely to tear during movement) and chronic back and neck pain (as tightness in one part like the hip can result in too much pressure on the lower back). Back and neck pain are two of the most commonly listed disabilities across the world: these are often a consequence of sedentary lifestyles.

I mentioned before the 'can you touch your toes?' test. It's a crude measure as it just examines one plane of motion, but it's a good way of gauging whether you should be doing more stretching around your joints and muscles. I find solo floor exercises boring, so will turn to a more social yoga or Pilates class, whether it's in person or online.

But I get a recurrent criticism when I talk to people about staying healthy, and also when I wrote about becoming a personal trainer in my *Guardian* column. It was that healthy choices are easier for those with time and money, and that an individualized approach brings blame. We already see this with the stigma of being obese, or of smoking. Certain behaviours become associated with being lazy or stupid, instead of with poverty, or lack of opportunity and life chances.

It's certainly true that there are challenges in building this kind of 'triangle' workout into a weekly routine. Aside from time, money and dislike of exercise, another factor in people not exercising is the idea that there's no good place to go to do this. This can be due to a range of factors, from women not feeling safe running outside (largely from the threat of harassment or assault) to people who think they are too old or out of shape to enter a gym environment.

Not moving enough is particularly acute in those aged eleven to seventeen, with 81 per cent of adolescents being insufficiently physically active; the rate among girls is even higher at 85 per cent. Girls face many barriers to being physically active: from safety concerns to the cultural barriers of sport being seen as a 'male' activity not done by girls or women. Girls often tend to drop out of sport around the age of eleven or twelve, when they might become self-conscious of their peer expectations or of their bodies, and when their parents might become protective of their activities and independence. It's estimated that 66 per cent of girls drop out of sport before or during puberty; this is true in studies whether from the UK, the US or India.

Tennis player Sania Mirza faced these challenges as a teenage star wanting to wear skirts and T-shirts in her matches. Soon after she broke into the tennis top fifty in 2005 (the first Indian woman to do so), a group of Muslim clerics issued a fatwa demanding that she cover up in matches, saying that her outfits were 'un-Islamic' and 'corrupting'. Haseeb-ul-hasan Siddiqui, a leading Sunni cleric, said: 'The dress she wears on the tennis courts not only doesn't cover large parts of her body but leaves nothing to the imagination. She will undoubtedly be a corrupting influence on . . . young women, which we want to prevent.' He suggested that she play in a long tunic and headscarf. Both extremely practical suggestions for a top tennis player needing to move around the court quickly with full visibility and agility.

An even more extreme example comes from the Taliban, who banned sports for Afghan female athletes after taking power in August 2021. Women and girls are expected to wear burqas – which cover their entire body and face with only a mesh to see through – and endure threats, and even beatings, for wanting to play sport and be active. The Taliban have also forbidden women from visiting parks or gyms, as well as attending schools and universities. Even before the Taliban, there was a deeply conservative view in Afghanistan that opposed women's sports, which were considered immodest and low status.

Cultural context plays a role in physical activity for young women and girls, particularly those from religious or conservative communities, and this creates an additional barrier. There are general challenges for both sexes, but some are unique to women around safety, cultural expectations and societal inclusion.

Making exercise environments inclusive and safe to all, regardless of gender, skin colour or age, is an important step. Practically, this can mean introducing zero tolerance policies for discrimination and harassment, training gym staff and coaches to modify exercises depending on individual need, offering women-only spaces and fitness classes, and ensuring that a wide variety of body types are used in advertising and marketing. Equally important are role models and support during childhood. I was lucky enough to have a dad who encouraged me into physical activity and sport from a young age.

Why Is Physical Activity So Good for Health?

We all know we should exercise more, but just how bad for our health is being sedentary? Many people I share this statistic with are surprised: those who are insufficiently active have a 20–30 per cent increased risk of death compared to people who are sufficiently active. That's huge.

A major physical activity study published in 2019 invited all residents in Norway aged twenty and older to participate at three points in their life (1984–6, 1995–7, and 2006–8). In total, 23,146 men and women were included. Their physical activity data was linked to information on deaths, and adjusted for other factors like body mass index, age, sex, smoking, education level and blood pressure.

Compared to the physically active group, people who were inactive in both 1984–6 and 2006–8 had a two-fold higher likelihood of dying from any cause, and a 2.7-fold greater risk of dying from cardiovascular disease. The principal investigator of the study, Dr Trine Moholdt of the Norwegian University of Science and Technology in Trondheim, said: 'My advice is to establish good exercise habits as early in life as possible. The health benefits extend beyond protection against premature deaths to effects in the body's organs and cognitive function. Physical activity helps us live longer and better lives.'

While of course starting sooner is better than later, getting moving at any age is beneficial. In March 2024, I attended the release of a London School of Economics and Vitality Health study tracking over a million people's activity levels and health outcomes. Positive impacts were seen in all age groups from increased activity levels tracked in the number of steps per day, but it was even more significant in older age groups. People over the age of sixty-five had a 52 per cent reduction in their mortality risk if they were able to routinely take 7,500 steps three or more times a week. Those aged forty-five to sixty-five saw a 38 per cent reduction in their mortality risk, which was higher than the total population's 27 per cent reduction.

In 2017, a study in US middle-aged and older adults looked at the association between sedentary behaviour (sitting) and all-cause mortality. The researchers collected data from 7,985 Black and white adults aged forty-five or older, and found a direct relationship between time spent sitting and the risk of early mortality from any cause. As total sitting time increased, so did the risk of early death. People who sat less than thirty minutes at a time had the lowest risk of early death. This was true regardless of age, sex, race, body mass index or exercise habits.

According to the principal investigator of the study, Dr Keith Diaz from the Columbia University Department of Medicine: 'Those who sat for more than 13 hours per day had a 200% greater risk of death compared to those who sat for less than about 11 hours per day. The study found that one behaviour change – taking a movement break every 30 minutes – reduces risk of death dramatically. Those who frequently sat in stretches less than 30 minutes had a 55% lower risk of death compared to people who usually sat for more than 30 minutes at a stretch.'

Physical activity also has significant mental health benefits. When muscles contract, they secrete chemicals into the bloodstream. Among these chemicals are myokines, so-called 'hope molecules'. These small proteins travel to the brain, cross the blood–brain barrier and act as an antidepressant. This has been referred to as 'muscle–brain cross-talk'.

The largest synthesis study (that is, a study which summarizes the main findings from multiple primary research studies) on the effect of exercise on major depressive disorder showed regular exercise had a significant impact on reducing depressive symptoms. The study's lead author, Dr Ben Singh, highlighted that physical activity is 1.5 times more effective at reducing mild to moderate symptoms of depression, stress and anxiety than medication or cognitive behavioural therapy. These findings have led to 'social prescriptions' from doctors such as more time outdoors and daily walks. It's part of a larger shift from a purely medical model of care to one best suited for the individual, mixing physical activity, community engagement and medicine when needed.

Myokines are not the sole chemical responsible for making us feel good: exercise also releases neurotransmitters such as dopamine, noradrenaline and serotonin that have a positive impact on our brains. They do this by improving our mood, our ability to learn, and our capacity for locomotor activity (complex movements that get us from one place to another), and they protect the brain from the negative effects of ageing. The hippocampus, the part of our brain involved in memory, learning and emotion, shrinks as we get older, leading to forgetfulness and possibly even dementia. A randomized control trial with 120 older adults showed that exercise training increased the size of the hippocampus by 2 per cent, effectively reversing the age-related loss by one to two years, and improving memory function.

We Know We Should Move but We Don't

Worldwide, around one in three women and one in four men don't do enough physical activity to stay healthy, and this is a problem getting worse in almost all countries. 'Enough' activity is doing per week at least 150 minutes of moderate-intensity physical activity (roughly twenty minutes per day), or seventy-five minutes of vigorous-intensity exercise (roughly ten minutes per day).

Insufficient activity increased by 5 per cent to 36.8 per cent of the population in high-income countries between 2001 and 2016. The World Health Organization (WHO) estimates that 4 to 5 million deaths per year could be averted if the global population were more physically active.

Take India. A survey in 2014 of 213 million people found that 54 per cent were physically inactive, with more inactivity in those living in urban areas compared to rural areas. If we extrapolate this pattern to the whole country, that's 392 million inactive people in India – more than the entire population of the US, active or otherwise. In contrast to the US and UK, physical inactivity in India was linked to having a higher income and belonging to an upper socioeconomic group, and with being older and having a higher BMI and waist circumference.

Most physical activity in India is linked to work and domestic requirements. When asked about recreational physical activity, the numbers dropped to fewer than 10 per cent overall: 86.7 per cent of those aged twenty to twenty-nine reported no recreational activity at all, increasing to 95.9 per cent in the over-sixties. In those saying that they did recreational physical activity, this was overall less than twenty minutes per day.

Here lies the problem in much of 'the developing world', although I don't like that term. (As my grandmother says, this implies that India should copy 'developed' countries instead of shaping its own trajectory.) In many of these countries, people have historically lived in rural communities and been sufficiently physically active through their jobs in farming, construction or domestic work. This was essential to survive daily life and was often linked to hardship and poverty.

As urbanization has happened and people have moved to cities, their lifestyle has changed. They don't need to walk long distances because they now have motorized options. They don't have physically laborious jobs but sedentary work. Not having to work in the fields or on a construction site is seen as a marker of success, which is why physical inactivity has become correlated to higher socioeconomic status in these countries. Plus people increasingly now have disposable income for 'high-status' products like packaged and fast foods. More on that later.

Rising income and GDP in a country correlates with decreasing physical activity: basically, as people become richer in low- and middle-income countries, they become more inactive. A major study in the *Lancet*, reviewing socioeconomic status and physical activity in low- and middle-income countries, found that upper socioeconomic groups were less physically active and consumed more fats, salts and processed foods than individuals of low socioeconomic status.

Health ministries have had to deal with the existing burden of 'poverty'-related infectious diseases like childhood pneumonia, measles and tuberculosis, while also confronting the rise of chronic disease from this lifestyle change. Trying to keep their populations alive longer and healthier has become a dual problem: one focused on reducing child mortality from preventable causes such as diarrhoea, hunger and childhood infections, while also trying to avoid premature mortality in adulthood (those under sixty) from chronic causes like heart attacks, cancer and stroke. It's somewhat understandable that governments have been slower in middle- and low-income countries to develop policies to promote physical activity.

But the 'essential' physical activity of labour hasn't been replaced by 'recreational' activity. Given how good exercise is for our bodies and how widely that is understood – even if some of the statistics in this chapter are surprising – why don't more people do it? A recent Ipsos survey pointed to: time, money, the weather being too hot or cold, and finally some people simply not liking exercise. For example, 51 per cent of people in Saudi Arabia said time was the biggest barrier, while 33 per cent in Turkey said it was lack of money.

In South Africa 38 per cent said it was too hot (or cold), while 37 per cent of Americans, and a third of Britons, said that there was no other barrier to sport beyond the fact that they just didn't want to do it in their free time.

In higher-income countries, the decrease in physical activity levels over the past two decades is linked to the rise in screen time. We are all spending more time on devices and taking less part in sport and other physical activities, and this includes children. This shift has significant ramifications for mental health: among fourteen- to seventeen-year-olds, those who used screens throughout the day were twice as likely to have been diagnosed with depression. A study of 40,000 children in the US found that after more than one hour per day of use, screen time was associated with less curiosity, lower self-control, less emotional stability and lower psychological wellbeing. More on mental health in a later chapter.

Governments are aware of the importance of getting their populations moving. Most recognize the links between physical inactivity and chronic disease and early death, and the impetus of doing 'something' to find a solution to this problem. But the policy solution implemented varies from more personalized options, such as individual exercise targets per day, to more society-wide changes such as redesigning cities to make them more cycle- or pedestrian-friendly.

Obviously just telling people to exercise more carries little cost, but does it change behaviour? And on the flip side, completely redesigning cities carries a large cost, but is there evidence that it's worth it?

I highlight examples of cities in this chapter because this is where half the world's population lives, and this is likely to increase to 70 per cent over the next twenty years. While cities have contributed to lifting people out of poverty and have provided employment and financial opportunity, they come with a set of challenges for health. For example, they often lack accessible green space, and physical activity levels of city dwellers are below recommended guidelines. There's a clear link between sedentary behaviours and urbanization. Except in the cities of the Netherlands.

Going Dutch

The Netherlands is the exception, not the rule, for a physically active population. It is the most 'fit' country in the world in terms of the mean hours of exercise per week. People in the Netherlands say they spend more than twelve hours per week doing physical activity, either as part of their daily life (getting to work, shopping, social events, school) or for fun (as part of a sports team or day out), compared to six hours per week in Britain. Only 4 per cent of people in the Netherlands say they don't exercise at all in the week.

The Dutch are the most active of all Europeans, according to the European Commission. About 80 per cent of them cycle, walk, garden or swim on a weekly basis, compared to 44 per cent of Europeans generally. They also like sport: 56 per cent of Dutch people play sports weekly, compared to the European average of 40 per cent.

The Dutch newspaper *Trouw* has covered extensively how the good infrastructure of cycle paths and footpaths is responsible for this active lifestyle. There's no explicit linking of activity or exercising for being in good health: it's linked to just living a happy and fun life in the Netherlands. It's the norm.

This has real consequences for health. Inadequate physical activity is not a main risk factor for early death in the country. The Netherlands has one of the lowest mortality rates from preventable and treatable causes in Europe. Mortality rates from heart disease, stroke and pneumonia are among the lowest in Europe. Life expectancy was high and going up until the pandemic, which increased excess mortality in 2020 and into 2021.

In 2019, about 75 per cent of Dutch people reported that they were in good health. This means that the health care system is also delivering. In the same year, only 0.2 per cent of the population reported unmet needs for medical treatment. Compare this to 13 per cent of the population of England waiting on routine hospital treatments in 2023. The Dutch focus their health care funding on long-term care and prevention, rather than acute care in hospitals. This is clear 'value for money' through preventing illness, and intervening at an early stage, rather than delaying to when health issues become costly in a hospital setting.

This is an argument made often: prevention is cheaper than cure. But prevention makes life a whole lot nicer too. Would you rather the society you lived in made it simple and normal to have an active, healthy lifestyle, with a lower chance of ever being unwell; or would you rather live in an inactive, unhealthy society, where there's a higher chance that you and those you know will suffer one or a mixture of the awful symptoms of ill health, not to mention early death? I know how I'd like my government to shape the society I live in.

Why Are the Dutch So Fit?

One word: cycling. The Netherlands is widely regarded as the world's most successful cycling nation and Amsterdam is now often referred to as the cycling capital of the world. But while some think that the Dutch have always had the city constructed around cycle paths, that's not the case.

In the early twentieth century – when cars were limited and expensive – cycling was indeed the main mode of transport. But during the 1950s and 60s, cycle paths started to be removed to make motorways for cars. Just as in other cities across the Western world, urban planners saw cars as the travel mode for the future, and the understanding at the time was that bicycles would disappear altogether, replaced by a higher-tech version of transport. Planners even destroyed entire Amsterdam neighbourhoods that interfered with the construction of major roads. City squares, once a central place for socializing and commerce, were replaced with city parking spaces.

In 1971, while cycling to school in the Netherlands, six-year-old Simone Langenhoff was killed in a traffic accident. She was one of 450 children killed that year by motorists, and one of 3,000 people affected by 'unsafe streets'. Simone's father was a well-known senior journalist at the national daily paper *De Tijd*. Full of grief, he wrote a

1972 front-page article entitled 'Stop de Kindermoord', which translates as 'Stop the Murder of Children'.

Langenhoff wrote: '[The country] chooses one kilometre of motorway over 100 kilometres of safe cycle paths . . . There's no pressure group? Let's start one. Parents of little victims, worried parents of potential little victims should unite!' Given the large number of children who had died that year, and the broader concern from parents of young children, this call was well received and soon after the activist group 'Stop de Kindermoord' was created. Their goal was 'to break through the apathy with which Dutch people accept the daily death of children in traffic'.

The organization was first led by Maartje van Putten, who made the rallying call 'protect children from motorists', and while the initial focus was on the need for school buses, it changed to street design and safe pedestrian areas. Van Putten said at the time: 'I was a young mother living in Amsterdam and I witnessed several traffic accidents in my neighbourhood where children got hurt. I saw how parts of the city were torn down to make way for roads. I was very worried by the changes that took place in society – it affected our lives. The streets no longer belonged to the people who lived there, but to huge traffic flows. That made me very angry.'

Stop de Kindermoord was strategic in offering practical solutions to city planners and to the Dutch government. For example, they recruited traffic engineers to put together child-friendly street designs and sent these to local authorities for consideration. The core idea here was *woonerf*, streets with speed bumps and bends to force cars to drive slowly. To ensure politicians were listening, they organized demonstrations largely by children and their parents. For example, they cycled in front of the house of the then Prime Minister Joop den Uyl with an organ, singing songs about safer streets. One of the most effective protests was outside Amsterdam's Rijksmuseum, when children and adults laid down their bicycles and pretended to be dead on the street.

Month by month, the activists managed to convince those in charge to extend and improve the cycling infrastructure. Stop de Kindermoord's creation was followed two years later by the First Only Real

Dutch Cyclists' Union demanding a city orientated around bikes, not cars. Tom Godefrooij, who was involved with this movement, said: 'Somehow we managed to strike a chord. First we would be arrested by the police, of course, but then the whole thing would be in the newspapers and municipal politicians would eventually listen. We had a great fighting spirit and we knew how to voice our ideas. In the end, we would get our bicycle lane. Even in the 70s, you know, there were politicians who understood that the general focus on cars would eventually cause problems.'

Changes began to happen: in 1973, the government started 'Sunday car-free days'. Political and public opinion shifted towards the benefits of cycling in the 1980s and 90s. All because a group of activists, driven by increased child deaths due to cars, said 'no more'.

One of the first major changes was to create entire networks of cycle paths, rather than single bicycle routes. This eventually led to 22,000 miles of cycle paths across the country. These paths are well trodden: 25 per cent of all trips were made by bicycle in the Netherlands in 2015, 38 per cent in Amsterdam and 59 per cent in the university town of Groningen. Only 2 per cent of trips in Britain are by bicycle.

In 1989, Stop de Kindermoord changed its name to 'Kinderen Voorrang', meaning 'Priority for Children'. In 2001, it became part of a general road safety campaign called 'Veilig Verkeer Nederland' or Safe Traffic Netherlands.

Just as a side note, while the Netherlands is the most active nation globally, their diet isn't great. Adults in the Netherlands have among the lowest fruit and vegetable consumption in Europe, with around six out of ten reporting that they do not eat even one portion a day. Only about a quarter of fifteen-year-olds reported eating at least one piece of fruit per day. But more on that later.

Building the 'Fifteen-Minute City'

France has struggled with low physical activity across its population over the past two decades. A study comparing physical activity in

2006 and 2016 found that sedentary screen time had become a major part of leisure time, and this resulted in less physical activity, especially in children. Observing these trends, city planners in Paris, driven by new mayor Anne Hidalgo in 2014, decided to take another route rather than just telling people to move.

In her first term, Hidalgo made it a priority to create bike lanes, raise parking meter prices, and move the city away from being dominated by cars. Funded by a 250-million-euro budget, the city implemented a set of measures to make cycling more accessible through adding 112 miles of new, permanent segregated bike lanes between 2023 and 2026. In 2021, Hidalgo committed to making the city '100 per cent cyclable'. The new 'Bike Plan' (Plan Vélo: Act 2) launched in 2021 was driven by a focus on sustainable travel, exercise and congestion. The plan had several goals.

First was to create enough lanes to ensure that more bike journeys of over a mile could be carried out on segregated paths. Having physical separation from cars, trucks and other motor vehicles is an important factor in whether people decide to cycle – especially for women, the elderly and children. Second was to have new lanes connecting the suburbs with central Paris, to ensure that the transition could be made to commuting into the city network safely. Third was creating enough storage and parking spaces for bikes so that they could be safely left when going about daily life. The mayor pushed this plan, saying that cyclists should be able 'to ride without doubt, without danger and over long distances'.

It's not been without problems, though. Pedestrians have been angered by cyclists jumping onto narrow sidewalks and endangering them. Many busy roads only have paint markings to separate cycle lanes rather than physical barriers that offer more safety from collisions. Car drivers have also been frustrated by 70 per cent of car parking spots being removed for bike space and other uses.

The oil and car industries have also lobbied against these measures (broadly seen within the umbrella of climate-related action), given the negative impact on their core businesses. In 2019, a study by independent research group InfluenceMap identified thirty-three companies that were the strongest opponents of action: six car companies (Fiat Chrysler, Ford, Daimler, BMW, Toyota and General Motors), with the rest from the oil, gas and energy industries. Julia Poliscanova, the clean vehicles director for an NGO in this space, said: 'The car industry has always maximized its profits from its existing models and products for as long as is possible to make their money and delay and work around the regulations.' These companies have focused their efforts on lobbying politicians to block, delay and dilute policy initiatives.

Professor Carlos Moreno from the Sorbonne University, who has been advising Hidalgo, said: 'The drivers were radically very noisy, saying that we wanted to attack their individual rights, their freedom. The motorist lobby said [Hidalgo] cannot be elected without our support, that they are very powerful in France . . . [but Hidalgo] often says "I was elected two times, with the opposition of the automotive lobby." In 2024, nobody requests to open again the highway on the Seine, no one wants the Seine urban park to be open for cars.'

He's right. Mayor Hidalgo was elected for a second term after successfully introducing many pro-cycling measures, and launched a campaign for President of France off the back of them. Referring to the lockdown period in France during the pandemic, David Belliard, the deputy mayor for transport, said: 'For the first time, people experienced the city without cars . . . and they understood we can live without cars and . . . it's better.' But not all publics are as welcoming of these kind of measures, as I'll come onto soon.

Investing in cycle lanes has been successful in increasing the number of people cycling – not for exercise, but for commuting. So much so that there's an everyday Parisian word for it: *vélotaf*. In the first year of the mayor introducing these measures, cycle use in both the centre and suburbs of Paris rose by 54 per cent. After separate cycle lanes were introduced, the proportion of women cycling in Paris increased five points to 41 per cent.

The larger idea behind Paris's drive has been the controversial 'fifteen-minute city', meaning that a city should be designed so that most of people's daily errands, work, education and life can be carried out within fifteen minutes (by foot or bicycle) from their home. This concept, heavily designed by Moreno, was primarily driven by a focus on climate change and sustainability. By April 2024, Paris had fifty fifteen-minute neighbourhoods running and plans to increase even further.

In March 2022, Oxford city council approved a twenty-year urban plan to adopt the fifteen-minute city model, falling in line with other British cities such as Bath, Bristol, Canterbury and Edinburgh. Similar to Paris, there was major pushback in Oxford. Roughly 2,000 people attended a rally in February 2023 against these 'Stalinist-style' measures, claiming that they would infringe individual freedom. Right-wing commentators said: 'You will only have fifteen minutes of freedom here in the UK.' In the House of Commons, Tory MP Nick Fletcher portrayed fifteen-minute cities as a 'socialist concept' to 'take away personal freedoms'. Sadly it became a divisive right-wing/left-wing issue, rather than a policy proposal about building a healthier future.

When partisan mudslinging starts, it's good to come back to the facts. The simple goal for these cities is to create neighbourhoods where essential services are accessible by walking or cycling less than fifteen minutes, which could be seen as providing more freedom of choice. Moreno said: 'Today 80 per cent of urban mobility is forced, because people have to get up early and commute to school, to workplaces that are far from their homes. In a city of proximity in which services are always close by, mobility is a choice: on foot, by bicycle, by public transport or electronic vehicle, you go where you want because you want to.'

But with the online world of conspiracy theorists feeding each other misinformation into a state of hysteria, and other lobbies such as the automobile and oil industries pushing to maintain the status quo, a reasonable, balanced discussion becomes harder to have. Moreno commented: 'This kind of fear-mongering is, to me, something very fascist. But it's also so absurd that it shows that the people . . . are gullible, terribly ignorant, in line with flat-earthers or those people who think the world is controlled by lizard people.'

Coming back to Paris and Mayor Hidalgo, the side effect of more people walking and cycling has been increased physical activity and less chronic disease. Numerous studies have shown the links between walking and cycling and lower risk of cardiovascular disease, cancer and death. The WHO estimates that regular cycling, such as commuting to work, reduces the total risk of mortality by about 10 per cent.

In many ways, it's not rocket science. People need to get about their daily lives, and walking and cycling are an efficient way to do so. I focus on cycling specifically in this chapter, given how striking the Amsterdam and Paris examples are, but making walking and public transport more accessible would have similar effects. The core idea is a move away from having individually owned cars as the only option for travel within a city. It's about more freedom, not less.

#Dubai30×30

Dubai Crown Prince Sheikh Hamdan bin Mohammed bin Rashid Al Maktoum gives a big smile as he shares his daily workout on Instagram. In the clip he holds a kettlebell as he stands on a balance board, hashtag #Dubai30×30. Using social media to broadcast this across the nation in October 2022, he kicked off the sixth Dubai Fitness Challenge to get people to complete thirty minutes of fitness training for thirty days.

For the month, thousands of classes and gym facilities were offered for free to make exercise as accessible as possible. Fahim Armar, a new expat in Dubai, welcomed this approach to fitness: 'Even my friends are willing to join me now. All thanks to Sheikh Hamdan bin Mohammed bin Rashid Al Maktoum, who has been the driving force of this city-wide event.'

The Crown Prince has made this one of his landmark initiatives. He tweeted: 'I look forward to having the whole community unite to turn Dubai into the world's most active and dynamic city'; and later, at the end of the thirty days, he celebrated: 'Together, we are well on the way to becoming the fittest city in the world.' To his credit, Dubai is (so far) the only city in the world to offer its citizens and visitors an entire month of free fitness classes, activities and events. The widespread media coverage, and leadership by the Sheikh, increased public awareness about the importance of physical activity in improving health and reducing chronic disease.

Yet physical activity levels in the United Arab Emirates are some of the world's lowest and continue to decline. More than 80 per cent of waking hours are spent in sedentary activities such as driving, working on screens, watching television, or eating. Correlated with this, obesity among children and adolescents is very high and rising, which many link to a sedentary lifestyle. A survey in 2019 found that nearly 84 per cent of children in the country didn't reach the minimum goal required per day for exercise.

How to reconcile the flashy, heavily publicized 'exercise for thirty minutes a day' campaigns with the reality of declining physical activity in the population? Quite simply, people struggle to incorporate physical activities into their daily routine, as 'exercise' time needs to fit within their leisure hours. Yes, part of this has to do with climate – as Dr Hesham, a local paediatrician, said, 'One reason for the low activity levels is the UAE's hot climate. People go outside less, so there are more indoor activities and more screen time, which is the opposite of what we want.' Dr Osama, another local paediatrician, added that children in the UAE don't usually exercise unless they have easy access to a pool or shaded outdoor space.

But it's not only climate: there's a lack of walking or bicycle-friendly pathways near most schools and communities, and given road design, parents have expressed concern about the safety of their children walking to school. This feels similar to the 1970s moment in the Netherlands, where child safety concerns prompted city redesign. Studies have shown that neighbourhoods with high walkability (low levels of traffic, safe routes) have higher levels of children walking to school, and higher levels of physical activity. Amsterdam is the clearest case study here.

Despite educational and marketing efforts to 'get moving' across the UAE, a study on physical activity of adolescents in Abu Dhabi noted that the city was not seen as conducive to walking by girls or boys. They pointed to streets being too narrow, no clear crosswalks, no pedestrian sidewalks, and unsafe driving behaviour at high speeds. If children can't walk to school easily, or play outside, then they end up taking cars and buses, where they sit. Which is more sedentary behaviour. To get to school where they also sit.

Just telling people to move doesn't work if they can't implement this advice within their daily life and routine. Every day, parents and children make a choice whether they should walk or drive to school, which is heavily affected by environmental factors such as safety and accessibility. The responsibility lies with government, whether at national or city level, to change the infrastructure around schools.

YouTube Fitness Campaigns

To return to India, in August 2020 the Delhi city government launched the 'Healthy Body, Healthy Mind' fitness campaign, triggered by the 'stay at home' orders of the COVID lockdown. This involved a YouTube channel where fitness videos were uploaded weekly.

But while the push has been on awareness, this hasn't been supported by infrastructure changes to make physical activity more accessible. A study of outdoor school environments in Delhi found that the majority of schools examined did not have cycle lanes, marked pedestrian crossings or traffic calming measures such as school warning signs.

Another problem in India that prevents increased physical activity is the dirty air. Delhi often has toxic levels of air pollution, which means that outdoor activities are advised against unless medical-grade masks are worn. I'll come to air quality in India later in this book, but it's a real challenge as very poor air quality means that even with the awareness that people should be exercising in parks or walking outdoors, it's harmful to health to be outside breathing this air without filtration. Estimates show that the optimal time to cycle in typical Delhi pollution levels is thirty minutes, where the health benefits of physical activity outweigh the harmful effects of pollution. Once ninety minutes of biking is reached, the total workout becomes a net negative to one's health.

This concern about outdoor air quality forces physical activity into indoor spaces such as homes which are already crowded, or into expensive gym facilities, which means exercise becomes a purely recreational activity, and one that can only be accessed by a subset of the population.

If we look at the trends over the past twenty years, physical activity has decreased in Delhi, and this was accentuated by the COVID lockdown. In the first lockdown there, people's activity dropped by 40 per cent. A similar trend happened in children. But a survey of children has found that activity hasn't bounced back after restrictions were lifted: it was still about 13 per cent down compared to pre-pandemic levels. Sedentary time also increased, compared to pre-COVID levels. This could also be due to the shift towards using screens as the main method of working, education and recreation.

When Being Sedentary Is a Sign of Wealth

If we head south on the globe and hit Accra, Ghana, we can see a similar challenge to what I've described about India. Most physical activity until recently came from walking long distances and domestic chores – carrying water, cleaning, washing clothes, building, digging, planting. But this is shifting with rising wealth and education and a move towards motorized transport and sedentary activities. As one Ghanaian adolescent said, 'I have a friend who always says I wasn't brought up walking, my daddy always picks me up wherever I want to go whenever, so even if the car is not available I have money to pick taxis.'

Not having to do domestic chores or walk long distances – which are both physically taxing – has become a sign of wealth. In this 'physical activity transition', there's not been the shift towards doing exercise as leisure which has happened in elite communities in the Western world. As researchers studying this have noted, 'Because of the labour-intensive nature of most occupations in society (e.g. farming and fishing), people in general do not necessarily perceive the need to instil a habit of intentional physical activity within the socialization process.'

Given that physical inactivity as a risk factor for chronic disease is seen as a 'new' phenomenon of the past decade or so, government action has lagged behind. In Africa, roughly half of national chronic disease policies are about tobacco. Only 16 per cent address physical inactivity. Physical activity policy is almost non-existent in most African nations: exceptions are awareness campaigns that touch on physical activity launched in Ghana and Cameroon.

In Ghana, Vice President Dr Mahamudu Bawumia launched National Fitness Day in September 2022 at Accra Sports Stadium as part of a new campaign to encourage exercise on the second Saturday of each month. This is similar to Dubai's efforts in trying to raise awareness of the importance of exercise through political leaders, and portraying it as something which is good for your mind and body, and which should fit into leisure time.

But there are questions as to how effective these kinds of 'awareness-building' campaigns are without wider integration into the daily rhythm of people's lives. So far, physical activity has continued to decline in Ghana despite these efforts.

Looking across Dubai, Delhi and Accra, a similar pattern of decreasing physical activity is observed, which shows the difficulty in using educational or motivational fitness language to change physical activity at a population level. I say this with some trepidation, given that I moved into being a personal trainer to help motivate individuals to get moving. But that's the reality.

Overcoming the Laziness Gene

Here are a few things we've learned from decades of research on physical activity and policy examples from across the globe. First, people are intrinsically lazy: when they don't have to do physical labour for domestic, travel or work reasons, they tend not to want to immediately transition into doing it 'for fun' or 'for health reasons'. From an evolutionary perspective, this makes sense. When it was difficult to gain access to food, conserving energy through sedentary behaviour was a survival trait. Having a neural predisposition to minimizing physical activity (i.e. a 'laziness gene') would be selected for, as these individuals were more likely to survive and pass on their genes to offspring.

Especially in low- and middle-income countries, physical activity has been interlinked with poverty and labour to survive, whether it's working in crop fields, walking with heavy water jugs, or cooking, washing clothes and cleaning. As people get richer in these contexts, they prefer to transition to less physically demanding jobs.

On the flip side, in richer countries, exercise has come to be linked with higher socioeconomic status, which means more free time and available resources. Fitness and sports brands have tried to link physical activity with a certain 'luxury' lifestyle that includes clothes, bags, and gym trends. All this means is that inequality in physical activity becomes more pronounced – the fit get fitter, and the inactive become more inactive – and the real benefits of movement to the entire population are lost.

Another lesson, as shown by various awareness campaigns over the years, is that just telling people to exercise, and explaining the associated health benefits, isn't sufficient to shift daily physical activity patterns. Going for a run or to the gym shouldn't feel like a punishment, or martyrdom to the 'health cause'. This linking of exercise to the idea of 'doing it for your health' through YouTube and Instagram videos is a good marketing tool, but doesn't seem to shift behaviour in a sustainable way.

If you've bought this book, you're more likely than the population at large to be interested in staying fit and healthy. Good for you! But on a population level – that is, being realistic about what will work for most people – the onus for increasing physical activity shouldn't be put only on individuals, but on governments and policy-makers looking to help support physically and mentally healthy behaviours. There are obstacles, sure. Governments are battling limited time, limited money, people not wanting to spend their free time exercising, and the accessibility challenges such as safe parks to run in, or the distance to the nearest leisure centre. But this obstacle course can be beaten.

The way to shift physical activity at a population level, as shown by Amsterdam and Paris, is to build it into daily life so that it becomes practical, invisible, free (or cheap) and social. People cycle in Amsterdam not for their health, but because it's the simplest way to get to work or to school, and because it's made safe, accessible and easy. Some may even say fun.

This means rethinking the entire design of cities, away from cars and towards bicycles and walking, supported by public transport. Public transport is an important component, because even taking a bus and sitting on it requires someone to walk to a bus stop, and then walk from the end stop back to their home. (For the pedants out there, yes, you walk to and from your car, but the journey is almost always shorter.)

However, this approach requires real infrastructure change, as well as a critical mass of the population moving in that direction. This means building up a strong public transport system, safe pedestrian walkways, and separate cycle lanes linked to cycle networks.

High-income governments are generally aware of the burden of health conditions linked to low physical activity, and are making attempts to move beyond awareness campaigns towards infrastructure and city design. Barcelona, Edinburgh, Austin, London, Munich – there are countless examples of governments working towards more active populations.

Politicians championing this cause face pushback from online conspiracy theorists as well as the automobile and oil lobby for obvious reasons. For example, the ten biggest carmakers and automotive associations employ around seventy lobbyists and spend 20 million euros a year in Brussels lobbying for car-friendly legislation by the European Parliament. But we have also seen mayors, for example in Paris, who are willing to stand up for long-term health and wellbeing objectives instead of short-term profit-driven interests.

I've exercised regularly for as long as I can remember. While exercise is a powerful intervention, some might say the most powerful, to living longer, my personal training education reinforced what I'd learned during my brief time in a medical programme, and in my research career. Physical activity isn't enough. It's also about diet. As the saying goes, 'You can't outrun a bad diet.' (Unless you're Dutch, it seems – but even they would be healthier if they had better diets.)

3. What's a Balanced Diet?

As I mentioned earlier, my personal life goal is to live to 100 with good health. To get there, I've tried to learn from the lifestyle of people who've made it to 100, and beyond. In 2019, Kane Tanaka received a certificate from Guinness World Records for being the world's oldest person. At that time, she was 116.

Tanaka was born in 1903, the year that Orville and Wilbur Wright launched the world's first successful flight in a motorized airplane, which travelled 852 feet in fifty-nine seconds. It was also the year that the Tour de France was launched, Pierre and Marie Curie won the Nobel Prize in physics, decaffeinated coffee was created, and the first trip by automobile across the United States was completed from San Francisco to New York.

Tanaka died in April 2022 at the age of 119 after living through two world wars, the 1918 influenza pandemic, two rounds of cancer and the COVID-19 pandemic. When asked the secret to her longevity, she replied with two words: 'Being myself.' On her diet, she responded, 'Appreciate anything I eat.'

Until the day she died, Tanaka kept her mental agility, humour and personality. In January 2022, when asked by a reporter what kind of a man she preferred, she cheekily said, 'A young man like you.' The president of the Japan Foundation for Ageing and Health said: 'She had a clear mind, took care of herself and lived to an advanced age . . . And she gave hope to others, making them think, "Oh, we may be able to live to that age, too."'

Her life wasn't especially privileged. She only completed an elementary school education and then had to work for the family until being married at age nineteen. She ran a *mochi* shop (sweet rice cakes) with her husband until he was drafted and sent to fight in the Solomon Islands during the Second World War. Two of her four children died before the age of two. Her oldest son Nubuo was sent to fight on the Korean Peninsula and in Mongolia, where he was taken prisoner. To support herself during the war, she ran the mochi business on her own and opened an udon noodle restaurant on the Japanese navy base in Fukuoka, including after the US occupied it in 1945.

She experienced the death of many loved ones, including several children and her husband. It wasn't as if she was in perfect health throughout her lifetime: she had colon cancer, pancreatic cancer, cataracts and paratyphoid. In the last years of her life, she was constantly in and out of hospital with various issues.

Tanaka was interviewed in her final years and pointed to family, sleep, hope and faith for her long life. Of course genetics also plays a role. Stephen Coles, co-founder of the Gerontology Research Group, said in 2014: 'I've interviewed more supercentenarians [those that live past 110] than probably anyone else, trying to find out what they have in common. The answer is almost nothing.'

That's not entirely true. They largely live in Japan.

It's Common to Live to 100 in Japan

Japan has more centenarians than any other country, with the average Japanese lifespan reaching ninety. Living to 100 is increasingly common: one Japanese person in every 1,450 is aged over 100. On the islands of Okinawa in 2015, there were almost double the number of centenarians per 100,000 people as there were in Japan as a whole.

Okinawans have a saying: 'Live far enough away from your family so you're not running into them every day, but close enough to take them a warm bowl of soup on foot,' and some point to this close-knit community as a key factor in longevity. But could there be more going on?

In 1975, Dr Makoto Suzuki started the Okinawa Centenarian Study, looking at over 1,000 100-year-olds to understand the various factors responsible for the long life expectancy on the islands. The findings aren't surprising: low cholesterol, clean arteries, low risk of cancer (80 per cent less breast and prostate cancer than North Americans), strong bones (half the risk of hip fractures of North Americans), and overall lean and fit bodies.

How do they manage to age in such a healthy way? A big factor is the Okinawan diet, which is largely plant-based and heavy on vegetables, fruit and legumes. Instead of bread, they eat sweet potato, which is considered a better source of carbohydrates because it contains more fibre, vitamins and minerals and is less processed and less calorific. Okinawans also have high standards of quality of food ingested into the body: the cultural belief is that the body is a temple which shouldn't be polluted.

They also practise *hara hachi bu*, a phrase that roughly translates into English as 'eat until you are eight parts (out of ten) full' or 'belly 80 per cent full'. This means that an average Okinawan consumes 1,800–2,000 kilocalories (kcal) per day, resulting in a BMI of about 18–22 for those over sixty. This contrasts with a BMI of 26–27 for people over the age of sixty in the United States.

Eating to more than 80 per cent full is considered over-eating and puts stress on our cells. Over-eating, especially foods such as sweets, sodas and heavily processed meats such as sausages, bacon and salami, increases the number of free radicals (molecules with unattached electrons) in the body. Free radicals accumulating within the body damages the structure and function of our cells. For example, they can lead to cell mutation and new cell growth, which is why they're implicated in health problems such as cancer, diabetes and hardened arteries.

But in our modern world, how does one stop at 80 per cent instead of feeling completely full after a meal? The Okinawans have several ways to do this. First, they eat slowly to allow the stomach to send signals to the brain that it is full. Meals aren't rushed – they are social occasions to see people and eat, with no pressure to drink alcohol heavily. Second, they focus on food, which means turning off the TV and devices like smartphones and instead savouring each mouthful of food and enjoying the taste and experience.

Third, they eat on smaller plates and with small drinking glasses, which means eating less without thinking about it. This tricks the brain into thinking it's eaten a large meal and a full plate. A meta-analysis which reviewed over fifty studies on whether smaller plates help with portion control found that they do indeed make a difference.

Reducing the area of a plate by half lowered caloric consumption by 30 per cent. This is particularly true if people help themselves to food on the smaller plates, as they then take less, and also if those eating aren't aware that their consumption is being limited in this way. So my advice to you in your journey to living to 100 is to use smaller plates – but forget why you're doing that . . .

From Fad Diets to Simple Advice

Diet is complicated because we eat for a variety of reasons beyond nutrition. For many years, my emotional state was reflected in my dietary patterns. I would eat out of boredom, or because I was sad or stressed and wanted to be comforted. I would eat because it felt social to join in, or because I was alone and wanted the company of food. I stopped eating for months after my dad died. I ate too much while studying for exams, using cookies as an incentive system. It's taken me years to become aware of the emotional reasons behind why I eat, and I'm still working on turning that awareness into shifting my actual habits towards a healthier and more balanced diet.

If you visit the diet section of a bookshop, read diet tips online or even download one of the thousands of dieting apps, you'll see a full range of fad diets. I remember reading a book by Coleen Rooney, wife of former footballer Wayne Rooney, that said not to eat bananas, as a key tip in trying to lose weight. Then there are 'diabetic diets', 'fasting diets', 'intermittent fasting diets', 'personalized diets based on your blood type', 'the paleo diet' – the list goes on. Each week seems to bring a new set of rules and ways of structuring what to eat.

As humans, we're not good at processing complexity and navigating difficult choices when it comes to food. Especially when we're hungry, tired and short on money. Especially when we find ourselves in places like a grocery store, in a restaurant with friends, or in an airport or highway gas station. Too much information is almost as bad as no information because of our cognitive inability to filter what's relevant.

I've read a huge amount of the advice being given, both in a professional context – large epidemiological studies – and in a private context of wanting to keep my growing waistline in check, and avoid diabetes. I would simplify what we've learned over fifty years in nutritional and obesity research to this: limit your intake of ultra-processed foods. They are designed to be addictive and are heavily implicated in the rising number of people who are overweight and obese. Yet they have become the main component of our diet in Britain and the United States, including in school lunches.

The problem is that identifying ultra-processed foods is not straightforward. The only easy way I've found is to look at the label, where you'll see ingredients with long names that you wouldn't use if you had made the item at home. These ingredients include chemical additives for taste, colourings, sweeteners and preservatives. Ultra-processed foods occupy shelves in grocery stores and in our kitchens, given that they include industrialized bread (in processed sandwiches or sliced in squishy loaves), pre-packaged meals (like frozen pizza), breakfast cereals (such as Rice Krispies and Cocoa Puffs) and sausages and processed meat products. They also include soft drinks (like Coke), crisps (chips in the US), industrial chips (French fries in the US), factory-produced biscuits, chocolate and candies.

These all seem like food to us, but the difference between eating real bread and ultra-processed bread is not only in the ingredients but in how it's made. Bread made from wheat flour, water, salt and yeast is fine. It's processed, but with few ingredients, and baked. But often loaves in supermarkets have those ingredients plus emulsifiers, colourings, preservatives and other chemicals added so that they stay edible for weeks, months or even years. Also these additives make them cheaper and more appealing to our taste buds. These are ultra-processed products, with a long list of ingredients including those you'd struggle to pronounce.

The shift towards ultra-processed foods in our diet has consequences for health. Numerous studies now show that the higher the proportion of ultra-processed foods that are consumed, the greater the risk of becoming overweight or obese. This is especially true for children. Professor Christopher Millett from Imperial College London said: 'We often ask why obesity rates are so high among

British children. Our findings show that an exceptionally high proportion of their diet is made up of ultra-processed foods – with one in five children consuming 78 per cent of their calories from ultra-processed foods.'

Commenting on the study, Kiara Chang, Research Fellow at Imperial College, said: 'During the 17 years of follow up, we saw a very consistent increase in all measures of unhealthy weight among children who consumed greater amounts of ultra-processed foods as part of their diet. Their BMI, weight gain, and body fat gain was much quicker than those children consuming less ultra-processed foods. We actually see it making a difference from as young as 9 years old, between those consuming the most compared with those consuming the least ultra-processed foods.'

There is also a strong correlation between eating ultra-processed foods and increased disease and early death. A study from Brazil looked at the number of deaths in the population and their relationship to the intake of ultra-processed foods. Depending on age demographics, Brazilians were getting between 13 and 21 per cent of their total energy intake from ultra-processed foods. The study showed that consuming such foods was responsible for 10.5 per cent of all premature deaths in adults aged thirty to sixty-nine. Researchers further noted that ultra-processed food intake was responsible for 21.8 per cent of all preventable deaths from non-communicable diseases.

I'm also increasingly convinced by the link between higher rates of cancer in people under the age of fifty and consuming an ultra-processed diet. Between 1990 and 2019, cancer rates increased by 22 per cent in people aged twenty-five to twenty-nine in G7 countries. Rates of cancer in the next age group, thirty to thirty-four, have been at the highest level ever. Cancer incidence is projected to keep going up in each generation of people born subsequently. Why? Professor Shuji Ogino from Harvard University thinks that increased cancer incidence in younger age groups is linked to early-life exposure to a diet that wasn't around for older age cohorts. He suggests that eating ultra-processed foods negatively alters the composition of the microbiome (the roughly 100 trillion microbes that live inside us, largely in the gut, and that help regulate our immune system). He's now launching studies looking at children's diet composition, how this changes the microbiome, and the link to early onset cancer.

The signals are clear from looking across the emerging evidence. Having a large part of our diet come from ultra-processed foods is likely making us die too early. We can see a clear correlation with increased obesity, and increased risk of chronic disease and early death.

Perhaps the health advice to individuals and governments should be simply to reduce ultra-processed foods within our diet. The problem is how to do this at a population level given that these foods are often chosen because they are cheap and non-perishable, and also that there's a lot of money to be made for companies through sales. The products come packaged with cartoon characters, heavy branding, marketing and product placement. They often have labels on the front of the box such as 'fortified with vitamins and minerals' or 'low-fat', which make them look like products with benefits for health, rather than with labels warning about the links to poor health outcomes.

Ultra-processed foods now make up 56 per cent of calories that the average person in the UK eats, and 57.9 per cent in the United States. School lunches in Britain have 75 per cent of their calories from ultra-processed foods. Most countries are facing a shift towards a larger part of people's diets coming from these types of foods instead of home cooking, including Italy, Ghana, India and Denmark.

In India, the ultra-processed food sector grew at a compound annual growth rate of 13.4 per cent from 2011 to 2021, according to the WHO. In June 2024, Professor Carlos Monteiro from the University of São Paulo in Brazil warned that these foods are displacing healthier diets across the world and causing major health issues, based on research studies he had conducted. He called for clear labelling on the packaging of these foods indicating the danger to health, taxation to make them less accessible, and bans on advertising and marketing.

But we can't talk about taking away one part of our diet without looking at how to increase the consumption of unprocessed foods (vegetables, grains, fruit, nuts) and simply processed foods (like cheese, olive oil or certain types of freshly baked bread) in a way that is affordable and accessible. Processed foods are relatively simple products made up of two to three ingredients usually. Compare this to ultra-processed foods, which typically have five or more ingredients including chemical additives, and high levels of refined carbohydrates, saturated fats and salts.

Why is it cheaper to eat ultra-processed foods than healthier options? They're cheap to make in a factory using machines, cheap to distribute (not requiring a cold chain or special handling) and they last a really long time. Compare this to bringing fruit and vegetables to market, which requires an agricultural workforce doing difficult, manual labour on little pay, resilience against extreme weather events, and careful distribution not to bruise or damage the produce and ensure people buy it before it goes bad.

The consequence is that fruit and vegetable prices are high, and increasingly unaffordable for most families. Britain has seen a fifty-year steady decline in the consumption of vegetables. In contrast, ultra-processed food consumption continues to increase. The unhealthy option has become the affordable, accessible and attractive option. The profits are made by large multinational corporations, and the costs are borne by our health systems crumbling under the weight of increased obesity and chronic disease, and by each of us in the toll to our own health and the health of our children and loved ones.

Why Is Being Obese Bad for Health?

The main consequence of a poor diet and eating too much is obesity. Calories are a standard unit for measuring the amount of energy our body gets from consuming food or drink. If we eat too many calories compared to what we expend, we gain weight. If we create a caloric deficit, we lose weight. But weight alone isn't a good measure of health: it doesn't say anything about a person's height, amount of different types of tissue such as muscle mass, or where fat tissue is located, which are all important considerations.

Weight is generally converted into a simple number such as body mass index, which is weight/height squared, largely because it's a free and accessible metric to assess obesity. Internationally, as I mentioned before, overweight is classified as a BMI between 25 and 30. Obese is 30–40. Severely obese is over 40. Some countries modify these categories: for example, in South Korea a BMI over 25 (not 30) is considered obese. The country uses this standard for obesity because of research showing that health risks rise significantly in South Koreans with a BMI of 25, rather than 30.

While BMI is the main assessment of 'how fat' a population is, it has major limitations. For example, two people could have the same BMI but one could have a lot of muscle mass and a low body fat percentage, and many world-class athletes would fall into the 'overweight' or 'obese' category for BMI. NFL football players are some of the fittest and fastest in the world, but based on players' height and weight, there is no Denver Broncos player within a normal BMI, and on average, their BMIs fall into the obese range of over 30.

Another critique of BMI is that it's not a good predictor for health conditions in Asian populations or older people. Type 2 diabetes, which is linked to body weight, is a classic example here. A study of more than a million people found that diabetes is more likely at a BMI of 30 if you're from a white background, at 28 if you're Black, at 24 if you're South Asian, and even at 21 if you're of Bangladeshi heritage. I see this in my own family: my Chennai-based grandparents aren't overweight but both developed diabetes. I recognize it in myself: the 'healthy weight' BMI is much lower for me given my Indian heritage, compared to my white colleagues and friends.

In South Asian ethnic groups, waist circumference is often a better way of assessing if someone is overweight, as it measures abdominal fat which is tightly implicated as a risk factor for disease. Basically, it's much worse to have fat stored on your belly and internal organs, than on your legs or bum. This is also why having a pear shape is better for health than having an apple shape. A study of 200 diabetic men and women indicated that rather than BMI or weight, an apple-shaped figure with more abdominal fat could better predict risk of heart disease.

What we're trying to assess through these measurements is the amount of fat tissue in the body (body adiposity) and where it's located. More fat, located more centrally in the body around the organs, is linked to metabolic syndrome, which is a cluster of conditions that occur together and increase your risk of heart disease, stroke and type 2 diabetes. Metabolic syndrome is diagnosed when someone has three or more of five risk factors: high blood glucose (sugar), high levels of triglycerides, high blood pressure, large waist circumference, and low levels of HDL (good) cholesterol in the body.

Diabetes as a 'Lifestyle Disease'

Metabolic syndrome is linked to insulin resistance, which causes high blood glucose levels. Insulin is a hormone that helps sugar enter the cells to be used as fuel. Insulin resistance means cells don't respond normally to this hormone and glucose can't enter the cells. The result is that blood sugar levels rise as the body produces more and more insulin to try to lower blood sugar. Insulin resistance can lead to type 2 diabetes, which is quite simply a disease of too much glucose, or sugar, in the blood. Uncontrolled high blood sugar can lead to vision loss from eye disease and eventually blindness, hearing loss, gum disease, heart disease, kidney disease (which requires dialysis or kidney transplantation) and nerve damage in the legs and feet.

Diabetes is common: in the United States, 9.4 per cent of the population have it, or around 30 million adults and children. An estimated 84 million more people have pre-diabetes, a condition where blood sugar levels are higher than normal, but not yet high enough to be diagnosed formally with diabetes. Diabetes is the leading cause of blindness in those between the ages of twenty and seventy-four in the US. The same story holds true for Britain, where diagnosis of diabetes has doubled over the past fifteen years. This means that by 2030, up to one in ten adults in the UK could have the disease.

But the place to really watch is India, which is often called the 'diabetes capital of the world'. India already has 17 per cent of the total number of diabetes patients in the world (around 80 million) and this is expected to increase to 135 million by 2045. It's becoming a health problem in young people too, with children and adolescents one of the groups most affected: this is linked to more ultra-processed and fast foods in their diet, and rising obesity. As I noted before, Indians are more genetically predisposed to diabetes. Studies have shown that Indians have a greater degree of insulin resistance, and that their blood sugar levels rise higher for a longer period of time when eating carbohydrates, compared to Europeans.

For this reason, diabetes is often referred to as a 'lifestyle' disease, linked to diet, body fat and weight. Similar to most chronic diseases, the response and funding has gone into treatment and acute services, rather than prevention.

Boris Johnson's Efforts to Lose Weight

The impact that high body fat and weight has on health was clearly visible during the pandemic. Studies on hospitalization risk, death and weight found that young patients (those under sixty) with a BMI over 30 were twice as likely to need acute hospital admission and almost twice as likely to need critical care than patients with a BMI under 30. Based on this data, the authors recommended that obesity be classified as a risk factor for severe disease from COVID. Going further, it was recommended that people with severe obesity (BMI over 40) were classified as a vulnerable group.

In England, a study of over 6.9 million patients indicated that above a BMI of 23, there was a linear increase in risk of hospitalization and death from COVID. This was particularly true for Black people and those under forty. A meta-analysis of 208 studies published before July 2021 concluded that overweight individuals were at greater risk of being hospitalized but not of death, obese individuals were at greater risk of both hospitalization and death, and those with severe obesity were at even greater risk of both hospitalization and death. Certainly in terms of the association between BMI and COVID-19 outcomes, there is now strong evidence from multiple countries that those above the normal weight range are at increased risk of hospitalization, ICU admission and death.

After suffering from COVID himself and ending up in ICU in March 2020, former UK Prime Minister Boris Johnson said he was 'too fat' and hired celebrity personal trainer Harry Jameson to help build up his fitness. Johnson also started speaking about how 'losing weight, frankly, is one of the ways you can reduce your own risk from coronavirus'. Working with a personal trainer is of course a good route for those who have choice and control over their diet, time and finances. It's not a realistic solution for the entire population. Also, while fitness and physical activity have many benefits, as I noted earlier, obesity itself is more directly linked to diet and caloric intake.

How I (Try to) Eat

Regardless of where we live, diet is something we have some control over, although there are major obstacles like cost, availability and time. What have I learned about eating and maintaining a healthy weight? Quite simply, and despite some recent popular books that challenge this based on faulty readings of data: gaining excess weight is a caloric imbalance. When we eat more calories than we expend each day, we gain weight. And in today's food ecosystem with condensed calorific foods, it becomes impossible to outrun a bad diet.

Running three miles might burn (depending on speed and body weight) 300–400 kcal. Eating one slice of a cake, also roughly 300–400 kcal, can take sixty seconds. We tend to overestimate the calories we expend on physical activity like walking or running, and underestimate the calories in the foods we eat. This is especially true of ultra-processed foods, where chemical processes to improve taste, texture and appearance mean that foods have incredibly high caloric density.

We also eat for multiple reasons, as mentioned earlier: out of boredom, stress, sadness, frustration, to fit in socially, and because we're evolutionarily programmed to consume and store calories. Storing fat reserves had major advantages historically when food was scarce and hunger was a daily reality. Our relationship with food is complex, emotional and personal. It's also linked to our childhood experiences and the meaning that food, or lack of it, had within our homes.

One of the challenges in eating 'better' is to not feel like we're being deprived or 'dieting', which is linked to sacrifice. Not having what we would like to have is unsustainable. My approach to diet is about a general, and long-term, shift in how and what we eat, rather than fad diets and extreme rules for a short period of time. Here are some simple things I've learned.

Ultra-processed foods trick our bodies into overconsuming and override our normal 'satiety' signals from the stomach that tell the brain we're full. If you want a biscuit, then bake it from scratch with basic ingredients. Even if each biscuit has the same number of calories as the shop-bought ones (in reality, the shop-bought ones likely have more), you probably won't be able to eat the same number of them – ultra-processed foods are designed to be ultra-palatable. Read the labels of packages and if there are names you can't pronounce, then it's better to avoid.

If you over-eat and drink too much at a dinner with family or friends, then just eat less the next day. These ups and downs then equal out at the end. It's about an overall balance in your diet that works also for your social life.

I've stayed within a normal weight range since a young age and done my best to eat a balanced diet wherever I've lived on the globe. I try to follow the Okinawa rule of eating until 80 per cent full, using smaller plates, and filling up with plant-based foods first before moving on to more calorie-dense options.

Our caloric needs also decrease as we age, so we need to eat less, and move more, as we get older. For example, a normal-weight, inactive Canadian man is estimated to need 2,635 calories a day between the ages of nineteen and thirty, which decreases to 2,227 by the age of fifty-one and to 1,982 by seventy. Someone of the same size who is active would still see this decrease in caloric need: for a very active man this decreases from 3,337 at nineteen to 2,896 by fifty-one and 2,630 by seventy. Working this out per year, it means consuming roughly fifteen fewer calories per day after the age of nineteen. It may not seem a lot, but this caloric difference contributes to gradual weight gain over the course of months and years. Our caloric needs decrease with age due to slower metabolism, the brain shrinking in size and requiring less energy, and the natural loss of muscle (which burns calories). It sucks, I know, but it's a scientific fact if you want to avoid a growing waistline.

The problem with the advice above is that it sounds like *Women's Health* magazine, geared towards affluent, time-rich people who have the bandwidth to focus on a good diet almost like a full-time job. It requires enough money to buy raw ingredients and time to go shopping regularly and cook or bake. It requires kitchens with adequate space and hopefully a dishwasher to save on time washing up. It requires a job that gives time for lunch, and doesn't leave you feeling exhausted and stressed by the end of the day. We know we make poorer health choices when stressed or tired: choosing the biscuits instead of the broccoli, the frozen, ultra-processed pizza instead of making dough, rolling it out and baking our own pizza.

This is why there's a strong socioeconomic correlation between BMI and wealth in the West: the richer you are, the easier it is to be in a normal weight range. It largely comes down to resources.

I was asked at a conference in 2024 whether the new anti-obesity drugs should be rolled out to everyone who is overweight as a population-wide intervention. They were referring to the drug Ozempic, which roughly 2 per cent of the US population is taking to lose weight. Ozempic, through its active ingredient semaglutide, works by suppressing appetite and making you feel full. Semaglutide mimics the role of a natural hormone called GLP-1, which is produced by the body when we eat. This hormone tells the brain we've eaten and makes us feel full. Semaglutide also helps the pancreas produce insulin, which is why it was previously approved to help manage type 2 diabetes.

While hailed as the main medical breakthrough of 2024, with its producer Novo Nordisk becoming Europe's most valuable company off the back of it, it's not without challenges. The cost of a thirty-day supply of Ozempic is close to $1,000 in the US, and £160 in the UK, putting it out of reach for most people. It also carries side effects such as nausea, stomach pain, gallbladder issues, kidney damage, pancreatitis and thyroid cancer, as well as 'Ozempic face' where the skin on the face sags and wrinkles. The drug also needs to be taken continuously, otherwise the weight-loss effect (through suppressing appetite) is lost. For example, one study found that once individuals stopped taking semaglutide, they regained two thirds of the weight within a year.

While acknowledging that these medicines have an important role to play in a small subset of the population with underlying metabolic or genetic issues, especially those with type 2 diabetes, they're clearly not the solution for the general population. Most obesity in the population is preventable through environmental, economic and lifestyle changes in combination. At the conference, I asked why children living in deprived areas of Britain were twice as likely to be obese as those in more affluent areas. It's impossible to ignore the distribution of obesity across the country. It's not a medical issue. It's a political and economic one.

We have created a society and economy where eating a 'healthy' balanced diet, and staying within a normal weight range, is an expensive and luxury lifestyle requiring time, money and space. A Food Foundation report in 2023 found that the poorest 20 per cent would need to spend more than 50 per cent of their disposable income to eat in line with UK government recommendations on eating a balanced diet. For the same number of calories, the average cost of a healthy food (like fruit or vegetables) in 2019 was around £7.68 compared to £2.48 for poorer dietary options.

Anna Taylor, the executive director of the charity, said: 'Unhealthy food is cheap because the prime ingredients can be mass produced and these products can be created in non-perishable form. We have this situation where it is very easy to buy very cheap calories with low levels of nutrients. Whereas the same is not true for some of the more nutrient-rich food like fruits and vegetables.'

So, yes, education and awareness are important in recognizing obesity as a problem, but they aren't enough. They're first steps, along with regular surveys and identification of at-risk communities and groups. But we also have to acknowledge that it's practically impossible in Britain or the United States for most families to follow an 'Okinawa' life, because even if an individual has the information, they don't have societal support and reinforcement in making healthier decisions.

While we have some agency over what we eat, our circumstances play a major part too. This is where the responsibility shifts to governments: to recognize what a healthy diet entails and the barriers that individuals face in following advice. Governments have varied in how seriously they've taken this health issue, and tied to this is their relative success in stemming rising obesity. Let's take a look at some positive examples of public policy affecting diet.

Make Fruit and Vegetables Accessible

Compared to major OECD nations, South Korea has the second-highest life expectancy at 83.5 years, trailing only Japan (84.7 years). Overall, baby boys and girls born in South Korea in 2020 are anticipated to live an average of 80.5 and 86.5 years. In 2025, the country is predicted to become a super-aged society, with the number of people aged sixty-five and over reaching 20 per cent of the total population, compared to 6.9 per cent in India, 18.6 per cent in Britain and 17.3 per cent in the US.

In 2019, chronic disease accounted for 79.9 per cent of the total mortality worldwide, and eight out of ten leading causes of death were related to chronic disease. This makes sense, as we all need to die of something. Cancer is the leading cause of death (158.2 deaths per 100,000 people), followed by cardiovascular disease (60.4 deaths per 100,000) and pneumonia (45.1 deaths per 100,000). Considering the rapid increase in the proportion of people aged sixty-five or over (expected to rise from 20.3 per cent by 2025 to 43.9 per cent by 2060), the burden of chronic disease is expected to increase steadily.

The public health aim is to extend quality life as long as possible. And South Korea is managing to do this, reversing the increase in early deaths from chronic disease. Compared to two decades ago, age-standardized deaths per 100,000 people for cardiovascular diseases and cancers have dramatically decreased from 150.6 to 57.3 and from 145.2 to 89.0 in 2019, respectively. Furthermore, the avoidable mortality has dropped from 329.2 to 138.1 per 100,000 people.

Much of this relates to the underlying health of their population, obesity being a key metric of this. According to international standards, South Korea has an obesity rate of 6.2 per cent in men and 5.5 per cent in women. Compare this to the obesity rate in men in other countries in 2019: 43.5 per cent in the US, 26.7 per cent in Canada, 31.5 per cent in Australia, 27.0 per cent in the UK, 18.1 per cent in Germany, and 13.5 per cent in France.

Diving deeper into these low obesity rates, how does it tie into diet? A study of thirty OECD countries looked at their consumption of vegetables. On average, 59.1 per cent of people aged fifteen and over across these countries consumed vegetables each day in 2019. Of them, Australians consumed the highest rates of vegetables (99.2 per cent), followed by South Koreans (99.0 per cent) and New Zealanders (95 per cent).

The South Korean government has been proactive in health promotion since the mid-1990s, focusing policy on the broader range of factors that affect health, from food to housing, income and work conditions. In 1995, the National Health Promotion Act was first enacted, and the Health Promotion Fund was created in 1997. In 2002, the first National Health Plan was announced, and a systematic foundation for the improvement of public health was established.

From 2002, periodic planning was performed every ten years, with additional plans every five years. This longer-term planning helps look at the population challenges emerging and moves to mitigate them. Compare this to the planning of Western countries, which can operate election to election and be driven by populist policies to win votes rather than taking a longer-term view of health and wellbeing.

The South Korean government closely tracks the consumption of fruit and vegetables. In its annual report, 'Korea Health Statistics 2020', the health ministry noted that while fruit consumption had dropped over the past decade, the mean vegetable consumption was maintained above 70 per cent between 2010 and 2020. In 2021, the government announced the 'Dietary Guidelines for Koreans' to encourage people to consume more than 500g (the recommended intake) of fruit and vegetables daily.

History and culture are also important to what people eat. Traditionally, the Korean diet evolved from its geographical isolation as a peninsula surrounded by oceans and mountains. Preserving food resources became essential in life, and countless fermentation techniques were developed. A traditional South Korean food is *kimchi* – salted cabbage or radish.

Growing evidence shows that although kimchi contains high levels of sodium, it helps prevent obesity and strengthens the immune system. High sodium intake is inevitable as a lot of salt is used for the fermentation process, which could partly explain the prevalence of hypertension or stroke in South Korea, even with a lower average BMI. Yet despite this, overall chronic disease in South Korea is relatively lower than in other high-income countries. Experts have pointed to the high consumption of vegetables from land and sea, legumes and fish, and less red meat.

Studies have demonstrated that the Korean diet helps prevent obesity and mitigate insulin resistance. In one study, mice were fed a high-fat diet for seven weeks and then switched to one mimicking the Korean diet. Several weeks after the change in intake, the blood glucose levels of the mice had improved, as well as their overall health. These findings indicated that the traditional Korean diet would be beneficial in preventing chronic disease development.

Government efforts also tie into a society which judges harshly those who are overweight. South Korea has high levels of 'anti-fat' stigma and pressure to look a certain way, even to be considered for a job. South Korean studies have looked at the impact of job applicants' outward appearance throughout the hiring process. Many firms need applicants to submit pictures, and some even ask for their height and weight.

A study published in the *Korean Journal of Health Economics and Policy* in 2015 looked at whether employment rate differed by weight and gender. In the case of obese female college graduates, 6.25 per cent found employment in well-paid jobs, such as office workers at large corporations or in the public sector. When all other conditions were equal, this was significantly lower than for those who were overweight (17.7 per cent), normal weight (15.6 per cent) and underweight (11.9 per cent). The employment rate of obese male college graduates was 40.2 per cent, lower than those who were underweight/normal weight (54.7 per cent) and overweight (53.9 per cent).

The 'body size' judgement can be even harsher on women. South Korean beauty standards are a well-known feature of the culture. *Seoul* magazine reported that extreme dieting is common among South Korean women. Another study on 'lookism' noted that young adults tend to consider external appearance as an important determinant of relationships and achievements. One of the authors noted: 'Men can get away with being overweight or unattractive much more easily than women. If you are a woman who is overweight or unattractive, people will judge you harshly.'

Since 2018, the social standard of a certain external appearance in South Korea has been challenged through a feminist movement called 'Escape the corset'. Women are pushing back against extreme weight standards, some of which idealize a girl's body shape instead of the normal curvy development of women after puberty. Even so, South Koreans negatively judge their own bodies and health status: they tend to think they're overweight (even when they're not according to international standards) and that they're not in good health (even when they are by various health metrics). This constant pressure to stay a certain weight and keep a certain body type comes with its own set of negative mental health consequences.

But like most Western countries, obesity is linked to socioeconomic status and inequality. In women, low income and low education levels were associated with obesity prevalence, and the gaps have become more pronounced since 2007. It's not only lack of knowledge, but lack of ability to implement the advice given.

Make It Easier to Eat Well and Harder to Eat Badly

In 2014, the WHO ranked the Nordic countries, including Denmark, with some of the lowest obesity prevalence out of fifty-two high-income countries. But even in a country seen as relatively 'healthy' on the world stage, obesity is a challenge in Denmark. Between 1987 and 2003, the prevalence of obesity among Danes increased by 75 per cent. In 2003, 10–13 per cent of the population was obese, with 30–40 per cent considered overweight. The numbers continue to go up. In 2016, 19.7 per cent of Danish adults were obese and 55.4 per cent were overweight.

These trends since the end of the twentieth century didn't go unnoticed by the Danish authorities. In 2001, the Danish National Board of Health established an external working group to develop a proposal for a national action plan for the prevention and treatment of obesity. In September 2002, when Denmark was EU President, the National Board of Health held a conference on obesity where the urgency of tackling this challenge was stressed.

The National Action Plan for Obesity was adopted, aiming to increase awareness about normal weight development, prevent people becoming overweight, and help those at risk of obesity to start reducing their body weight. The recommendations focused on food, with proposals such as higher excise duties on soft drinks, and subsidies for food with low fat and sugar contents. In total the plan included sixty-six recommendations, and this was followed by national guidelines in 2014 by the Ministry of Health, and a Danish National Centre for Obesity in 2020.

One distinctive Danish policy was to introduce a 'Keyhole' label to help consumers identify healthier choices when buying food. The label identifies healthier food products that contain less fat, sugar and salt, and have more fibre. It was especially tailored for those with a low level of practical education to be able to read complex food labels and make informed shopping decisions.

An evaluation showed that the campaign had a positive effect on the number of Keyhole-labelled products sold, which increased by 9.6 per cent. The largest positive effect was identified for fresh fish, frozen fish, and fresh fruit and vegetables. However, the higher relative price of Keyhole-labelled products was flagged as a significant reason why a consumer wouldn't buy them. After the campaign, men over thirty-five with a low level of practical education were more likely to mention health as a reason for purchasing Keyhole-labelled products. Making healthier choices identifiable in a supermarket seemed to have a real impact within the limitation of price.

In 2004 an artificial trans-saturated fat ban was introduced in Denmark. Trans fats raise bad cholesterol (LDL) and lower good cholesterol (HDL) and are hazardous to health. The Danish law mandated that 2g of TFAs (trans fatty acids) per 100g was the maximum allowed content of artificial trans fats in oils and fats. In 2000 most margarines had been reduced to less than 1 per cent, after voluntary agreements signed by the Danish Nutrition Council and the Association of Danish Margarine Producers. However, trans fatty acids were still found in (mostly) imported, ultra-processed foods.

In 2002 the incoming Minister of Food, Mariann Fischer Boel, stressed the need to regulate trans fats given their significant health risks, and the government extended the voluntary agreement to all food produced and marketed in Denmark. The trans-saturated fat ban seems to have led to a moderate decrease in obesity rates among children, and a potentially large effect on adolescents, while the effect on adult obesity rates remains uncertain. Additionally, the ban seems to have decreased cardiovascular disease deaths by thirty fewer deaths per 100,000 inhabitants.

Following on from the success of that ban, in 2011 Denmark introduced a 'fat tax' for foods high in saturated fats. The tax was levied on all foods containing more than 2.3 per cent fat, including milk, butter, cheese, oil and meats, as well as processed foods. Per kilogram of saturated fat, sixteen Danish krone (£1.70 at the time) was added.

But the fat tax was repealed only one year after its introduction for political reasons. It was opposed by farmers and food companies, who complained that the tax was a bureaucratic nightmare and increased administrative jobs while putting other jobs at risk. Additionally, the tax was unpopular among consumers, who decided to avoid it by shopping in Germany and Sweden. In 2013, a sugar tax was supposed to be introduced, but after repealing the fat tax, plans were shelved.

The Danish government has continued to try to shift the population's diet towards healthier sources of food. To be fair, it's doing better than comparator countries. All the policy measures above mean that the government has taken this seriously for decades and continues to do what it can to reverse the trend towards unhealthy foods. The full story of Denmark's health isn't simply in its diet: it's also a country with a government actively promoting physical activity and movement in daily life and in schools.

But we shouldn't overstate Denmark's overall success. It's still struggling with rising obesity and the consumption of unhealthy foods. I doubt anyone could look at the increased prevalence of chronic disease and think the country has the ultimate solution or a silver bullet. Obesity almost feels like a tidal wave engulfing the world, one which certain governments are trying to counter by building seawalls in the policy steps they take. Some of these might be seen as 'nanny state' intervention, but doing nothing isn't in the public's interest.

Prevent Childhood Obesity

The South Korean and Danish governments have both focused on the diet of children. It makes sense to focus on what kids eat, because overweight children become overweight adults. Losing weight becomes harder as we get older, given that our caloric needs decrease with age, as mentioned earlier.

A meta-analysis on the impact of childhood obesity on adult obesity found that obese children and teens were five times more likely than those of normal weight to be obese as adults. It found that roughly 55 per cent of obese children become obese teens and around 80 per cent of obese teens become obese adults. Ensuring children stay within a healthy weight range is an important short- and long-term public health objective, and children are best reached through schools.

In 2008, the South Korean Ministry of Health and Welfare created and financed the Special Act on Food Safety Management for Children, implementing it on the 22nd of March 2009. It has certain key policies relating to schools within it. For example, to protect children by creating a safe and healthy food environment around schools, the 'Green Food Zone' or Children's Food Safety Protection Zone was designated within a distance of 200 metres around the school. Within this boundary, merchants cannot sell junk food, high-calorie, low-nutrition food, or high-caffeine food or drink.

Of 9,053 schools, 8,051 were selected and managed as Green Food Zones by December 2009. Initially, there were some sceptical assessments of the policy's effectiveness, suggesting that it was not enough to bring noticeable changes to children's food safety and dietary behaviours. But since then, local governments have strengthened the monitoring of supermarkets and retailers by increasing the number of inspectors, and those that violate regulations have faced fines and legal action. The policy has become more effective with stricter penalties for violations, and in this way the government has protected children from the targeted branding and marketing of ultra-processed foods.

Children have also been a focus of Danish government intervention. Danish children can receive seven preventive health examinations free of charge during their first five years of life at the GP. These include measurements of height and body weight and assessments of weight for length (below age two) and BMI for age (above age two).

Schools are important in the Danish strategy for the prevention of children becoming overweight. Since 2009, data on children's height and body weight during their first year of life and during school years has been collected by the National Register of Children's Health. From 2011, it has been mandatory for health services in the municipalities to monitor and report the data to the register. This means that an overall picture on child obesity can be built, supported by guidelines on early identification and support for those who are overweight and obese among school and pre-school children.

In 2014 the Children's Obesity Clinic received a lot of attention, as international newspapers wondered if Denmark had cracked the problem of childhood obesity. In the treatment programme, children are admitted to hospital for twenty-four hours and have a series of tests and body composition measurements. Additionally, they must complete a detailed questionnaire on diet and lifestyle, with the support of parents.

Based on the tests and questionnaire outcomes a tailored protocol is developed. This includes a set of rules aimed at improving the child's diet, increasing exercise levels, and reducing sedentary time. Initial results published in 2011 showed significant reductions in BMI after eighteen months.

When the Obesity Clinic protocol was adopted in another clinic, a substantial reduction in BMI was found among children aged five to eighteen after one year, and an even greater reduction after two years. The protocol was also effective in a community setting. Results led to Danish clinical guidelines, set in 2014, for examining and treating overweight and obese children and adolescents in paediatric settings.

Denmark and South Korea show that certain policies can reduce the increase in childhood obesity that most countries across the world are seeing. When I am asked how to approach the public health challenge of rising overweight/obesity rates, I point to children and schools. These are where interventions can be implemented at an early stage for relatively low cost. The benefit, not only in reducing future health care costs but also in increasing quality of life, is massive. These are the kinds of proposals we (scientists) need to be putting in front of politicians, showing concrete examples of how policies were introduced, implemented and funded in other settings, and the impact they've had.

The (Second) Fattest Country

For many years, the United States was the fattest country on the planet. This distinction has now been taken by the UAE. But the US is a federal system with fifty states which differ considerably in their politics, local economy, epidemiology and climate. The 2019 Obesity report from the Trust for America's Health, a non-profit organization, highlighted that the obesity crisis was getting worse almost everywhere across the country, with nine states having obesity rates over 35 per cent in 2018 – Alabama, Arkansas, Iowa, Kentucky, Louisiana, Mississippi, Missouri, North Dakota and West Virginia – compared to 2012 when no single state had an adult obesity rate over 35 per cent.

The president and CEO of the Trust, John Auerbach, said: 'These latest data shout that our national obesity crisis is getting worse. They tell us that almost 50 years into the upward curve of obesity rates we haven't yet found the right mix of programs to stop the epidemic. Isolated programs and calls for lifestyle changes aren't enough. Instead, our report highlights the fundamental changes that are needed in the social and economic conditions that make it challenging for people to eat healthy foods and get sufficient exercise.'

But it's not a hopeless situation, as the city of Huntington in West Virginia shows. In 2008 Huntington was named the fattest city in the US. At the time, approximately 45.5 per cent of its adults were obese. In the following thirteen years, however, Huntington turned a corner and cut the number of obese adults down to 32.6 per cent.

After being named 'fattest city', Huntington implemented various strategies to tackle high obesity. For example, a collective 'walk to the Moon', and later to other stars and planets, was organized. Additionally, hospital programmes were introduced, focusing on helping children lose weight. A new local, affordable farmers' market, which partnered with food banks and accepted Supplemental Nutrition Assistance Program benefits, was also set up. The farmers' market filled an important void in the city, given its few grocery stores and the many convenience stores not selling fresh produce or meat.

The most notable change was due to the unfavourable attention of being called the fattest city. This led the local government and community to prioritize diet and health. As Steve Williams, Huntington's mayor, said, 'When the students started getting involved, once the families started getting involved, once the institutions started getting involved, it wasn't: "Watch." It was: "Join in." '

The US Food and Drug Administration (FDA), which helps regulate food products, supports city policy efforts. As part of a new strategy on diet in 2018, the agency launched 'The New Nutrition Facts Label: What's in It for You?' The campaign was aimed at raising awareness about the changes to the Nutrition Facts label, increasing its use, and helping consumers, health care professionals and educators learn how to use it as a tool for maintaining healthy dietary practices. The agency also issued voluntary sodium reduction targets for industry in a wide variety of processed, packaged and prepared foods as part of an ongoing effort to reduce sodium in the food supply.

The FDA has begun the process of developing a symbol that industry can voluntarily use to label food products that meet its updated 'healthy' definition. This is similar to Denmark's efforts to provide shortcuts to consumers identifying better options for food products.

Much of the federal government effort in the US has focused on awareness and education. For example, an initiative called MyPlate encourages healthy eating and proposes small steps towards achieving this. The MyPlate food guide icon is found on food packaging and shows a place setting with a plate divided into five food groups recommended as part of a healthy diet. These are 30 per cent grains, 40 per cent vegetables, 10 per cent fruit, 20 per cent protein, and a glass of milk/dairy on the side.

Its five further recommendations are first to choose a variety from different food groups (along the lines of the percentages above), make half your plate fruit and vegetables, make half your grains whole grains, vary your protein routine, and move to low-fat or fat-free dairy milk or yoghurt. The objective of these recommendations is to increase fruit and vegetable consumption, given that these are rich in vitamins, minerals and nutrients with clear health benefits, to encourage diversity in diet, and to shift dietary choices towards higher-quality foods.

Former First Lady Michelle Obama launched MyPlate in June 2011 at the White House, noting: 'Parents don't have the time to measure out exactly three ounces of chicken or to look up how much rice or broccoli is in a serving . . . And we're all bombarded with so many dietary messages that it's hard to find time to sort through all this information . . . But we do have time to take a look at our kids' plates. And as long as they're eating proper portions, as long as half of their meal is fruits and vegetables alongside their lean proteins, whole grains and low-fat dairy, then we're good. It's as simple as that.'

But again the onus here is on individuals and families to find time and money to support their chosen eating habits. Information is only useful in behavioural change if you have the practical ability to implement it.

In terms of US taxation policies, there is no federal or state-wide tax on sugary drinks. Recognizing the problem these drinks present, various cities have introduced a sugary drink tax. The first to introduce such a tax was Berkeley in California, with 75 per cent of voters voting in favour in November 2014. The tax was introduced in January 2015 and imposed a one cent per ounce tax on the distributors of specified sugar-sweetened beverages such as soda and sports drinks, while fruit juice, milk drinks and alcohol were excluded.

A self-reported study showed a 21 per cent drop in consumption of sugary drinks a few months after the introduction of the tax. However, it's not clear if the reduction was due to increased prices of soda, or increased awareness of the health consequences of sugary drinks. A year after the introduction, sugary drink sales had decreased by 9.6 per cent. Other places that introduced the sugary drink tax following Berkeley's experiment were: Philadelphia, San Francisco, Oakland, Albany, Boulder, Cook County, the Navajo Nation and Seattle. Simple policy steps by city and state governments have made a difference in lowering the consumption of unhealthy beverages, which is another step towards a better overall diet.

650 Per Cent Increase in Obesity: Guess Where?

You might be surprised to hear that obesity is a problem in low-income countries too. Take Ghana, where 24 per cent of the population live below the poverty line. It ranks 140th out of 189 countries on the Human Development Index, falling between a low-income and lower-middle-income economy. Historically, levels of chronic disease have been low in sub-Saharan Africa, with infectious diseases and childhood illnesses the dominant health concerns.

Over the past two decades, sub-Saharan Africa has seen a persistent rise in levels of chronic disease, specifically in non-communicable diseases like cardiovascular disease, respiratory disease, diabetes and cancer. By 2030, non-communicable diseases are projected to become the primary cause of mortality in the region, eclipsing infectious diseases, maternal and child illnesses and nutritional conditions combined.

This is also true in Ghana: in 2000, non-communicable diseases like cancer, diabetes and heart disease accounted for 29 per cent of deaths. By 2019 it was 45 per cent. This is projected to increase even further. While reduced deaths from malaria, HIV, tuberculosis and other infectious diseases is a positive development, the rise in chronic disease is linked to obesity and changes in diet.

Ghana has experienced a 650 per cent increase in obesity since 1980. Not 65 per cent. 650 per cent. In 2016, almost 43 per cent of the population was overweight or obese, putting it on a par with many Western countries. This has put a huge strain on the health care system, with 51 per cent of obese men and 27 per cent of obese women in Ghana having hypertension and requiring medical support.

The numbers have only increased with time, especially in children. In 2019, 19 per cent of Ghanaian children were overweight or obese, with the majority in the nine to eleven age group. This has been linked to what children are eating at home. Wealthier, urban Ghanaian residents are more likely to purchase supermarket food that is largely ultra-processed and imported, instead of buying local produce. Roughly 40 per cent of the population consume sugary drinks, and 67.1 per cent of the population don't consume the recommended daily allowance of fruit and vegetables.

This phenomenon is called the 'nutrition transition' – a shift in diet from traditional local foods to one dominated by foods with higher energy content (high fat and sugar) that are popular in Western countries. But in Ghana, this is not a transition away from undernutrition to overnutrition: it's an objective increase in overnutrition alongside the undernutrition crisis.

Unlike in Britain and other Western countries, high socioeconomic status is positively correlated with BMI: the richer your family is, the more likely you are to be overweight. Consuming internationally branded fast food is also seen as a display of social status, given its high relative price. While this perception is slowly shifting with social media and Hollywood movies, large body size is still associated with affluence, high social status and eating well.

The Ghanaian Ministry of Health is largely seen as successful in its efforts to halve the number of clinically underweight children and improve access to health services and clean water. Ghana was one of the first countries in Africa to meet the Millennium Development Goals in 2015, which were UN targets for countries on various development objectives. More on those soon.

But the government seems to ignore the fact that there's a chronic disease problem. In the 2020 National Health Policy, the words 'obesity' and 'overweight' did not appear once. The policy did talk about healthy eating and physical activity, but with no specific measures or policy recommendations. The 2022 National Policy for the Prevention and Control of Non-Communicable Diseases focused on tobacco and alcohol measures and how best to treat certain diseases like hypertension, diabetes and breast cancer, but again did not confront the larger issue of rising body weight.

For example, cancer is already one of the leading causes of death in Ghana. Incidence is increasing, with the most common types being breast and cervical cancer in women, and liver, prostate and lung cancer in men. Public health efforts focus on increased screening, the development of cancer registries, and funding treatment and technologies. This is within a context where the entire country has only twelve oncologists. There's no way that Ghana can currently 'treat' its way through rising cancer incidence: there needs to be a parallel shift towards addressing the main risk factors.

But diet (as well as physical activity) is largely ignored, not only within Ghana but throughout sub-Saharan Africa. Unsurprisingly, Ghana has shown no progress towards obesity targets or the reduction in chronic disease-related deaths, which continue to increase year by year. There's no high-level or political interest in these issues, and almost no money to address this agenda. As Dr Gertrude Nsorma Nyaaba says in a 2020 article: 'The donors are interested in the communicable ... TB, malaria and HIV/AIDS have a lot of funding so the health system is focusing on that because that is what donors will fund and they are prevalent.'

This is within the wider context of sub-Saharan Africa where health ministries remain focused on infectious disease causes and tend to ignore what are considered 'lifestyle' factors, such as what someone chooses to eat. If there are any policies on chronic disease risk factors, these focus on tobacco rather than diet or physical activity. The WHO also has lagged on this, with salt reduction the main measure endorsed as a target for reducing an unhealthy diet. South Africa is probably the most advanced in terms of developing policies for diet: the health ministry has proposed mandatory tagging of salt, fat, sugar and calories on food items, but no policies have been implemented yet.

Sadly, it looks as if countries like Ghana will first follow the path of the US and UK in rising obesity before having to develop policies to help regulate a better diet, instead of learning from the mistakes made in the Western world and being proactive in trying to reverse the flood of ultra-processed foods.

The Maharaja Mac

Earlier in the book, I mentioned heading to India for my fieldwork on public health. During a trip in 2005 to New Delhi, I picked up a copy of *Frontline* magazine. The cover article described the destitution, and severe undernutrition, of the tribal communities in Maharashtra. That same day I attended a presentation on cholesterol at the India International Centre. The presentation was by an official from the World Health Organization and was sponsored by the Almond Board of California in honour of World Heart Day.

Like Ghana, India is experiencing a rapid health transition with a dual burden of under- and overnutrition. A 2006 WHO study of employed Indian adults shows that the prevalence of individuals who are overweight in urban areas is high. It was estimated that 30.9 per cent of men and women were overweight. Government data indicates that about 25 per cent of urban women are either overweight or obese. As noted earlier, India already has the largest number of individuals suffering from diabetes, a comorbidity of obesity: a 2023 Lancet study estimated that 101 million people in India (roughly 11.4 per cent of the population) have diabetes and another 136 million people (or 15.3 per cent of the population) could have pre-diabetes. Even in poor areas this is a problem. A 2001 study in the urban slums of Delhi found high rates of diabetes among dwellers.

Along with the rising rates of those overweight and obese, there exist huge rates of undernutrition. India alone has 204 million individuals who are facing starvation on a daily basis. More than one third of women aged fifteen to forty-nine have a BMI of less than 18.5, indicating undernutrition. Undernutrition and poverty are concentrated among the historically marginalized groups such as scheduled castes and tribes (officially designated groups among the most disadvantaged in India), the elderly, women, and individuals with disabilities.

As I discussed in my first book, *The Battle Against Hunger*, undernutrition is a manifestation of several underlying factors such as infectious disease, drinking dirty water, lack of food security, intra-household gender inequality, and poor caring practices. According to a 2018 UNICEF report, a third of Indian children were classified as stunted, meaning that they were more than two standard deviations under international standards for height-for-age. Stunting is seen as a good measure of long-term undernutrition (reflected in short stature) while wasting is a reliable measure of acute undernutrition (reflected in being underweight).

In contrast, diet-related diseases such as obesity, diabetes, cardiovascular disease and stroke have been traditionally viewed as diseases of the upper classes, simply confined to elite groups in India. High levels of obesity are attributed to an unhealthy diet (e.g. ghee, cream, dairy, oil, deep-fried food) and inactivity, as well as a genetic predisposition, sometimes referred to as the 'thrifty genotype'. Basically, this means that populations used to surviving in a low-energy environment become thrifty at converting energy into body fat.

Despite the high prevalence of being overweight in the upper classes, in the general population, as of 2021, only 3.4 per cent of children under five were classified as overweight. Overnutrition is not yet a public health concern comparable to undernutrition.

However, this is changing. The past thirty years, especially since India's economic liberalization in the early 1990s, have resulted in rapid changes in diet and lifestyle among almost all sectors of the population. Liberalization policies have included reducing tariffs and duties on imported goods, opening up state-controlled industries to the private sector, and transforming the banking and investment sector. In terms of economic development, between 1991 and 2023, India's GDP grew on average 6.2 per cent per year, making it a fast-growing economy. One in three Indians are 'middle class', with the number expected to double by 2047.

Both in terms of demand (higher income per capita) and supply (greater access to market), the opening of India's economy has resulted in changes in dietary choice. The diet has shifted away from traditional foods (e.g. rice, ragi, wheat, lentils, vegetables) towards high-energy-density, high-fat and low-fibre diets (e.g. animal products and ultra-processed foods). If taken in sufficient quantity and diversity, the traditional diet is extremely healthy, especially when fish or chicken is included. For example, pulses and dried fish are comparatively cheap sources of protein.

When exploring the issue of nutrition, I asked women in my study area in New Delhi about their usual diet. One woman's response was telling. She said: 'All we have is rice, chapatti, dahl, we cook with mustard oil, we're not rich. We have vegetables – yellow gourd, spinach, potato, tomato, pumpkin, but we cannot afford a healthy diet.'

When I pushed her as to what she viewed as healthy, she said, 'We cannot afford sweets, ghee, milk, Pepsi,' and she added: 'I worry about my children's health, about them not getting enough energy.' It might seem surprising that she was aware of Pepsi, but there was fairly widespread knowledge of drinks such as Pepsi, Fanta, Limca and Thums Up, and companies such as McDonald's and Pizza Hut. Several other women repeated her desire for these goods as well.

The simple explanation is that poor women want to have the products that the wealthy have. This is not a new observation. Rather, the interesting phenomenon was the widespread knowledge of different brands of Western foods and products and the belief that these products were healthier and better.

Transnational companies have taken advantage of the new environment to launch targeted marketing campaigns aimed at branding. To illustrate how rapidly the branding has occurred, it is worth noting that Coca-Cola opened in India in 1993 and McDonald's in 1996. Since then, these companies have reached segments of the population that the government has been trying to reach in a concerted public health campaign for over fifty years, with messages such as boil your water, have fewer children, use iodized salt, and vaccinate your children.

Marketing campaigns of transnational companies project an image to the middle and lower classes regarding what wealthier individuals consume. The media projects that what the wealthy do is Western. If a product is labelled in English or associated with being American, even if it is expensive, consumers are satisfied to pay more because there is the belief that due to its cost, it must be a good product, and healthy. Having a label in English gives the product legitimacy.

The perception exists that wealthy individuals eat outside the home. This creates the desire to eat non-traditional foods, and can be viewed as part of the general aspiration for a better life. As a reporter remarked, 'Make good money and get cars, get houses, get servants, get meals, get diabetes.' In one advertising campaign, the MW fast food and ice cream restaurant in Chennai had a special offer: 'Overweight? Congratulations.' The promotion offered consumers discounts equivalent to 50 per cent of their weight in kilograms. The heaviest diner weighed 135 kilograms and ate for 67.5 per cent off.

Unlike the middle classes of India who can consume these Western products and eat outside the home, the slum community does not yet have the disposable income. Rather the aspiration for certain types of food exists. Among women who are illiterate, there is knowledge of Western brands and an association with these brands. As an employee of a marketing company said, 'We are dream merchants basically . . . we are writing to a [people] that cannot easily afford these things but who'd like to.'

In Western countries, eating ultra-processed foods and fast foods is linked to their cost and taste. The 'health-wealth' explanation for the occurrence of obesity in high-income countries such as Britain is that poorer people are forced to eat energy-dense processed foods due to monetary, time or structural constraints.

This is not the case in the poorer communities in Delhi. For example, during my fieldwork there, although women said that they would like to eat sweets and more energy-dense products such as dairy or meats, they did not have access to these due to cost constraints. Energy-dense products are very expensive. Traditional diet items such as green leafy vegetables, spinach, lentils and rice were not considered healthy foods or nourishing goods.

Many women held strong opinions about the world. For example, one of them asked me where I was from. When I replied 'England', she said: 'Oh yes, England is where they do not take baths and wear skimpy clothes.'

She had learned about England from the television, a ubiquitous presence in urban settings. The influence of TV and smartphones is pervasive. Almost every household I visited owned one or both. There are more mobile phones than toilets in India. Soap operas and advertisements are watched daily by families, especially children.

Many individuals, particularly children, cannot distinguish between programmes/posts and advertising on TV and social media. In fact, TV has been a negative factor in primary education efforts. One teacher who works in a state school attended by many children from poor households complained that unregulated TV in the household was causing many of the children not to complete assignments and to do poorly in school. This is now being seen in all socioeconomic groups with the ubiquitous use of mobile phones.

Being on various screens also contributes to reduced activity levels. In this particular field site, over 90 per cent of women did not work outside the home. Their day was occupied by housework, caring for children, visiting neighbours, cooking and watching TV. This was viewed as a healthy lifestyle, perhaps because it is linked to a wealthy lifestyle. When I asked one woman why she does not work and why she is not educating her teenage daughter, she said: 'When I ask my husband to work he says, "Do I not earn enough?"'

Not having to do manual labour or physically exert oneself is viewed as a sign of being better-off. While I was in the slums, I entered a tiny home. There was a bed, a little stove on the side of the house and a medium-sized TV. The woman of the household said that they had saved for many months to buy it. Physically and symbolically it was in the middle of the house and viewed as their prize possession. TV plays a central role even in poor communities.

What are the forces promoting unhealthy foods and driving the rise in obesity in India? Take McDonald's, for example, which was one of the first foreign chains to move to India; its first store was opened in 1996 in Mumbai. Onlookers noted that the store had mile-long lines and hundreds of people fighting for burgers and fries.

As of 2024, India now has 400 McDonald's, with plans to expand further. A McDonald's press release noted that India is viewed as the company's most promising new market. Because of the sensitive market, McDonald's tailored its menu to India when it first opened. There was no beef on the menu and no eggs in the mayonnaise. There were two separate burger cooking lines, one for vegetarians and one for meat-eaters. The workers in the vegetarian line wore green aprons and those in the non-vegetarian section were forbidden to cross over without showering first.

In terms of pricing, McDonald's employed a ladder strategy, with prices starting at Rs. 29, going up to Rs. 89. This broad range of prices for value meals was to ensure that most sections of customers were catered for in terms of affordability. As a McDonald's managing director in India said, 'Our clear strategy is to bring the customers in initially and to provide a range of entry-level products so that they can try new items and graduate to the higher range.'

While these prices might seem low compared to international standards, relative to local foods they are expensive. McDonald's has marketed itself as a luxury good and targets a different demographic in India, the upper and upper-middle class, compared to the West. In India, McDonald's delivers through its service McDelivery. It also caters parties.

The provision of services aimed at the upper classes can be viewed as brand creation. While McDonald's is seen as fast food in the UK, meaning it is cheap, affordable and unhealthy, in India it has come to symbolize wealth, excess, and being part of an elite. In its association with being expensive and American, it is also perceived as healthy and good for children.

In fact, outlets are called 'McDonald's Family Restaurants' as opposed to just 'McDonald's' as in other parts of the world. The restaurants provide a clean, comfortable and stress-free environment, and, especially important in India's hot climate, most outlets are air-conditioned.

In addition, as one woman noted, 'What attracts me to McDonald's? The ability to give my children a slice of America.' McDonald's has also come to be associated with certain American traits such as success, productivity and a good life. This growing acceptance corresponds to the big impact of American influence on Indian entertainment, business and diet.

However, I should note that this is changing among the upper classes, who are facing a diabetes epidemic. As a doctor in India remarked: 'I say you haven't made it in society until you get a touch of diabetes.' As the media attention to chronic diet-related disease increases, there is a general awareness of lowering intake of cholesterol, saturated fats, sugar and sodium. But because of the social aspects of food, there remains a tension between the public health messages to slim down and eat healthily, and the social context of needing to provide and consume Western products.

There is a conflicting statement: eat more but weigh less. There is also the general acceptance that obesity and chronic disease are inevitable, just another part of life. One gets old, and one gets sick. A friend who is twenty-nine and works as a reporter in Delhi recently emailed: 'I think we youngsters should also plan a Himalayan expedition (adventure cum spiritual) before we get really old and all the ailments strike us – BP, diabetes, hypertension to name a few.'

Child obesity is still not a policy priority in India, given that 35.5 per cent of children younger than five have stunted growth, and 32.1 per cent of under-fives are underweight. For this reason, the flagship programme for improving nutritional outcomes in children, the National Nutrition Mission, does not list child obesity among its key targets.

In fact, overweight children are seen as a success. As Dr Anurag Agarwal, a professor in Delhi, said: 'In India, social norms among most families lead to a positive attitude towards overweight children. We are seeing obesity even among children from lower socio-economic groups who come to government hospitals.'

The annual increase of child obesity in India is projected to be 10.8 per cent, a concerning number given the implications for adult obesity and chronic disease. In certain Indian states like Delhi, Goa and

Tamil Nadu, more than 12 per cent of adolescents are overweight. Health experts feel like the government should be doing more. Much of the effort has focused on educational campaigns such as Eat Right India, without specifying what that means. Health experts in India have pushed for warning labels on ultra-processed products, indicating that they're harmful and helping parents make better choices for their children.

In terms of going further, Kerala, one of the most advanced states in India with health metrics comparable to European countries, implemented a fat tax in 2016. This was a tax of 14.5 per cent on unhealthy products (burgers, donuts, pizza, and food from chains such as McDonald's, KFC and Pizza Hut), and aimed to steer the population towards healthier choices. It was contested politically and by businesses, but the Keralan finance minister pushed back, saying: 'The fight against fat has just begun.'

Unfortunately, the federal government cancelled this tax with its own Goods and Services Tax, and so the fat tax was only implemented for a year. Because of this, no assessment was made of the impact it might have had on health, or on raising additional revenue. The additional concern was that a fat tax needed to be implemented alongside a subsidy on fresh fruit, vegetables and unprocessed foods.

Politicians also faced anger from the Indian population over making products that were for so long inaccessible to the middle class, such as burgers and pizza, more expensive and again out of reach. Citizens wanted access to Western foods and fast-food chains, rather than government intervention restricting choice – an understandable view for those who grew up without the ability to eat what they wanted. This is the delicate line between individual freedom and public health measures to protect individuals from products that have negative health consequences.

Taking on the Ultra-Processed Food Industry

While diet is an area we each have agency over, governments through public policy definitely shape the food ecosystem we are part of in terms of what's available, what it costs, and our exposure to advertising and marketing, which is why we see such stark differences among countries. If governments know what to do, why don't they just do it?

The answer is clearly political and economic: governments choose not to do it because it entails hard choices in spending money on schools and children, regulating certain products, engaging in unpopular debates and decisions with the public over choice, pushing back against lobbying by transnational corporations, and taxing and labelling ultra-processed foods.

Countries reversing the tide such as South Korea, Japan and Denmark target their efforts at children and through schools. This can be through regular screening, nutritious school lunches, creating 'safe' food zones' around schools and making fruit, vegetables, plants and protein sources affordable and accessible to all families.

Keeping children within a healthy food environment, and within a healthy body weight, is crucial to them growing into healthy adults. We seem to be going the other way in Britain and in parts of the US: feeding children ultra-processed calories at lunch, making fast food and packaged foods the cheapest option while fruit and vegetable prices increase dramatically.

If government ministers are protected from the impact of ultra-processed foods, and obesity, because of wealth and resources, and because their children go to private schools with healthier options, then they don't feel a personal impetus to act on this issue. It requires leadership that prioritizes the broader health of the public, including a real concern on improving diet.

The challenge is taking on large multinational corporations that produce ultra-processed products and deploy questionable marketing tactics aimed at children, and – through lobbying politicians – avoid scrutiny and regulation. These companies spend millions on reaching consumers with slick advertising linking their products to wealth and success, and governments are too slow to recognize the coming tide of obesity. For example, in Ghana and India, child obesity is rising and the health impacts will only be felt in the decades to come. By then, implementing policies to regulate the marketing and branding of products will have minimal impact on that generation.

At the same time, this effort needs to be careful not to tip into stigma towards those who are overweight, and to move away from 'lookism'. There's already discrimination towards overweight and obese people, which affects employment prospects and can result in poor mental health. It's not the fault of individuals that they struggle in a calorie-dense food environment that pushes them towards unhealthy choices. It's closely tied in richer countries to poverty, low wages, and stressful employment. There is such a close connection that the president of the Royal College of Paediatrics and Child Health in Britain said that a child being overweight is a sign of child poverty. Similarly, a population being overweight is a sign of government inaction, rather than an individual lack of discipline.

4. Don't Smoke

Smoking is something that never held much interest for me personally – largely because my father (a lung cancer doctor) showed me slides, projected onto the walls of our home in Miami, of blackened lungs, hearts and livers. He was ahead of his time: if you now go to buy cigarettes, you'll see the same kinds of images on the outside of packages trying to deter people from smoking.

My dad figured out this was an effective strategy with his five kids early on. Just gross them out. I guess it worked because none of us has taken up smoking. The closest I got was holding on to a cigarette (trying to look cool) in a parking lot full of my friends in high school. I couldn't bring myself to go any further: the image of black smoke flowing through my lungs was vivid in my mind.

Each day, including most weekends, my dad would drive to Sylvester Cancer Center in downtown Miami and see patient after patient suffering from lung cancer. Almost all were smokers who regretted the decision now that they faced disease and imminent death. While his academic research was on novel treatments, including a lung cancer vaccine, he also pushed anti-smoking public initiatives.

Sebastien is an orange and white ibis and well known in the United States as the University of Miami mascot. Why an ibis? Folklore says that the ibis, a native bird of the Everglades National Park, is the last animal to take shelter before a hurricane, and the first to reappear once the storm has passed. The name of the University of Miami sports team is the Hurricanes. Sebastien dances around the sidelines of American football pitches and basketball courts, and he's the cornerstone of the multimillion-dollar merchandizing empire of the University of Miami, whose football team is always in the top ten in the US.

But Sebastien had a major problem, according to my dad. Sebastien smoked a corncob pipe. My dad was concerned that this promoted smoking to impressionable young people and was irresponsible, given the links between smoking and cancer. He saw people each day dying from taking up smoking in their teens, who had been told back in the 1940s and early 1950s that it was 'safe'. The man inside the Sebastien costume, John Routh, was also concerned and said: 'Like everything else, kids are persuaded by cartoon characters. This is not the example we want to be setting.'

Why did Sebastien even have a pipe in the first place? Some thought it represented being tough like Popeye. A University of Miami spokesperson explained: 'The bird really isn't smoking. It's just part of that Popeye nonsense. Remember how he used to smoke spinach and blow steam out of his pipe? It's steam, really. Not smoke.' After lobbying from concerned groups, Sebastien quit smoking after thirty-five years in 1992. Luckily my dad was able to see that change happen within his lifetime.

How Does Smoking Affect Our Body?

Today, it's universally accepted that smoking is bad for health. Yet, cigarettes still cause one death every five seconds around the world. Smoking accounts for almost 90 per cent of lung cancer risk in men and 80 per cent in women. But it's not just lung cancer: smoking causes a range of other health issues and harms nearly every organ in the body.

For example, smoking increases the risk of macular degeneration, which is the leading cause of blindness in those over sixty-five. Smoking also causes rheumatoid arthritis, a chronic inflammatory disease of painful swelling in the joints of the hands and feet. Smoking contributes to type 2 diabetes and poor blood flow to legs and feet. It causes narrowing of the blood vessels, including those that supply blood to the penis, resulting in erectile dysfunction.

Ectopic pregnancy, when a fertilized egg implants somewhere other than the uterus, is more likely in smokers and can be life-threatening. Smoking during pregnancy also causes birth defects like orofacial clefts when a baby's lips and mouth don't form properly.

Smoking is linked to hip fractures because it causes the loss of bone density at a faster rate than for non-smokers. It's also linked to colorectal cancer, the second-leading cause of cancer deaths in the United States. Smoking is a major cause of tooth loss in adults through causing periodontitis, a gum infection that destroys the bone that supports teeth.

Back in September 1950, Richard Doll and Tony Bradford Hill published a report on smoking and carcinoma of the lung which stated that smoking was causing lung cancer. When pushback from industry came that the data wasn't clear, the two researchers did a major cohort study (a type of health study where a group of people are followed over time to track specific behaviours) of 34,000 male British physicians to record their smoking status. The study showed that smokers were dying at a higher rate than non-smokers, and that lung cancer couldn't be caused by general air pollution.

While Doll and Bradford Hill were conducting large epidemiological studies in Britain, across the pond at Washington University School of Medicine, researcher Adele Croninger wanted to see the impact of cigarettes more directly on cells. Croninger, with her colleagues, did an experiment showing that tumours could be triggered by painting tar found in cigarette smoke onto the shaved backs of mice.

Croninger's work showed clearly that tobacco was dangerous to health. This finding was covered broadly by the media and caused stock prices of American cigarette manufacturers to plummet. But industry pressure meant it would still take until 1964 for the US Surgeon General to point to smoking as a cause of lung cancer in men.

What's the exact biological mechanism that makes smoking harmful? Tobacco smoke is a toxic mix of more than 7,000 chemicals and compounds. These enter the body through the lungs and then spread across every organ and cell. The smoke harms our DNA, as well as the cells that repair DNA damage, causing inflammation and cell damage. The build-up of these DNA mutations over time leads to cancer and also reduces our body's ability to fight cancer. In short, smoking cigarettes shortens our life.

Playing Trumpet in Smoky Jazz Clubs

Fortunately, rates of smoking continue to decline in most parts of the world, driven not only by scientific research but also by passionate individuals. A key figure in Britain's tobacco story is a fascinating guy called Roy Castle. Roy could tap dance faster than anyone in the world (twenty-four taps per second). He also could play the same tune on forty-three different instruments in four minutes. The son of a railwayman, he was born in 1932 in Yorkshire and had a diverse arts career in music, stage and film as well as TV presenting. He became a household name as the longest-running presenter of the children's series *Record Breakers*.

But if you google Roy Castle's name, that's not what appears first. It's the Roy Castle Lung Cancer Foundation, which is the only British charity solely dedicated to defeating lung cancer. Castle was diagnosed with lung cancer in 1992, the same year he was awarded an OBE in recognition of his talents and services to charity. He was told that he would likely die of the disease within six months.

Castle was shocked by this diagnosis because he had never smoked a cigarette in his life. In fact, even when others were smoking in the years before the link to cancer was found, he stayed away from tobacco, thinking it was a disgusting habit. But Castle believed he had damaged his lungs from years of playing trumpet in smoky jazz clubs early in his career. In a documentary about his disease, he said: 'Whilst playing the trumpet in smoky rooms I inhaled great gulps of air – you have to fill your lungs.'

Castle was one of the first to talk about secondary or passive smoking. His widow Fiona said in an interview in 2010, 'When Roy was first diagnosed people were very disparaging about the prospect of passive smoking doing any harm.' She continued: 'The specialist who had diagnosed Roy said his condition had to come from passive smoking – up until then no one would have believed that passive smoking was a killer.'

After receiving his diagnosis, Castle decided to do all he could to raise awareness about passive smoking and lung cancer before he died.

Fortunately, his time alive was extended due to a mix of chemotherapy and radiotherapy. Despite his deteriorating health, he carried out a high-profile 'Tour of Hope' to raise funds for his Lung Cancer Foundation, and he pushed for standards to protect people from the effect of others' smoking. For example, he inspired the Roy Castle Clean Air Award to be given to smoke-free venues, like restaurants and cafes, which voluntarily agreed to stop indoor smoking. He also fundraised for the International Roy Castle Lung Cancer Research Centre in Liverpool.

He died two days after his sixty-second birthday, in 1994, having brought national attention to the dangers of cigarette smoke. Fiona Castle continued campaigning for a smoking ban in indoor public spaces, which was finally passed in 2004 in the Republic of Ireland, in 2006 in Scotland and in 2007 in England and Wales. His biggest achievement, continued by Fiona, was that 'Roy made people aware and take notice.'

In Britain and parts of the United States, where cigarette smoking rates have reduced dramatically in recent decades, it's easy to be dismissive of this issue and to forget how far we've come. It's the classic story of public health: if we do our jobs well, people don't notice our influence; if we do our jobs poorly, people die.

The UK's success contrasts with India and China, which continue to see increases in cigarette consumption. With reduced sales in some countries due to public health measures, multinational tobacco companies have simply shifted to a different part of the world to grow their business and stay profitable. Deaths caused by smoking around the world are still a massive issue, and so we would do well to think more deeply about the success of public health measures to tackle smoking in places like the UK as well as in certain parts of the United States like New York City.

Making It Expensive and Difficult to Smoke

Smoking peaked in Britain in 1948, with 82 per cent of men and 41 per cent of women smoking. But concerns started to be raised about the impact of cigarettes on health, triggered by Doll and Bradford Hill's research linking smoking and lung cancer. In response, the industry pushed back, saying that it was uncertain and ambiguous whether tobacco was truly harmful. Confusion manufactured by industry led to significant delays in people recognizing the harms of tobacco.

It was only in the 1960s that the UK's Royal College of Physicians alerted the world to the dangers of tobacco. Derek Yach, a prominent anti-tobacco activist, said: 'Within months many people started quitting. This was not because of taxes or legislation. It was because of the debate around the dangers of tobacco.'

Slowly, thanks to the efforts of people like Roy and Fiona Castle, the public perception around smoking shifted, and there was a push for governments to do more to keep their populations safe from this health risk. Here are a few examples of what Britain led on. First, on making it more difficult to buy tobacco through taxation and raising the minimum age. The price of tobacco in the UK increased by 80.2 per cent between 2003 and 2013. By 2014, a twenty-a-day smoker of a premium brand would have spent about £2,900 a year on cigarettes. By 2017, the cheapest packet of cigarettes cost £8.82. In October 2007, the minimum age for legal purchase of tobacco increased from sixteen to eighteen in England, Scotland and Wales.

Second, Britain has led on making it more difficult to smoke around other people. In July 2007 the smoking ban was introduced in England, making it illegal to smoke in almost all enclosed and substantially enclosed public places and workplaces. Scotland had already introduced the ban in March 2006, with Wales and Northern Ireland following in April 2007. In October 2015, it became illegal to smoke in a car (or other vehicle) with anyone under eighteen, to protect children and young people from second-hand smoke.

Third, Britain pushed back against the advertising and marketing efforts of large tobacco companies to target youth. In March 2015, the House of Commons voted overwhelmingly in support of plain cigarette packing without branding. Promotional words like 'lite', 'natural' and 'organic' were not allowed to be used, and health warnings had to cover 65 per cent of the front and back of the packaging of cigarettes and rolling tobacco.

Soon after, shops were banned from selling small bags of rolling tobacco and ten-packs of cigarettes, as part of a move to make smoking more expensive, and thus unattractive and inaccessible, for young people. Packets of ten were referred to as 'kiddy packs' because they were more affordable to buy from pocket money, compared to minimum pack sizes of twenty. In May 2020, menthol cigarettes with a minty flavour were banned in Britain, several years after fruit-flavoured cigarettes, with flavours like vanilla, spices and sweets, were made illegal. These flavoured cigarettes were falsely seen as less harmful than non-flavoured cigarettes and were often the route into teens taking up smoking. The ban aimed to reduce youth uptake of smoking.

Fourth, Britain invested in free medical cessation support through the NHS, using the community outreach of pharmacies. This meant that those wanting to stop could approach a linked pharmacy and get behavioural support as well as nicotine replacement therapy. This could be through skin patches, chewing gum, tablets or sprays, or even through using vapes, as I'll talk about soon.

Have these measures worked in reducing the number of people smoking regularly, or taking up smoking? In the UK in 2007, 25 per cent of all British adults smoked. In 2015, 18 per cent. In 2021, roughly 13 per cent of adults smoked cigarettes, which is the lowest proportion of smokers for decades. The numbers continue to fall. This is true also of young people. In 1982, 53 per cent of eleven- to fifteen-year-olds had tried smoking; this was down to 16 per cent in 2018.

Smokers under eighteen are a major focus, both for industry trying to sell them products and for public health authorities. 'Two-thirds of smokers start before the age of eighteen, so it is vital that everything is done to put tobacco out of sight to protect future generations,' said Hazel Cheeseman, policy director at Action on Smoking and Health. Eighty per cent of smokers start before the age of twenty, and 40 per cent start smoking regularly before the age of sixteen. Much of this is linked to living with parents or siblings who smoke: among regular smokers, 98 per cent have friends who smoke and 78 per cent have family members who smoke.

Which of the tobacco policies introduced have been the most effective? A study in 2012 in the *European Journal of Public Health* used a 'SimSmoke' model to examine the effect of tobacco control policies over time on smoking initiation and cessation in Britain. It looked at the effect of policies between 1998 and 2009 on smoking prevalence, which had reduced by 23 per cent.

About 30 per cent of the reduction in prevalence by 2009 was explained by price increases, whereas smoke-free air and cessation treatment policies each accounted for roughly 20 per cent of the reduction. 'Public health' approaches, such as tax increases and smoke-free air laws, were shown to primarily increase quit attempts, while treatment policies suggested by the 'medical' model made those quit attempts more successful. The study estimated that 210,000 premature deaths would be averted by the year 2040 because of policies implemented between 1998 and 2010. These didn't include the tens of thousands of deaths averted because of reduced second-hand smoke exposure.

In 2017, Japanese public health experts reflected on the political dimensions of the British success model. 'One of the key determinants for the UK's success was the government's leadership and commitment to legislate control policies, accompanied by robust scientific evidence, and strong support from health-care professionals to improve population health.'

While Japan is a model for healthy ageing and good nutrition, it looks to the British policy model when it comes to managing tobacco. This shows how each part of the world can learn from another, and that governments are constantly learning international best practice.

In 2017, the Japanese Ministry of Health, Labour and Welfare tried to introduce a smoking ban in public indoor places with the goal of a smoke-free 2020 Tokyo Olympics. But the policy was fiercely opposed by the tobacco industry and retailers selling tobacco products, both concerned about maintaining their revenue.

At the time, the Japanese Ministry of Finance owned about a third of Japan Tobacco, which created inter-ministerial tension on how best to manage this concern: whether through awareness, education and voluntary participation, or legally imposed government mandates.

Fortunately the Japanese prime minister at the time, Shinzo Abe, banned indoor smoking and the country's smoking rates have continued to decline. In 2001, 48.4 per cent of men smoked, which was reduced to 25.4 per cent in 2022, while the female smoking rate was 7.7 per cent that year.

Cigarettes Are Eating You Alive

In 2006, approximately 7,000 adults died from smoking-related illnesses in New York City. This was 14 per cent of all adult deaths, or one in seven people. Observing that the prevalence of smoking among adults (22 per cent) hadn't declined in a decade, the city health department came to the conclusion that more action was needed by government.

Years earlier, in 2002, a Five Point Plan for tobacco was enacted, which had five pillars: an increase in the price of cigarettes; comprehensive smoke-free air legislation; access to cessation support; mass media campaigns on the negative health outcomes of smoking and second-hand smoke exposure; and finally, evaluation after a year of key interventions to assess impact. Sound familiar to the British approach?

The first step in 2002 was increasing the tax on cigarettes, as previous studies had shown that this reduced new young smokers who were sensitive to price. Officials raised the price of a pack of cigarettes from $5.20 to $11, which consisted of $6.86 tax. Soon after, comprehensive smoke-free legislation was passed, which banned smoking in workplaces, including more than 20,000 restaurants and bars. Evaluation showed that 95 per cent of venues complied, including hospitality, and that there was no negative impact on sales or employment.

The success and popularity of this measure triggered the expansion in 2009 to banning smoking within fifteen feet of hospitals, health care centres and care homes. In 2011, outdoor smoking was banned in all of the city's 1,700 public parks, beaches and pedestrian areas, including around Times Square. Linked to these policies was messaging to the public on why restrictions had come into place, and the benefits it would bring to public health and the city. These measures had a real impact: evaluation a year later showed a two thirds decrease in smoking in parks, as well as reduction in smoking-related litter in parks and on beaches.

Linked to these regulation efforts was awareness-raising on the dangers of tobacco. Data from Australia indicated that campaigns that showed the health effects of smoking seemed to be the most effective at changing behaviour. In 2006, the health department started producing emotionally provocative material based on the stories of real people and families.

For example, there was the campaign 'Cigarettes Are Eating You Alive', which showed cigarette smoke entering the body next to images of organ damage in adults and children. Other advertisements such as 'Suffering Every Minute' and 'Pain' extended the messaging to the effect on family members of second-hand smoke. Each advert ended with the line 'Quit Smoking Today' and an invitation to call 311, the city's information line. From there people would be connected to the New York State Smokers' Quitline and provided with free nicotine replacement therapy.

How effective were these interventions? Adult smoking rates decreased from 21 per cent in 2002 to 15.5 per cent in 2012. Smoking among state high school students decreased from 52 per cent in 2001 to 8.5 per cent in 2011. Between 2002 and 2012, the average number of cigarettes smoked by daily smokers decreased from 14.6 to 11.8 per day. Annual calls to 311 for help quitting smoking increased from 43,000 in 2005 to 164,000 in 2008 when the campaign was in full swing. Future projections estimate that nearly 50,000 people who quit smoking in those years are predicted to avoid premature death before seventy-five. In 2010, life expectancy at birth in New York City reached 80.9, three years higher than in 2001, and a bigger gain than in other parts of the United States.

While the campaign cost roughly $10 million to run each year, the revenue generated from tobacco taxes since 2003 is more than $1 billion. Based on the success of that campaign, the battle against tobacco continued. In 2013, New York City became the first city to raise the minimum sale age for tobacco, including vapes, from eighteen to twenty-one years old. It continues efforts to keep those gains in the interest of broader population public health.

The New York City approach is remarkably similar to the UK's. That's because there is a widely understood toolkit on how to tackle smoking at a population level, and proven interventions and steps. I could have also talked about New Zealand, the Netherlands, Brazil, or a number of other countries, and the story would have been the same. But this progress isn't universal. Some parts of the world are still struggling to reduce tobacco consumption.

Regulation Only Works If It's Enforced

India is the second-largest tobacco consumer with 267 million users, and the third-largest tobacco producer in the world. In 2020, tobacco was responsible for more than 1.2 million deaths, and contributed to an estimated 27 per cent of cancers in the country.

While tobacco use has been recognized as a problem since the 1960s, it was the Framework Convention on Tobacco Control which spurred global action. This convention was agreed by all World Health Organization member states in 2005. It committed governments to implementing key measures to limit demand for tobacco, to support cessation, to regulate tobacco products and to limit the negative influence of the tobacco industry. Key control strategies included pricing and taxation measures, smoke-free air policies, appropriate labelling of products (including health warnings), awareness-raising on the negative impacts of tobacco, banning of marketing and sales to youth, and support for alternative employment strategies for tobacco workers. In short, it was a toolkit for governments to reduce the prevalence of smoking.

The Indian government soon after created the National Tobacco Control Programme, which committed to those measures. The key policy measures have been referred to as MPOWER:

Monitor tobacco use and prevention policies;
Protect people from tobacco smoke;

Offer help to quit tobacco use;
Warn about the dangers of tobacco;
Enforce bans on tobacco advertising, promotion and sponsorship;
Raise taxes on tobacco.

Progress on each of these measures must be reported at the national level to the WHO as part of its monitoring of the impact of the Framework Convention on Tobacco Control.

The Indian government seems to have met several of these targets, such as health warnings on cigarette packs and developing cessation programmes. They've made progress on monitoring prevalence, implementing advertising bans, enforcing smoke-free environments, and introducing taxation. Roughly 57.6 per cent of the total price of a pack of twenty cigarettes is tax.

But there have been challenges in the Indian context and a gap between stated policy ambitions and the reality on the ground. In 2022, almost twenty years after the Framework Convention, tobacco use had declined relative to before but remained at an absolute high level. India has a federal government, which means that budget and policy decisions are devolved to individual state governments, which have their own chief minister and plans. This is reflected in variability in tobacco use, from 9.7 per cent in Goa to 64.5 per cent in the north-eastern state of Tripura. Tobacco use is higher among men (42.4 per cent) than women (14.2 per cent), and higher in rural areas and among those with lower socioeconomic status and lower levels of education.

Why is reducing tobacco use proving such a challenge? Several factors help explain this. One is that implementation on the ground isn't working. For example, in 2003, India banned the sale of tobacco products to anyone under eighteen, yet these laws are ignored at the neighbourhood level. Studies have shown easy access in local shops for adolescents, with the average age of starting to buy tobacco eleven to twelve years old.

Another challenge is poverty and low education levels: poor and less educated people are less aware of the health risks of tobacco, more likely to find themselves around others who use tobacco, and more likely to have a sense of fatalism, i.e. higher risk-taking behaviour and less concern for the consequences, given other stresses in their lives. Forty-six per cent of those who smoked were illiterate in a 2018 survey.

In addition, while the focus in Britain and the United States has been on cigarette smoking (or, in India, on *bidis*, which are hand-rolled cigarettes), smokeless tobacco use (chewing, sucking, sniffing tobacco products) is much higher among Indians. Roughly 100 million people aged fifteen and older smoke tobacco, while around 200 million people in the same age group use smokeless tobacco. It's a unique problem to India, which accounts for almost 75 per cent of the global burden of disease attributable to smokeless tobacco. Just focusing on cigarette smoking (by raising taxes on cigarettes and creating smoke-free air policies) doesn't address a large chunk of the tobacco use in India.

Another factor is that tobacco use rates among women, while low already, have not declined as rapidly as for men. A factor here is the stigma faced by women if they admit that they use tobacco and come forward for medical cessation support. This gender dynamic isn't visible in the British or American context, and it plays into stereotypes of what a 'good woman' is in India. But stigma isn't helpful in public health, and the example of tobacco in India shows the limits of public health intervention when individuals don't feel comfortable admitting to their loved ones or health professionals that they are taking part in a risky behaviour.

Despite the challenges outlined above, the Indian government continues to press on this issue. Parliament has discussed banning sales of loose cigarettes and doing away with smoking zones in airports and other public buildings. It is also considering increasing tax from 53 per cent on cigarettes and 64 per cent on smokeless tobacco to 75 per cent.

The Indian example shows, in comparison to Britain or New York City, that national context matters, and that even with high-level political leadership to create policies on an issue, whether those policies are implemented depends on daily buy-in at the community level, as well as awareness of barriers. A major barrier in India is illiteracy and low levels of education: making progress on tobacco also requires a joint effort to improve overall education and literacy, especially in rural parts of the country. A socioeconomic gradient is also clear with tobacco: it is linked to poverty.

Where Even Doctors Smoke

Yet illiteracy and low levels of education don't explain every country's situation. Take China: a local newspaper estimated that nearly 60 per cent of male doctors in China are smokers, the highest in the world, compared to 3.3 per cent in the United States and 6.8 per cent in Britain. Most would consider medical doctors one of the most highly educated groups, especially on health topics.

One surgeon in Kunming said: 'Smoking is such a big part of being a doctor here. The director of our hospital smokes. The party-secretary smokes. The chair of my department smokes. And whenever I walk into the duty office, most of my colleagues are smoking. And to tell you the truth, with such a pressure-filled job, smoking is extremely helpful, at times soothing, at times energizing, at times helping me focus my attention when preparing for a complex surgery or facing a stack of paperwork at 10.30 at night.'

When the health ministry banned indoor smoking in hospitals, doctors were found hiding in the toilets of wards smoking away. One patient said: 'If I know doctors smoke, why would I quit?' Wang Chen, head of the Beijing Chaoyang Hospital, commented: 'Many other doctors think smoking is a habit and not an illness.'

If even doctors are smoking, it's clear that China has a tobacco problem. The country is the largest producer and consumer of tobacco in the world, with 26.6 per cent of people over fifteen smoking regularly. More than 300 million people in China smoke, which is nearly one third of the world's total. Roughly one in every three cigarettes smoked in the world is smoked in China, and over 700 million non-smokers in China, including 180 million children, are exposed to second-hand smoke on a weekly basis.

This translates into a major health burden of more than 1 million people dying each year in China from diseases linked to tobacco use, and an additional 1 million dying from the effects of second-hand smoke. This is roughly 6,000 deaths a day from a preventable cause. The government is aware of the impact that the high levels of tobacco consumption are having on population health and reduced life expectancy.

In 2005, China signed on to the Framework Convention on Tobacco Control alongside other World Health Organization member states like India. This was followed by a decade of small, incremental changes. In October 2016, President Xi Jinping announced the 'Healthy China 2030 Blueprint', a national strategy for improving public health, including the target of a decrease in the rate of smoking by 20 per cent by 2030.

While China does not have one comprehensive tobacco control law, several national laws and regulations cover tobacco. For example, smoking is banned in at least twenty-eight types of indoor public places, including medical facilities, restaurants, bars and most public transportation. However, there is no law to punish those who violate the smoking ban. It's more advisory than legally enforceable.

Advertising of tobacco is banned in films, on TV and radio, and in newspapers and magazines. However, online advertising, tobacco sponsorship and point of sale advertising are permitted. Text-only warnings are required but only cover a maximum of 30 per cent of the pack, and they are created by tobacco companies themselves.

It's a start, but much more could be done to strengthen key policy levers to reduce demand for tobacco and help smokers quit. For example, smoke-free air policies are the least implemented measure nationally. A modelling study estimated that smoke-free policies alone could reduce the rate of smoking by almost 3 per cent by 2030, which would be almost 38 million fewer smokers in China than if nothing was done.

Tobacco taxes have also remained low, and the government has been reluctant to increase the cost of a pack of cigarettes. This impacts demand: several studies have found that a 10 per cent increase in real cigarette prices in China reduces total cigarette consumption by 5 per cent. If China were to implement the full MPOWER package by 2030, smoking would be reduced by an estimated 17.4 per cent.

Why doesn't the Chinese government implement policies, and enforce them? Because it's a key revenue stream, with tobacco sales generating 7–10 per cent of government revenue. China produces 42 per cent of the world's cigarettes. The China National Tobacco Corporation is, by sales, the largest single manufacturer of tobacco products in the world and has a monopoly in mainland China. Yang Gonghuan, deputy director of the National Centre of Disease Control in China, said at a conference that the tobacco industry generates a lot of tax and employs a large number of people, which is why progress in tobacco control is painfully slow.

From a distance, it seems like the health ministry in the Chinese government is aware of the detrimental impacts of tobacco in the population, as well as the commitments made to the Framework Convention on Tobacco Control. However, there are real barriers – namely, lack of political will at the highest level in government – to take substantial steps to reduce tobacco consumption. This is because instead of reducing private profits from tobacco, as in the case of the US and UK governments, reduced cigarette sales would also decrease the revenue of the government itself.

In addition, tobacco control policies are being implemented within a cultural context of smoking as a 'social activity'. But, as recent surveys in Chinese urban settings have shown, popularity for smoke-free air policies, and for more medical support for cessation, has grown with time and with specific cities implementing stricter policies.

For example, the city of Shanghai has had a sustained campaign for no smoking either indoors or outdoors, moving towards a tobacco-free environment with heavy fines for rule-breakers. This has successfully reduced the rate of adult smoking to just under 20 per cent, and smoking in no-tobacco zones to 12 per cent. Culture isn't a static concept; it ebbs and flows as people in China look to cities like Shanghai and wonder what their cities and communities could look like if more was done to limit the impacts of smoking, including second-hand smoke. Change looks feasible. It's been done elsewhere in their country.

Taking on the Tobacco Industry

Tobacco control is probably the clearest (and one of the simplest) public health challenges to overcome, largely because there is consensus that smoking is harmful to health in any amount, and strong evidence that government action works to reduce smoking rates. In addition, decades of research have shown the dangers of secondhand smoke, and why we can't leave this issue to individual discretion completely. The UK government over the past few decades has provided a template on the combination of public policy and medical interventions that is effective in reducing smoking rates. What are the lessons for the world?

First, make it harder to smoke through taxation, minimum purchase age, bans on 'kiddy packs', and ensuring cigarettes aren't visible in shops. Second, reduce the ability of people to be able to smoke in social or work settings. Third, counter the marketing and advertising of tobacco companies which are selling a dangerous product that literally kills. Fourth, support those wanting to quit through offering free community-level comprehensive cessation services without stigma or judgement. These types of therapies have been shown to nearly double the chances of quitting smoking without relapsing.

These are the four proven policy steps that reduce smoking rates through making it harder to smoke, and easier to quit. Britain has implemented these effectively, and so have several cities like New York and many countries such as New Zealand and Switzerland. It seems obvious that this is an easy way to live longer for individuals, but also an easy way to improve overall population health, which begs the question why more countries aren't taking more proactive steps in this direction. Most are on the journey, just not as advanced as Britain is.

It's a political decision not to adopt and implement these policies, and this is often influenced by lobbying from tobacco companies or tobacco sales being a major contributor to state revenue, as in China. The profit interest here runs completely counter to public health's objective to improve people's health and wellbeing.

This isn't like food manufacturers or pharmaceutical companies, which create and manufacture products that have arguably beneficial effects on health and wellbeing. The tobacco industry directly kills people. In markets where they've been heavily regulated, they've just switched their focus to e-cigarettes, which carry less harm than regular cigarettes, but come with their own negative health impact.

Vaping: How Bad Is It Really?

My dad didn't live to see the start of the vaping (e-cigarette) epidemic and two University of Miami students advocating for giving Sebastien a Juul, a popular e-cigarette used to vape.

E-cigarettes are electronic devices that heat a liquid (which usually contains nicotine, flavourings and other chemicals) and produce an aerosol, and using one is called 'vaping'. Some e-cigarettes look like regular cigarettes, cigars, pipes, USB flash drives, pens and other everyday items.

Juul is the top-selling e-cigarette brand in many countries including the US. It is shaped like a USB flash drive and has a high level of nicotine. A single Juul pod contains as much nicotine as a pack of twenty regular cigarettes. It comes in flavours like cotton candy, mango and crème brûlée, and while heavily used by young people, roughly two thirds of Juul users aged fifteen to twenty-four don't even know that the product contains nicotine.

Returning to Sebastien, a petition launched in 2018 reads: 'We, the undersigned students of the University of Miami, advocate the Board of Directors to let our school mascot, Sebastien the Ibis, hit the JUUL.' But wasn't Sebastien happy enough just being a bird without a pipe? One of the students behind the petition, Alex Castillo, disagreed: 'That'd be so lame. I would be so ashamed to go to a school with a mascot that's just a bird. But a smoking bird? That's dope.'

This push towards vaping is one that the industry has welcomed, because it creates a new stream of revenue. British American Tobacco and Philip Morris have seen the global e-cigarette market as major places of profit, given that it's estimated to be worth $22 billion. In the UK, Philip Morris Ltd invested £15 million into the expansion of VPZ, the UK's largest chain of vape stores, and has begun to craft its own e-cigarettes. In 2018, British American Tobacco bought Highendsmoke, the largest chain of vape stores in Germany.

Since 2021 in Britain, children between eleven and seventeen years old have been more likely to vape (7.2 per cent) than smoke (5.1 per cent), while in adults, the vaping and smoking rates have been roughly the same. Roughly 11.5 per cent of those vaping have never smoked cigarettes, which indicates it's a new market for companies to target. It appeals to youth because it's much cheaper than cigarettes. Smoking is expensive in Britain, given the high percentage of tax put on it (as discussed earlier) and the strict regulations on sales, advertising and marketing.

Industry's marketing efforts are working: the use of e-cigarettes among adults in Britain tripled between 2012 and 2014, from an estimated 700,000 to 2.1 million. In March 2023, the proportion of children trying vaping had grown by 50 per cent in just a year, from one in thirteen to one in nine. NHS figures for 2021 show that 9 per cent of all eleven- to fifteen-year-olds use e-cigarettes regularly, up from 6 per cent in 2018. Half of all children report seeing e-cigarettes being promoted in shops, while nearly a third report e-cigarette promotion online. It is illegal to sell e-cigarettes to children under eighteen in the UK but this has been poorly enforced. Until recently there's been a loophole in that giving vapes out to children for free has been legal.

In the US, similar targeting to young people has happened through, for example, e-cigarette companies offering scholarships (from $250 to $5,000, some with no minimum age for applying) that involve students writing essays on topics like the potential benefits of vaping. Companies like Juul also pay for campaigns on social media, including YouTube and Instagram, promoting vapes as part of a fun, free and sexy life. These campaigns were found to be highly correlated with retail sales. E-cigarette companies have also sponsored music festivals and events featuring vaping lounges, free samples of new flavours, performances from trending artists and interactive social media stations to expand the reach.

These companies have also marketed kid-friendly flavours such as gummy bear and cotton candy, and even designed the vaping devices themselves to look like candy. A study of teens in the US found that appealing flavours was the main reason that they wanted to try vaping. Just ask any high schoolers you know about what they smell when they go into school bathrooms: it's probably the latest vape flavours. In terms of companies' marketing behaviour and the range of products being sold, it's clear that the target market by industry is those under eighteen.

The message towards vaping is more ambiguous from a public health perspective than towards cigarettes, which are seen as simply bad. E-cigarette aerosol is not harmless 'water vapour'. The aerosol contains nicotine; ultra-fine particles that go deep into the lungs; cancer-causing chemicals; flavourings such as diacetyl, a chemical linked to serious lung disease; and heavy metals such as nickel, tin and lead. The Royal College of Paediatrics and Child Health has talked about the dangers of vaping for lung development. The WHO has warned about the impact of vaping on child brain development as well as the adverse health effects of nicotine. Vaping can often be a gateway to smoking: the Irish Health Research Board found that teenagers who use e-cigarettes are three to five times more likely to start smoking cigarettes than those who never vaped.

Grace Kearney, who works with young people through the Bridgeways Family Resource Centre, is concerned about the harms that vapes bring. 'It's not a problem, it's an epidemic and it is ruining young people's lives. I have never seen a craze like this, it is so accessible, so cheap. It's completely geared for young people, with all the different flavours. I feel that parents and kids don't realize the impact these highly addictive vapes are having on their lungs, their capacity and their concentration because they are so addicted to them. A disposable vape is only a little wider than a pen, you can just put it down your bra or you can put it at the side of your shorts. It is so easy to transport and it is so instant.'

From a health perspective, it's clearly better not to vape. But if the choice is cigarettes or vaping, vaping is the less harmful choice. In April 2023, the UK launched the first national 'swap to stop' scheme aimed at encouraging smokers to swap cigarettes for vapes. Those wanting to quit smoking are provided a vape starter kit alongside behavioural support, which is seen as a key component of the UK's ambition to be smoke-free by 2030.

But again, industry motives for profit and increasing sales conflict with the government's objective to use vaping in a narrow way as a smoking cessation tool. Vapes are being deliberately marketed to younger people through online promotion on TikTok, Instagram and Snapchat and through creating products that are cheap, colourful and with child-like flavours such as bubblegum.

If you're a parent or family member of a child who vapes, it's worth pointing out to them that they largely do contain nicotine, are likely bad for their lungs and health, and when the concrete research on health harms emerges in the years to come, they'll have been the guinea pigs. Like the smokers in the 1950s and 60s.

The cat-and-mouse policy game between industry and government continues with a new product. In May 2023, the UK government announced new policies to close the loophole allowing the vaping industry to give free samples of vapes to children in England. It also announced increased education and dedicated school police liaison officers to keep illegal vapes out of schools, and stricter rules around the sale of nicotine-free vapes to under-eighteens, as well as fines for shops selling illicit vapes.

Returning to the University of Miami and Sebastien, the non-smoking ibis mascot, the students' efforts to grant him a vape were denied by the board. Instead, staff and administrators organized the first 'Canes Against Vaping Week' ('Canes' is short for Hurricanes, the team name for the University of Miami) in August 2019 to raise awareness about the health impacts of vaping. The university also enforced a strict no smoking policy on campus, which includes e-cigarettes, with a $250 fine.

Fortunately, vaping rates among students at the university are decreasing, likely due to more awareness of the negative health impacts as well as policies banning smoking on campus. As Whitney Platzer O'Regan, assistant dean of students, said: 'It really comes down to thinking twice about what substances you are putting into your body and making an educated decision on what effects it may have.'

How has the University of Miami managed such strict no smoking and no vaping policies? Political leadership is essential. The university was led from 2001 to 2015 by Donna Shalala, who was my mentor when I was an undergraduate studying medicine, and who continued to support and advise me in the years after. From 1993 to 2001, she was US Secretary of Health and Human Services in the Clinton administration, making her the longest-serving health secretary ever. Tobacco regulation was one of the priorities during her tenure, and this individual interest in public health as well as her long-running governmental leadership on this topic informed her presidency at the University of Miami.

The next UM president was Dr Julio Frenk, who was Minister of Health in Mexico from 2000 to 2006 and later Dean of the Harvard School of Public Health. He brought his expertise in this area to inform his university leadership, including during the pandemic.

I caught up with Julio when I was back home in Miami one Christmas. Over tea in the garden of his university home in Coral Gables, he recounted the efforts he made during the pandemic to set up a test and trace system within the university, to support students isolating and to promote public health policies within a state led by a governor who wanted to pretend that the disease was a hoax. We had a fascinating discussion until a brown lizard fell out of a tree into my teacup, then scurried off. I felt lucky it wasn't a larger iguana. That's Miami for you. You'll be happy to know that under both Julio and Donna's leadership, Sebastien remained cigarette-, pipe- and vape-free. And under my dad's influence, so have I.

Not smoking is one of the simplest ways to live a longer and healthier life. While cigarettes are legal to buy and smoking is an individual decision, a population's smoking rates are heavily shaped by the policies put in place by governments to make it harder to smoke and easier to quit.

5.   Struggling to Cope

So you don't smoke, you exercise pretty regularly and your diet is balanced. But there's more to the story of living longer. Stress is implicated in being more vulnerable to getting sick, and the past few years haven't been easy, dealing with the fall-out of the pandemic. One of the things I've found hardest to manage is the public abuse and threats that come from doing public-facing work. Usually these are restricted to the virtual world, and easy enough to tune out. I just have to stay off social media, ignore newspaper commentary and focus on my real day-to-day routine in the university. But every once in a while, it's impossible to block out.

One day in August 2023 when I was working in my office, a notification popped up on the right-hand corner of my laptop screen. It was Marie, down in reception, letting me know that a package had arrived. I assumed it was probably a newly published book, or an academic report. I get sent quite a few books, and I was expecting one from a friend, Dr Amir Khan, who had just finished his first novel. I popped down to pick it up and make myself a cup of tea.

The package was sitting on Marie's desk, and I asked about her next holiday while opening it. When I looked down my hands were covered in a clay-coloured powder and there was a typed note in CAPS. Another death threat. I've experienced quite a few since the start of the pandemic, largely from anti-vaxxers. I ran to the nearest bathroom to scrub my hands free of any particles. I returned to reception and asked Marie, 'Should we call uni security?'

Marie and I had been through this before. She said, 'Sure, I'll take care of it, go make your tea.' I went to the kitchen and looked out of the window as the kettle boiled: the city was in full swing with the annual festival and bustling with life. My back pocket buzzed and it was Marie calling. 'Devi, we need to evacuate the building. The police are on their way.'

The next few hours passed by in a whirlwind. The police arrived and cleared the building. They were worried that the powder could be either explosive or toxic. Hundreds of people left the area without being told much. I gave my statement about coming down to reception, opening the package, finding the powder, and the history of these threats. Soon after, a team arrived dressed head to toe in hazmat suits. Fire engines were by now blocking the road. An ambulance pulled up and the police pointed the crew in my direction. My main feeling was guilt that all these people's work was disrupted because one person was angry that I spoke about vaccines.

The paramedic then took some vitals to ensure I wasn't affected by the powder. He talked to me in a friendly way, probably to make the entire situation less bizarre. 'How do you become a professor? What's the track?' I gave some drawn-out answer about grants, research and academia. He commented that my blood pressure was high, then asked: 'How are you doing? Feeling okay?' I responded, 'I'm fine. I don't think anything is wrong with me. It's just a hoax, I bet.' He pushed back: 'I mean mentally, are you okay?'

I Struggle Too

Like everyone else, I've had periods of feeling low or struggling to find joy or happiness in life. I can also feel anxious, which is built into my genes: both my grandmother and mum are quite anxious people too. My grandmother (I'll talk more about her approach to life in the final chapter) has managed her anxiety through daily meditation, being strict over her diet (including caffeine and sugar consumption) and thinking and writing about philosophy, religion and spirituality.

My way of coping is exercise. Movement, in whatever form, and for however long, just makes life feel better. I see it as moving meditation because I don't have the patience to sit still and reflect without picking up my phone, wanting to eat something, or making to-do lists in my head. After thirty-eight years, I know that if I'm feeling low, I will feel better if I get my body going. This could be a jog around the block, a hike in the hills, heading to the gym, or booking in for a hot yoga session.

I've already written an entire chapter on the benefits of physical activity for our health and for living longer. We know it helps lower blood pressure and reduce the risk of diabetes, cancer and stroke, and that it contributes towards ageing in a healthy and independent way. I talked about myokines (the 'hope molecules') and the emerging research on their impact on mood, as well as neurotransmitters such as dopamine, noradrenaline and serotonin. This cocktail of chemicals seems to improve mood management, with participants noting they feel happier and more hopeful after exercise sessions, even those as short as ten minutes.

During my PT training, I ran a small group fitness class for friends at the Meadows in Edinburgh. Despite complaints about how hard it was during the session, my friends left feeling happier. Maybe because they were leaving!

Within population health, larger studies involving thousands of participants have tried to capture the effect of exercise on mental health. A meta-analysis in the *British Journal of Sports Medicine* in 2023 looked across forty-one studies (which were randomized controlled trials, which means one group exercised and one group didn't) to estimate the efficacy of exercise on depressive symptoms. The authors conclude: 'Exercise is efficacious in treating depression and depressive symptoms and should be offered as an evidence-based treatment option.'

The authors note that the other two options offered for depression are psychotherapy and antidepressant medication, or a combination of the two. These two options are cost-intensive, requiring one-to-one interaction with a trained professional, with antidepressants also carrying side effects. This isn't a realistic access option for the bulk of people living in the world. Because of this inaccessibility of care, the authors estimate that about two thirds of adults with depression do not receive treatment.

We can already see this in Britain with the NHS, where waitlists for mental health support can be upwards of two years. GPs (or primary care physicians) help provide mental health support. While they can make referrals for specialist care, the lengthy waitlists mean that patients keep on returning to their GP even in acute situations.

It's the same within the university I work for: the waiting list for staff to access mental health support from university services is roughly nine months. The support offered is a maximum of six therapy sessions, one per week. The offer is short-term support to help with a specific issue, not a longer-term way to manage poor mental health.

The links between physical activity and mental health are also true for children and young people, as growing evidence shows. With the stress of adolescence – whether peer pressure, post-COVID trauma, exams, isolation, or uncertain economic futures – physical activity, especially team sport, is a good protective measure for mental health. A large study from Norway showed that physically active teenagers in team sports had higher self-esteem and life satisfaction, particularly for senior high school girls. This was also true for university students, where a clear association was found between inactivity and poor mental health, self-harm and suicide attempts.

Within schools, we could do so much more to promote a healthy, lifelong relationship with exercise. This is especially true for teen girls who might be scrolling on Instagram and seeing posts about ideal body weight or getting a six-pack. Instead, exercise in schools should be marketed with the message that it's not just about staying a certain weight or being a certain size: it's about keeping our minds and bodies functioning and strong.

But the links between mental health and physical activity are rarely part of conversations about 'mentally healthy school environments', exercise in the education curriculum, or raising resilient adolescents. I've tried to emphasize the links between physical activity and mental health to those working in governments on schools policy, but it's not been an easy conversation. They're still seen as separate, unconnected issues.

In contrast, the growing use of social media has been shown to have a detrimental impact on mental health. In 2023, the US Surgeon General (and my Miami childhood friend) Vivek Murthy issued an advisory on the effects that social media use has on young people's mental health.

He said: 'The most common question parents ask me is, "Is social media safe for my kids?" The answer is that we don't have enough evidence to say it's safe, and in fact, there is growing evidence that social media use is associated with harm to young people's mental health. We are in the middle of a national youth mental health crisis, and I am concerned that social media is an important driver of that crisis.'

Research cited by Murthy shows that adolescents who spend more than three hours per day on social media have double the risk of depression and anxiety. Furthermore, 46 per cent of adolescents aged between thirteen and seventeen say social media makes them feel worse about their body image, and 64 per cent of that age group are 'often' or 'sometimes' exposed to hate-based content.

His words were reinforced by the president of the American Medical Association, Jack Resneck Jr, in even stronger terms: 'With near-universal social media use by America's young people, these apps and sites introduce profound risk and mental health harms in ways we are only now beginning to fully understand.'

A study by researchers at the University of Bath looked at the mental health effects of a week-long social media break, which on average freed up about nine hours of that week. One hundred and fifty-four participants were randomly allocated to either stop using social media (Facebook, Twitter, Instagram and TikTok) for one week or to continue using it as usual. Even after seven days, participants had significant improvements in wellbeing (up by 4.9 per cent), depression (down by 2.2 per cent) and anxiety (down by 1.7 per cent) compared to the control group.

There is growing consensus among health experts about the negative chronic health effects of social media use. But trends are going the wrong way. Young people are spending more time online and in the virtual world, and less taking part in sport and other physical activities.

One of the senators proposing US legislation to regulate social media, and a concerned parent of two children, Brian Schatz, said: 'The growing evidence is clear: social media is making more kids more depressed and wreaking havoc on their mental health. While kids are suffering, social media companies are profiting. This needs to stop.' Murthy's report highlighted that among fourteen- to seventeen-year-olds, those who used screens throughout the day were twice as likely to have been diagnosed with depression.

My personal approach to mental health, specifically depressive symptoms, is to think about it as a spectrum, where external factors can move us up or down that spectrum. Mood management. Certain factors push us towards feeling low and more hopeless: social media is a key factor here. Exercise, on the other hand, can have a protective effect and push us towards feeling happier and more hopeful.

Like most people, I have moments where I think about the past and mistakes that I've made and other paths my life could have taken, which is a recipe for feeling depressed; also I have concerns about the foggy future and what might go wrong, which is a recipe for anxiety. Part of my ongoing mental health 'workout' is to wake up each day, pull open the curtains and make the bed, stay positive, be actively engaged with my work and routine, build in activities that make me feel better, and try to limit the things that drain my energy.

If I think too much about the past or future, I start drowning. I have to limit my mind to what my plan is for the day, what will be meaningful and make me excited, and focus on that. During harder moments I concentrate on just getting to lunch, and then to my afternoon cup of tea, and then to dinner. I guess this is called mindfulness: I call it getting to the next meal with purpose. Mealfulness.

Nights can sometimes be the hardest to get through, given the lack of distraction and the deafening silence, and this is when I think about Victor Hugo's quote: 'Even the darkest night will end and the sun will rise.' He's right: the sun always rises in the morning, a new day begins, a new start in whatever direction we want to go in. Life has ups and life has downs, and we largely can't control those winds. What we can control is how we react to those moments, and how we manage the stress that we feel as we react to various life events.

There's no easy fix to staying mentally healthy, like there's no easy fix to staying physically healthy. It's about the daily habits and choices we make, and that our governments help us make, as we'll see.

Poor Mental Health Makes Us Die Sooner

Part of the challenge of even talking about mental health is that it's like talking about physical health without specifics: it incorporates a broad range of conditions from schizophrenia to anxiety to depression to eating disorders to autism spectrum conditions and more. These types of disorders are increasing with time: mental disorders increased by 48.1 per cent between 1991 and 2019. The pandemic in 2020 only accelerated this trend.

Overall health isn't a binary where we can identify: is it the mind or the body that's struggling? The mind affects the body, and vice versa. People with mental disorders experience disproportionately higher rates of disability and mortality. Those with major depression and schizophrenia have a 40 to 60 per cent greater chance of dying prematurely than the general population. This is likely due to physical health problems that are often left unattended (such as cancers, cardiovascular diseases, diabetes and HIV infection) and a higher propensity towards suicide. Suicide is the second most common cause of death among young people worldwide.

The links between the mind and body are clear. Depression predisposes people to heart problems and diabetes, and having these conditions has a negative impact on mental health and is correlated with increased depression. Many of the risk factors for heart disease, cancer and stroke, such as alcohol use, poor diet, stress and financial precarity, are the same as for mental disorders and other noncommunicable diseases. Addiction and substance abuse in particular are linked to mental disorders.

The inverse relationship is also true: those physically unable to exercise, due to disability or chronic pain, suffer from mental health issues. When the body doesn't feel good, the mind doesn't feel good, and vice versa.

In 2004, 13 per cent of the total global burden of disease (which is disability and death together) was linked to various mental disorders. Depression alone accounted for 4.3 per cent of the global burden of disease and was among the largest single causes of disability worldwide, particularly for women. The economic consequences of these health losses are equally large: a recent study estimated that the cumulative global impact of mental disorders in terms of lost economic output will amount to $16.3 trillion between 2011 and 2030.

In contrast to two decades ago, when I started looking at this health area, mental health is now a cornerstone of the WHO's technical advice and policy promotion to its member states. The WHO defines mental health as 'a state of mental wellbeing that enables people to cope with the stresses of life, realize their abilities, learn well and work well, and contribute to their community. It is more than the absence of mental disorders.'

In 2013, all WHO member states committed to implementing the 'Comprehensive Mental Health Action Plan 2013–2030', which lays out clear steps to providing care and support at a population level. Yet in 2020, when the WHO analysed country performance against the action plan, they found that most nations hadn't met the agreed targets.

This is exactly the issue we found when my team did research on global mental health support for the *Lancet* in 2007. We found that low- and middle-income countries, especially those suffering from a large infectious disease toll, prioritized diseases like measles, HIV, TB or malaria. Basically these were health problems that have simple 'silver bullet' public health interventions to tackle them, such as vaccines, bed-nets, condoms or drugs.

Ministries of health have to agree their public health priorities and plans with the World Bank if they want a package of financing. In many countries, per capita government health spending is very low. In Nigeria it's $15 a year, in the Democratic Republic of the Congo it's $13 a year and in Tanzania it's $35 a year. Compare this to the UK, where health spending was £4,188 per person in 2021, and the US where it was $12,914 in 2021. Low-income health ministries are dependent on external funders to help finance their health budgets, and these external funders just don't see mental health as a priority.

When we did the *Lancet* research, we asked World Bank officials why they didn't include mental health as one of the key priorities in countries, despite burden of disease data estimates showing the toll these conditions were taking. They noted that funding priorities were all aligned around the Millennium Development Goals (MDGs). These were a set of eight goals to be achieved by 2015, agreed at the UN by world leaders in September 2000. The goals were: to eradicate extreme poverty and hunger; achieve universal primary education; promote gender equality and empower women; reduce child mortality; improve maternal health; combat HIV/AIDS, malaria and other diseases; ensure environmental sustainability; and establish a global partnership for development.

These are all clearly important goals, but largely orientated towards infectious disease and poverty in low- and middle-income countries. In the process of simplifying the complexity of 'what is development?', they also didn't capture everything important to society. Mental health is a notable absence. The consequence was that countries were unable to support and fund mental health care.

After the MDGs expired in 2015, a new set of goals was agreed: the Sustainable Development Goals (SDGs). I was part of a large EU-funded consortium on the SDGs, looking at the impact these had on countries, and the strengths and weaknesses of this broad approach to development. To their credit, the SDGs included mental health. SDG target 3.4 says: 'By 2030, to reduce by one third premature mortality from non-communicable diseases through prevention and treatment and promote mental health and wellbeing.'

But this was just one target amid 168 others: the SDGs include seventeen goals, 169 targets and 230 indicators. Some have referred to the SDGs as 'senseless, dreamy and garbled', given their complexity, and the consortium I was part of found that it wasn't a useful way of steering local priorities. Our consortium did community consultations with marginalized groups in Uganda, Bangladesh, Australia and Guatemala. These groups were asked about their post-2015 priorities, and the key take-away was that communities wanted to determine their own health priorities based on their values and needs, and felt that these should determine local access to health services.

Reflecting on this research, I wrote in the *Lancet* that we must acknowledge that the SDGs are 'mostly vague, largely immeasurable, somewhat attainable, and definitely relevant'. In the end, local needs should determine local access to services: and if development agencies need to estimate how 'developed' a country is, there are simplified ways to do this.

Professor Francis Omaswa, director of a major health research centre in Kampala, Uganda, proposes maternal mortality as a measure of the strength of a health care system, the idea being that a good health care system doesn't allow women to die during childbirth because it provides adequate care. I've proposed from my PhD research that child malnutrition is a good measure of the impact of social determinants of health and the level of health inequality. This is true whether in India, where hunger is the major issue, or Britain, where child obesity can be seen as a marker of child poverty.

Journalist Laurie Garrett has proposed life expectancy as a measure of public health services. From the title of this book, you can see I'm sympathetic to her case. In the end, we want to live longer and healthier lives. Public health is largely how we do this, with medicine stepping in as needed.

It's Hard to Get Depression Taken Seriously

I won't be looking at the full range of conditions that sit within mental health, such as autism spectrum disorders, schizophrenia or eating disorders. I'm just going to tackle depression (and when it tips into people taking their own life) in this chapter, given that it constitutes the largest burden within mental health.

Feelings of chronic sadness, depression and anxiety are universal human experiences. Yet there are countries where the problem is worse than others, and where it leads to poor quality of life or even people ending their own life. Take, for example, Brazil, which leads the world in the prevalence of anxiety disorders and ranks in the top five for depression. The second-leading cause of death in Brazilians aged fifteen to twenty-nine is suicide. Most of those suffering from mental health illness don't have access to treatment or support. The result is that people with serious mental health disorders tend to die ten to twenty years earlier compared to the general population (even if the direct cause is preventable physical disease).

Within the Brazilian context, mental health disorders are highly stigmatized. In contrast, physical ailments, especially infectious diseases, are taken seriously. Those are seen as 'real disease' in contrast to 'just feeling sad'. Because of this cultural taboo around speaking about mental health issues, studies such as those by Professor Nancy Scheper-Hughes, an anthropologist, have found that Brazilian women channel their anguish into a physical ailment. For example, they will say they have a headache or stomach ache for it to be taken seriously. This results in a doctor treating the physical ailment without recognizing the real cause of feeling unwell. Although there are known treatments for anxiety and depression, more than 75 per cent of people receive no treatment even after seeing a medical professional. But stigma for mental health conditions isn't unique to Brazil.

Despite multiple studies from across the world quantifying the large global burden of disease due to mental health conditions, progress in mental health service provision at a population level has been slow. Why? In 2007, I worked with a team of researchers led by the WHO to understand why getting government attention to mental health issues including depression was pretty much impossible, and to identify the specific blocks in the system.

We interviewed mental health experts and leaders from many countries and found that one of the key universal problems was the stigma surrounding mental health issues. This stigma is often tied to discrimination: which means direct negative consequences for people acknowledging they have a mental health condition. While physical health conditions are often attributed to external factors beyond an individual's control (such as a virus), mental health is often seen as someone's 'fault' or 'weakness'.

Recognizing the importance of tackling stigma in mental health, the *Lancet* created a commission specifically focused on ending stigma and discrimination in this area. They spoke to people living with mental conditions and found that they often reported not being treated as equal to those suffering with physical health conditions. This is true not just at an individual level but at a global level: government spending on mental health is, on average, only 2 per cent of the total health budget.

The media was pointed to, by these *Lancet* commissioners, as having a powerful role in how mental health is portrayed. Celebrities, for example, can be influential in shaping how mental health is viewed: I think of athlete Frank Bruno and actor Robin Williams.

Frank Bruno is a British former professional boxer who won the WBC heavyweight title at Wembley Stadium in 1995. In September 2003, Bruno suffered a breakdown and was taken forcibly by police to a mental health hospital. The *Sun*, at the time the most popular tabloid in the UK, ran with the headline, 'Bonkers Bruno Locked Up' in its first edition; but this insensitive approach backfired due to public opinion. The paper was forced to recall the first edition, change the offensive headline and lead with a softer story referring to Bruno as a hero. Using his public platform, Bruno openly spoke about mental illness, trying to remove the stigma and shame towards those struggling.

In 2017, the Frank Bruno Foundation was set up to support young people with mental health issues. Bruno's vision was to help others suffering through sharing his own battles with mental health, and to show how exercise has helped him manage his internal battles. His foundation runs campaigns for public awareness of mental ill health and how it can affect anyone, and encourages adolescents especially to talk about their feelings openly and not feel like they'll be discriminated against.

Overcoming stigma is probably the greatest challenge for individuals sharing their struggles, as well as for public health researchers wanting to convince governments that this is an area worth investing in, and is not just people having a 'bad day'. Despite the daily impact on their health and wellbeing, most people with depression, especially in low- and middle-income countries, suffer without professional support.

We Know What Works with Depression

Research over the past few decades, and policy experiments within countries, have shown that we know what works to help treat and support those suffering with depression.

In 2018, the *Lancet* put together a commission on global mental health and sustainable development. The commissioners started with four key premises for their discussions and recommendations. First, that mental health isn't a low-income/high-income issue: all countries could be seen as 'developing countries' in terms of mental health services provision.

Second, that trying to assess whether someone has a mental health condition as a 'yes or no' doesn't reflect the real lived experience of humans. Instead, mental health problems exist on a spectrum from mild distress, which is time-limited and linked to a specific event and coping with it, to chronic and severely disabling conditions. The interventions necessary will differ based on where someone sits on that spectrum. The closest analogy is probably a 'triage' for what level of care is necessary, based on an initial assessment.

Their third premise was that a rights-based approach is needed to protect the welfare of those suffering from mental health problems. Governments need to see provision of mental health support as a basic human right, in the same way as access to health care is seen as a fundamental human right.

Finally, the *Lancet* commission noted that there are key interventions that governments can provide from the individual level to the policy level. For example, at the individual level, governments can increase access to mental health services and treatment, ideally through primary care systems, while also trying to reduce the stigma linked to asking for help.

This is supported by working with families, especially identifying at-risk families, to increase mental health help-seeking. Part of this is identifying and intervening in domestic situations with risky behaviours that are linked to mental health consequences: for example, violence or sexual abuse involving children, intimate partner violence, drug addiction, alcoholism, or coercive controlling behaviour. This shows the links between the health care and social care system within governments.

At the community level, interventions are necessary to 'activate' community leaders to reduce stigma against those with mental health conditions, ensure local media is contributing to local campaigns to seek help, and create multi-sector coalitions involved in the planning and implementation of mental health services.

Institutionally this can mean bringing mental health services into where people are located, for example prisons or workplaces, making it easily accessible for those who need support. We also know that pre-arrest mental health programmes could help many people avoid imprisonment completely.

In 2023, the WHO produced a report on public health in prisons. This found that the most prevalent condition among people in prison was mental health illness, which affected an estimated 32.8 per cent of those incarcerated. This incredibly high rate is due both to mental health issues developing while in prison, and also to prison becoming the place where people with mental health problems are sent when no mental health institutions are available.

The Royal College of Psychiatrists in Britain looked at this issue in 2021 and estimated that 10 per cent of the current prison population in England and Wales missed out on a community sentence, or suspended prison sentence with a Mental Health Treatment Requirement, because the required mental health services weren't available.

It's a false economy: the cost of sending someone to prison is £35,000 per year. If more funding was allocated to community support for those with mental health illnesses (the Royal College estimates that £12 million of funding for mental health services is required), thousands of people would avoid prison and the government would avoid that yearly cost. The Royal College estimates that £56 million could be saved. Prevention is generally cheaper than cure.

The lead author of the report looking at this, Professor Pamela Taylor, said: 'Too many people with mental disorders who get involved with criminal justice are being failed by a system that overlooks the use of Mental Health Treatment Requirements. Sending them to prison for quite minor offences may be dangerous for the offender-patients and may harm the wider community too. Re-offending rates are high when people are locked away for a short period while their problems remain unsolved or increase. Thousands of people could benefit from structured, formally supervised care and treatment in the community, but mental health services don't have the resources they need to deliver mental health treatment requirements at scale.'

What Causes Poor Mental Health?

Underlying the development of interventions to support those with mental health challenges is the question of what causes poor mental health. I mentioned a few behavioural situations above, but it's worth digging deeper and listening to those with extensive experience in this area. I think of the Reverend Chad Varah, founder of Samaritans, a volunteer-run service where those struggling, especially with suicidal thoughts, can call anytime, day or night, and speak to someone who offers emotional support.

Varah described how the idea for the organization came when he made his debut in the ministry by overseeing the funeral of a fourteen-year-old girl who had committed suicide. She had killed herself because her period had started, and she wrongly thought she had a sexually transmitted disease. She didn't know who to go to for help.

Varah said: 'In an emergency, the citizen turns to the telephone and dials 999. I looked at mine: FIRE it said . . . POLICE it said. But at the time suicide was a felony. AMBULANCE it said. There ought to be an emergency number for suicidal people, I thought.'

Nearly two decades later, in 1953, Varah set up Samaritans. By 2018, the charity was receiving over 5 million calls a year in Britain alone. Varah noted: 'Befriending has saved thousands of lives in Britain. My job now is to organise it all over the world, until suicide becomes unimportant as a cause of death.' The core of his approach is listening therapy – that is, just listening to someone talking about their troubles without offering advice or passing judgement. It's proved to be an effective approach to stopping people from killing themselves in their darkest moments.

After observing those with suicidal thoughts over several decades, Varah concluded that a few drivers were behind the bulk of those struggling with mental health problems. The first was abuse, most likely in childhood, of a physical, sexual, emotional or verbal nature.

Childhood trauma is often the cause of lifelong mental health problems including anxiety, depression, post-traumatic stress disorder (PTSD) and other mental illnesses.

Another key factor is genetic: the National Institute of Mental Health in the US estimates that 50 per cent of mental illness, such as bipolar disorder or schizophrenia, is caused by inherited factors. Mental illness runs in families. But it's not a simple causative relationship: genetics often requires an environmental trigger.

Certain development periods are implicated, with environmental factors interacting with genetic vulnerability to trigger psychiatric disease; for example, during pregnancy, early childhood, or adolescence. During these stages, our DNA is affected by chemical marks (the epigenome) that determine how much a particular gene is expressed. Studies in genetically identical twins have shown how even with the same DNA, gene expression varies by environmental influence (both positive and negative) in key stages of life. The interaction of genetics and environmental factors is called epigenetics. In lay terms, it's the combination of nature and nurture.

Other implicated risk factors are specific traumas, such as being sexually assaulted, serving in the military (this is why PTSD is high in those returning from active duty in conflict areas), or chronic pain, which can lead to difficulty reintegrating into society and feeling isolated.

Grief is also often listed as a key factor in depression. The death of someone loved, especially a parent or child, is one of the most difficult experiences a person can go through. Relationships are a key aspect of a meaningful life, and losing someone can make life feel empty.

Finally, financial stress, precarity, and feeling unable to cope with the pressures of modern life, such as rent, food bills and heating costs, can lead people to feel hopeless and unable to continue. In the movie *The Big Short*, Brad Pitt's character observes: 'You know what I hate about fucking banking? It reduces people to numbers. Here's a number – every 1 per cent unemployment goes up, 40,000 people die, did you know that?'

Suicide mortality increased during Greece's economic crisis of

2011/12, with unemployment significantly linked to suicide mortality especially among working-age men. Or just look to India, and the link between crop failure and farmer suicides, due to their inability to repay agricultural loans and their fear of letting down an entire family dependent on them for income.

One of the challenges of this area is that mental health issues are caused by a range of factors: it's not simply a pathogen that can be identified like cholera, or particles that we breathe in from pollution. It's a range of risk factors that are often beyond an individual's control, and these individuals are largely left to cope alone.

For most people, suicidal thoughts are not a regular occurrence, but feeling low or depressive might be. When government is absent or public mental health services are unavailable, the burden falls on the voluntary sector. Charities like Samaritans are a safety net for those in the depths of despair. This is mental health support in its most extreme form, with front-line staff all unpaid volunteers.

Most government approaches to mental health are focused on delivering treatment, care and support to those self-identifying as needing therapy or medication. Unfortunately, in no country, as the *Lancet* commissioners pointed out, is everything going well, so it's impossible to point to one place that's got it all figured out. Instead, I'll take a closer look at successful initiatives and policies to tackle mental health – some led by government, some by NGOs.

Provide Trained Local People to Listen

The rural Amravati district of Vidarbha, central India, was considered the epicentre of farmer suicides, largely by pesticide, in 2014. In a population of roughly 1 million people, spread across thirty villages, over 5 per cent of people interviewed that year had thought of taking their own life in the previous year, and of these, nearly half said they had depression. Two NGOs decided to implement an experimental intervention to see whether they could bring these rates down. The Vidarbha Stress and Health Program (VISHRAM) was launched in 2014 for eighteen months.

The core of the programme was using community health workers as a first point of contact for those struggling with their mental health. They visited households and held small meetings to increase awareness of mental health conditions and the services available to treat them. They also helped identify people with symptoms of depression, persuading them to talk to a lay counsellor for support. More serious cases were referred to psychiatrists working for the government's district mental health programme.

By the end of the project, the proportion of people with depression who sought care increased from 4 per cent to 27.2 per cent, the prevalence of suicidal thoughts in the previous twelve months fell from 5.2 per cent to 2.5 per cent, and the prevalence of depression fell from 14.6 per cent to 11.3 per cent. These changes were driven by each of the thirty villages involved having a local community health worker who was trained to detect depression, provide frontline support and refer serious cases to the medical system for further management.

Just a year later, in 2016, the *Lancet* published a key paper in which the authors argued that lay counsellors – community members who get three weeks of intensive training plus supervision – could effectively counsel people with depression. They pointed to an intervention in Goa, where lay counsellors were taught an approach called 'behavioural activation'. This means helping those suffering from depressive symptoms to identify and intentionally schedule activities that bring them joy, and using these as a pathway out of depression.

The Wellcome Trust's Mary De Silva funded these studies in Goa. She said: 'These robust studies prove there are cost-effective solutions to the shortage of trained mental health specialists in low resource settings. They also provide food for thought for high-income countries, where, despite their affluence, mental health service provision is frequently sub-optimal.'

The idea now gaining traction is that not everyone who needs treatment for depression needs to be seen by a professional psychiatrist or medical doctor. Some serious cases would need professional care from those who have spent years studying, but others might just need someone who listens and offers simple advice and support. This is probably the only realistic model of care for those living in low-income settings.

For example in India, less than 1 per cent of the national health care budget is allocated to mental health care. The result is that 90 per cent of people with depression have not received any care in the previous twelve months. Using community health workers to identify those at risk, lay counsellors to offer support, and mental health professionals for more serious cases could be a more accessible, and affordable, system to ensure that unmet need isn't eye-wateringly high.

Make It Harder to Buy Stuff That Kills People

Sri Lanka has had a problem with self-harm by pesticide poisoning going back decades. The 1980 Control of Pesticides Act, which ensures that only the least dangerous pesticides are available, was driven by concern over the suicide rate. Back in 1980, pesticide poisonings were responsible for more than two thirds of all cases. After the introduction of pesticide regulations, the country's suicide rate was reduced by 70 per cent by 2016, one of the greatest decreases in suicide rates in the entire world. People tend to kill themselves and others with what's available. Making pesticides less available meant that it was harder to commit suicide, and so fewer people died.

In 2004, Sri Lanka was heavily hit by the Indian Ocean tsunami, triggered by a magnitude 9.1 earthquake off the coast of Indonesia. With waves up to 30m high, it killed an estimated 230,000 people in the deadliest natural disaster of recent times. I was in India visiting family for the holidays when the 'Boxing Day' tsunami hit, and I remember how devastating it was to the region. In Chennai, where I was staying with my grandparents, water came 1 kilometre inland, while other districts in Tamil Nadu like Cuddalore and Nagapattinam were inundated up to 3 kilometres inland. Marina Beach (the longest urban beach in Asia), where we used to go for evening strolls, was destroyed by the high waves.

Sri Lanka was even worse hit, with tens of thousands of deaths. The government took a political interest in mental health off the back of this crisis, and worked with the WHO for immediate resources for emergency medical care. The Sri Lankan Ministry of Health worked with stakeholders to develop a national mental health policy: the goal was to ensure local availability of mental health services in all districts of the country. By 2022, every district had mental health services infrastructure, compared with a third before the tsunami.

How have they managed to build up this provision in every district? The government created the position of Medical Officer of Mental Health, who oversees the provision of mental health care in their district. Each officer receives three months of pre-service training in mental health after their first medical degree. They work closely with the primary health care team to ensure that mental health support is available at a community level.

However, stigma is still a major issue for those seeking care. Yolanda Foster, Amnesty International's Sri Lanka researcher, said: 'Mental health is not openly discussed in Sri Lanka. This is linked to cultural taboos.' This was reinforced by Dr Sherva Cooray, consultant psychiatrist in intellectual disability, who said: 'Stigma attached to mental disorders from a social and cultural perspective in both the Sinhalese and Tamil communities contributes significantly to the problem.' Stigma is a difficult thing to change, whether in Sri Lanka, Britain or the US.

Provide Universal Access to Therapy

In 2021, the French government released a public health study that surveyed 2,000 residents, asking about their mental health from March 2020 onwards. The survey found that 10 per cent of respondents had had suicidal thoughts over the first pandemic year, which was double the percentage in the years before, and that number was 20.9 per cent for those in school and 16.8 per cent for those unemployed.

French President Emmanuel Macron highlighted these results in a speech in which he noted: 'Mental health is a major issue that is insufficiently addressed in our country.' He announced that the government would cover the cost of eight therapy sessions for anyone over the age of three as part of a larger mental health initiative. This would help patients afford therapy visits, as well as provide a guaranteed market for mental health providers: he announced the creation of 800 jobs in psychological health centres.

Alongside Macron, Health Minister Olivier Véran announced the launch of a free national suicide prevention hotline, accessible 24/7, to help ensure that no one felt alone in their hour of greatest need. Macron reinforced this, saying: 'Talking about mental health, informing, preventing and treating it better, is also a way of living in a more peaceful nation.'

While this political leadership is essential, the same three challenges remain as in other countries: stigma around seeking help, enough mental health care professionals to provide therapy for every citizen, and adequate financing allocated to mental health within the national health care budget.

'Be Happy' Campaigns

In 2008, the state of Western Australia decided to do an outreach campaign called 'Act-Belong-Commit', built around three messages:

Act: 'Do something to keep physically, socially, spiritually and cognitively active'
Belong: 'Do something with someone to keep connected to friends, family and community'
Commit: 'Do something meaningful, important and valuable to provide a sense of purpose'

This was the world's first comprehensive population-wide public mental health promotion campaign. By 2018, 82 per cent of Western Australians were aware of the A-B-C campaign, 16 per cent of whom had taken action to improve their mental health as a result. The media campaign was supported by online resources and integrated into local schools. The campaign's school-based programme for mental health promotion had also trained teachers in fifty-one local schools, reaching 46,000 children and teens.

While seen as a valuable media tool to help people with their mental health, and adopted into other countries to help frame media campaigns, it has the limitation that it falls into the 'self-help' camp of outreach, and any campaign needs to be accompanied by support for people to undertake those actions. For example, those who are feeling isolated after a traumatic experience might know that they would feel better if they kept connected to others, but may not know how to overcome feelings of anxiety to do this.

It's the disconnect between knowing what needs to be done and having the support to do it. This is where the government needs to step in to ensure that it's not left completely up to individuals to 'help themselves'. While mass media campaigns are valuable in reducing stigma and raising awareness, they need to be supported by community health officers, lay therapists, or basically just someone who is available to speak to. The simple act of being listened to by someone calm, non-judgemental and trained to listen can often be the most powerful intervention.

Japan's Suicide Struggle

Throughout this book, I've covered the Japanese approach to various health issues because in general, they're a healthy society with long and high-quality life expectancy. At least that's what I assume you'll have taken away from their government's approach to diet. But they're a country that has a high suicide rate.

Japan is the only G7 country where suicide is the leading cause of death in young people aged fifteen to thirty-nine. Suicide made global headlines in October 2020 when it claimed more lives that month than COVID had in the entire year to date in Japan. In October that year, 2,153 people killed themselves, while Japan's total COVID death toll for 2020 was 2,087 at that point.

As an associate professor at Waseda University in Tokyo, Michiko Ueda, said: 'We didn't even have a lockdown, and the impact of COVID is very minimal compared to other countries . . . but we still see this big increase in the number of suicides.' Japan's suicide problem isn't new: in 2016, the country had a suicide mortality rate of 18.5 per 100,000 people, almost double the annual global average of 10.6 per 100,000.

What explains these high rates? Limited access to mental health support seems to be at the root, a mix of a lack of people seeking help and a lack of places to get help. In Japan, it's estimated that only 6 per cent of people facing mental health problems have relied on a therapist, compared to 52 per cent in Europe and the US.

Stigma around mental health issues is a key component. Ueda says: 'It's not something that you talk about in public, you don't talk about it with friends or anything, [which] could lead to a delay in seeking help, so that's one potential cultural factor that we have in here.' Even admitting to be struggling can be a source of shame. As one Japanese expert said, 'It's shameful for others to know your weakness, so you hide everything, hold it in yourself, and endure. We need to create the culture where it's OK to show your weakness and misery.'

The government has identified this as a problem and passed the Basic Act for Suicide Prevention in 2006, which was updated in 2012 and then again after the pandemic. The key slogan was 'Toward Realization of a Society in which Nobody is Driven to Commit Suicide', with the top priority being the expansion in support for mental health.

The OECD looked at Japan's mental health service provision and concluded that support is focused on institutional settings for in-patient psychiatric care. Mental health care provision is minimal in primary care and community settings, where it could address low to moderate-severe depressive symptoms and better identify those needing support.

In 2022, the first course on prevention and recovery from mental health challenges was added to the high school curriculum to help increase awareness of issues like depression and reduce the stigma around talking about it. In addition, NGOs have started increasing support through phone lines (like Samaritans), text-only lines (for those not wanting to use their own voice to speak about it), and AI chatbots to help provide emotional support in a completely anonymous way.

The main challenges for Japan are similar to those of other countries:

providing mental health support, even through lay therapists, at a community level, and destigmatizing the seeking of help. Sadly, there aren't any signs that the picture is improving in Japan; but just as other countries have much to learn from the Japanese, the Japanese have much to learn from other countries that have managed to reduce suicide rates and increase mental health support.

Making People Feel Cared For

We've learned a huge amount over the past few decades on how to improve mental health support. Stigma is one of the largest challenges to getting movement on this issue. But as I've tried to show, most causes of mental health struggles are beyond an individual's control: chronic pain, childhood abuse, serving in the military in active conflict, or losing a loved one. It's not someone's fault. Even for myself, someone who has worked and done research in this area, it took a while to recognize that it wasn't my fault or personal weakness that I was feeling low after being sent death threats or receiving daily abuse on social media.

Mental and physical health are interconnected. We should never see someone struggling with mental health as having less of a condition than someone with a physical one. We know that mental health challenges can shorten someone's life considerably, with suicide the most extreme form. In terms of all the ways to live longer, preventing and treating depression has the furthest to go, in my view. We still don't have universal acceptance of the evidence base or concrete progress in service provision and financing.

But there are clear lessons from research and policy experiments on how governments, and the wider community, can act on this issue. We know that daily physical activity has a positive impact on improved mood management and is an effective intervention for those suffering from depression. We know this won't work for those who can't take part in physical activity and might need more targeted therapy services.

We know that the inclusion of mental health services in primary care delivery, including therapy and access to further specialized services, is important. This could involve lay therapists who act as a first point of contact. Even the act of listening has a profound impact on rates of depression and suicide. We know that the media and marketing campaigns play an important role in reducing the stigma of having a mental health condition and increasing the likelihood that someone reaches out for help.

Life isn't only about not dying too soon. It's about enjoying and being happy with living. Mental health is a core part of overall health, and one that an increasing amount of attention is finally being spent on. Perhaps more than anything it's about people feeling that they're not alone, that they're part of a community that cares, and that they are able to ask for help and get it in a timely way. This effort can't be left only to charity organizations like Samaritans or kind-hearted individuals. It requires an overall government commitment to improving mental health and wellbeing, with clear policies put in place.

6. Guns, Guns, Guns

One of the most frequent questions I get asked while living in Scotland is: 'Why would anyone move from Miami to Edinburgh?' My response often points to how much safer Scotland is, especially for young people and children, who don't need to worry about mass shootings in schools or at music concerts.

Given the threats I have received for my public health work, at least I don't need to worry about being shot while doing public events. This contrasts with the experience of my public health colleagues in America. Unlike diet, physical activity, smoking and even mental health, which you have some agency over, where you live probably affects your risk (and your loved ones' risk) of dying from gun violence more than anything else.

Guns are a fact of life in Miami: I've known that for as long as I can remember. It's in the advice you get as a teenager starting to move around independently. Don't exchange cross words with someone in traffic, they might pull a gun on you. If someone grabs your purse on the street, just give it to them because they might pull a gun on you. Go through the metal detectors as you enter school, because it's better that guns are taken off children immediately and it's for the collective safety of all.

Guns, guns, guns. When I go back to visit the US, having lived in places with far fewer of them, it feels like guns are everywhere, and they are at the forefront of my mind. Several of my high school friends have been carjacked while waiting at red lights: someone just pointed a gun at them through the window and said give me your wallet and phone, and they did. Because they didn't want to die.

The Parkland school shootings happened close to where I grew up, at Marjory Stoneman Douglas High School in Florida. On the 14th of February 2018 at 2.20 p.m., the gunman arrived at the school carrying an AR-15 rifle, ammunition cartridges and smoke grenades.

He had bought all this legally in Florida. He set off the fire alarm so the students would leave their classrooms and flood the corridors. He fired multiple times and killed seventeen people, injuring another seventeen. He then walked out of the building, visited a Walmart, bought a drink at a Subway store, went to a McDonald's and sat down. Shortly after, he was captured by police in Coral Springs close to the school.

Four minutes. That's how long it took for him to kill seventeen people and injure seventeen more. The victims were a mix of students and teachers. Geography teacher Scott Beigel unlocked a classroom for students to enter and hide from the shooter, and was then killed. Aaron Feis, an assistant football coach, was shot while shielding two students. Student Peter Wang held doors open to let students get out quickly and was shot.

Students at Parkland founded Never Again MSD, an advocacy group that lobbied for gun control. They pointed out that the nineteen-year-old shooter had legally purchased the semi-automatic rifle in a Coral Springs gun store after passing a background check. At the time of the shooting, it was legal for those over eighteen to purchase guns from certain dealers (that's now been changed to twenty-one). Bizarrely, he passed these background checks to purchase weapons despite the local sheriff having received at least forty-five calls about his behaviour between 2008 and 2017, several anonymous tips describing him as a 'shooter in the making', and a school counsellor noting that he had spoken of his intent to buy a gun. He had also posted a comment online: 'Im going to be a professional school shooter.'

What changed because of this shooting? The school reopened two weeks later with a heavy police presence, as well as fewer entrances, security officers at each entrance, identification badges for students and staff, and a requirement that all backpacks be see-through. US President at the time Donald Trump offered prayers and condolences to the victims' families. He suggested that a solution would be arming up to 20 per cent of teachers to stop these kinds of crimes, tweeting: 'Highly trained, gun adept, teachers/coaches would solve the problem instantly, before police arrive.' Republican Florida Senator

Marco Rubio said that most proposals on gun regulation would not have prevented this shooting, and pointed to mental illness as the underlying cause.

The school community, especially the student survivors, pushed for stricter action on guns. They held rallies across the country, a seventeen-minute school walkout, and marches in Washington DC and in Tallahassee (the capital of Florida). The 'March for Our Lives' demonstration in Washington saw more than 200,000 people attend and inspired local marches across the country. One of the Parkland survivors' fathers registered a super PAC (Political Action Committee: these raise money from members for specific political campaigns), Families v. Assault Rifles PAC, to 'go up against the NRA [National Rifle Association] candidates in every meaningful race in the country'.

But not much changed in terms of concrete steps towards banning guns. In March 2018, Florida Governor Rick Scott signed a bill (the Parkland Bill) that allowed for the arming of trained teachers and the hiring of more school officers. It also raised the minimum age for buying rifles to twenty-one and established waiting periods of three days and background checks. Even this ridiculously small step to raise the minimum age and establish background checks faced major opposition. The National Rifle Association sued, challenging the legality of the ban on gun sales to under-twenty-ones, and lost in court. The NRA appealed this decision, and the case is still in court.

At the same time, a federal law was passed which increased funding for metal detectors, security training and similar protective measures (the STOP School Violence Act). But the Parkland students were sceptical. One said: 'You know the Stop School Violence Act doesn't even mention the word gun once. We need to fight the problem from the core, which is guns.' Another continued, 'You'll notice in all these shootings – not just the ones in schools and movie theaters, airports, churches, nightclubs – there's no specific mental health issue that you can tie to every single one. The only thing you could tie to every single one is weapons that belong in the hands of soldiers in the hands of citizens who are untrained.'

It somehow stuns me that a mass shooting (which the US Federal

Bureau of Investigation defines as when four or more people are killed, within one event and in close geographical proximity) happened in a school nearby to where I grew up. But it shouldn't have been surprising. Just a few months earlier in October 2017, there was a mass shooting in Paradise, Nevada; and then a month later, in November, another in Sutherland Springs, Texas. More and more shootings.

Moving to Britain in 2003 was a revelation: learning that school shootings don't happen regularly, that people shout at each other on the street without drawing weapons, and that gun deaths are in the low dozens rather than the tens of thousands. I probably have a group of parents in Dunblane, Scotland, to partly thank for that.

Andy Murray

Andy Murray, undoubtedly Britain's best-ever tennis player (sorry, Tim Henman), is well known for winning Wimbledon in 2013 in a tense final against Novak Djokovic. Murray became the first British winner of the men's singles tournament in seventy-seven years. He went on to win Wimbledon again in 2016, giving him a total of three Grand Slam singles titles, including the US Open in 2012. He also won two Olympic singles golds, in 2012 in London and in 2016 in Rio.

Yet all this could have disappeared within seconds during Murray's childhood in Scotland. When he was eight, and his brother Jamie was ten, a gunman broke into their Dunblane primary school gym and began shooting at a class of five- and six-year-olds. The shooter was armed with four handguns and 743 rounds of ammunition, all of which he had bought legally.

Murray's mum, Judy, described how horrible it was. 'Andy's class had been on their way to the gym. That's how close he was to what happened. They heard the noise and someone went ahead to investigate. They came back and told all the kids to go to the headmaster's study and the deputy head's study. They were told to sit down below the windows, and they were singing songs.'

Andy himself says he doesn't remember much about the day beyond being in a classroom singing songs. It was only later that he found out what had happened. In a BBC documentary about the murders, he broke down in tears, saying, 'You have no idea how tough something like that is, and then as you start to get older, you realize . . . It wasn't until a few years ago I started to research it and look into it a lot, because I really didn't want to know.'

Outside the school gates, parents started to show up wanting to know what exactly was happening, having heard there was a possible shooting. Judy says, 'I was driving there thinking I might not see my children again. There were too many cars on the road – everyone was trying to get there. I got angry, shouting, "Get out of the way!" About a quarter of a mile away I just got out and ran.'

As the children were released to their parents, Judy felt relief when she saw her two boys were safe, and then guilt as she realized another mother had lost her daughter that day. In total, sixteen children were killed along with their teacher. While this tragedy on the 13th of March 1996 wasn't the first mass shooting in Britain, it led to major change.

Dunblane's parent community mourned, but they didn't stay silent. As Dr Peter Squires from the University of Brighton explained, 'The notion that someone could use handguns to kill children, like shooting fish in a barrel, was just so appalling that it provoked a reaction.' Mick North's five-year-old daughter was killed in the attack: he made a career change from being a biochemist in academia to creating the first UK organization dedicated to gun reform, called the Gun Control Network.

At the same time, a group of Dunblane mothers launched the Snowdrop Campaign to collect signatures for a petition banning all handguns in Britain. In just a few months, they collected over a million signatures and brought the petition to Parliament. The UK government also conducted its own inquiry into the Dunblane shooting, and the resulting Cullen Report outlined several small changes on gun control related to stricter checks and limitations on ownership, but without moving towards a complete ban.

Like the grieving parents of the 1970s Netherlands, the Dunblane parents continued pushing a grassroots campaign for major changes on gun control, keeping the issue in the headlines and turning public opinion in their favour. Under huge pressure, Conservative Prime Minister John Major put forward the Firearms (Amendment) Act 1997 which banned large-calibre handguns, but permitted smaller ones, for example in licensed clubs where they could be used for target shooting. Allowing smaller-calibre handguns in certain venues was due to right-wing lobbying from those wanting to keep guns for sports shooting and hunting rather than personal safety. But what Dunblane sparked was a growing movement to limit the damage caused by guns, especially to children.

Are Guns More Dangerous Than Cricket Bats and Tennis Rackets?

In 1997, Labour Party leader Tony Blair campaigned to win the next election on the platform of extending the ban on large-calibre handguns to all handguns. After becoming prime minister, Blair proposed this legislation (the Firearms (Amendment No. 2) Act), which the House of Commons approved in June 1997. At that time, among industrialized nations, only Japan had such strict control over handguns written into law. Britain and Japan led the world in having the strictest gun-control laws at the end of the twentieth century. The components were banning private ownership of handguns and semi-automatic weapons, and mandatory registration for shotgun owners.

A core part of this legislation was compensating gun owners for turning in their weapons at the gun's market value. When this legislation was passed, the frequency of handgun use in robberies and crimes was on the increase, as a 'gun culture' continued to set in. This concerned MPs. As former Labour MP Angela Smith said, 'No one says this will dramatically reduce crime . . . But what we can do is everything we can to make it less likely.' Another Labour MP, Robert Marshall-Andrews, said that this wasn't about infringing on personal freedom, but rather to ensure that 'the horror of Dunblane is not visited on others'.

Since 1997, the British public has accepted that limiting the rights of a few to carry handguns is worthwhile to ensure the freedom of children to go to school without worrying about a mass shooting event. In 2003, Britain passed the Anti-Social Behaviour Act, which made it an offence to be in possession of an air weapon or imitation firearm in a public place. In 2014 a guide issued by the College of Policing required police to refuse or revoke firearms licences where the applicant/licence holder has a record of domestic violence, drug and alcohol abuse or mental illness, and in 2016, the British Medical Association required GPs to record firearms licence applications on patient notes and inform police of any factors that might be concerning. In 2016, a gun safety phone line was established to enable anyone with concerns about a gun owner to register these concerns anonymously.

There has not been another school shooting in the UK since Dunblane. By 2019/20, England, Scotland and Wales combined had only about thirty gun deaths per year, compared to almost 46,000 in 2020 in the United States.

Gun control worked in Britain. As the Gun Control Network says, it 'proved that good governments acting in the interests of the many, not the few, can overcome the rich and powerful gun lobby'. There was huge political opposition to stricter gun control in Britain from several large stakeholders: from those wanting full rein over civil liberties including the right to own and carry a weapon, from gun store owners concerned about lost revenue, from those wanting guns for hunting and hobby shooting, and from the royal family.

In 1996, Prince Philip criticized the proposed handgun legislation, saying that gun club members were no more dangerous than golfers or tennis players. He compared guns to cricket bats: 'I mean if . . . look, if somebody . . . if a cricketer, for instance, suddenly decided to go into a school and batter a lot of people to death with a cricket bat, which he could do very easily, I mean, are you going to ban cricket bats?' He continued: 'I think one's got to make a difference between what the weapons can do and what the people can do.'

The parents of Dunblane stood up to the prince. As one of the mothers who lost her daughter at the shooting said, 'I certainly cannot remember the last time a tennis player walked into a primary school and massacred sixteen children and their teacher.' It was the passion and dedication of these parents that made progress happen in Britain, including turning popular opinion against private gun ownership. They pushed for this right after Dunblane because that was the window to pressure politicians to do something.

In 2004, the Dunblane Centre – built on donations from around the world – opened as a site to remember the local tragedy. Glass etchings honour the seventeen victims in the building's windows: Sophie North's (killed aged five) shows a cat on a chocolate bar, Ross Irvine's (killed aged five) has a fox from his favourite TV show, Brett McKinnon's (killed aged six) has a Power Ranger. But the Dunblane Centre is not just about thoughts and prayers: it also stands to show what collective action can do to change policy. In 2013, it was here that locals gathered to watch Andy Murray become Wimbledon champion. Who knows what the school friends he lost could have gone on to achieve, had Britain's gun laws been amended sooner.

Contrast this with the number of school shootings in the United States: 2,032 since 1970 and 948 since 2012. Each day, twelve children die from gun violence and another thirty-two are shot and injured. Guns are the leading cause of death among American children and teens, more than car crashes, drug overdoses, poisoning or infectious disease. The UK's annual rate of gun deaths per 100,000 people was 0.2 in 2015, versus 12.09 in the US. Two countries separated not only by an ocean, but also by gun regulation.

Over 90 Per Cent of Gun Homicides Are in Stable Countries

Guns kill a lot of people – hundreds of thousands – across the world. The disability and death caused by guns is called 'firearm violence' in the public health community, and it's been a challenge to convince politicians and gun owners that gun control is about public health rather than personal freedom or civil liberties.

In 2022, one of my researchers, Jay Patel, wanted to investigate this area further so we worked on a *Lancet Public Health* paper, laying out the evidence on who dies from guns, where they live, and how many of these deaths are preventable. What we found is that in the past decade, firearms have taken more than an estimated 2.75 million lives, largely in men (88 per cent), in Brazil, Colombia, El Salvador, Guatemala, Mexico, the US and Venezuela. It's not just violence in conflict situations: over 90 per cent of deaths from guns are homicide (the killing of one person by another) in stable countries.

From 1990 to 2019, little progress was made globally on reducing the mortality rate from gun-related violence. It was 2.41 deaths per 100,000 people in 1990, and 2.29 deaths per 100,000 in 2019. This is an average across 204 countries and territories.

Deaths are concentrated in certain hotspots: largely low- and middle-income countries in Latin America, and the United States, which remains an outlier in deaths by guns compared to other wealthy countries. Guatemala, Venezuela and El Salvador have mortality rates from guns at around forty deaths per 100,000, compared to the global average of 2.29 per 100,000. Even within 'hotspot countries', deaths are concentrated within certain age groups (twenty- to twenty-four-year-olds) and those living in poorer areas.

The World Health Organization has attempted to take on gun control within the broader challenge of violence prevention. A 2009 briefing focused on three of the most lethal forms of violence: firearms, knives and pesticides (used in agricultural communities for self-harm, suicide and homicide). For reducing gun violence, the agency suggested public health measures such as bans, licensing schemes, minimum age for buyers, background checks, and safe storage regulations. But the WHO faced pushback from certain governments. These recommended public health measures were criticized for infringing country sovereignty.

In 2006, the United States was the only government not to agree to a UN vote to implement stricter standards on the arms trade using an international arms trade treaty. This built on the UN Protocol against the illicit manufacturing and trafficking of firearms, their parts and components and ammunition, in 2001. The US has tried to weaken international agreements on gun control policies, largely because they are a profitable export. Seventy per cent of trafficked firearms in Mexico come from the US, to the point that the Mexican government has sued American gun manufacturers for pushing the trafficking of weapons into their country and causing tens of thousands of deaths.

This points to the difficulty in looking at gun control at purely a national level: it takes multi-country collaboration to limit the transfer of guns, which flow largely from high-income countries into low- and middle-income countries, and often through black markets.

Mass shootings have happened across the world. Some governments have responded by putting in place key policies to limit the damage to populations from guns. Britain is a clear example here, but I could have picked out dozens of countries that went down the same path. I'm going to tell the story of four countries: two 'freedom-loving' countries and two with a history of violence and conflict.

I'm going to use the term 'freedom' quite a lot, within quotes, because it's often the main argument against gun regulation. That line of thinking goes that people should be free to choose what they have in their homes, including weapons, and the state shouldn't infringe an individual right to bear arms. But you could also make the argument that people should have the freedom to send their children to school without worrying about them being shot, and the freedom to live within a safe society.

What's the Point of Being in Office If You Can't Make Life Safer?

Modern Australians love their freedom, and it's a core part of their history: the country was a European colony in which guns played an important role in defending property, conquest, and the massacre of indigenous people. The Australian gun lobby had support in rural and conservative parts of the country, and opposed any kind of regulation on firearms.

This all changed on the 28th of April 1996 when a shooter killed thirty-five people and injured twenty-three more within twenty-two minutes starting in a cafe and gift shop in Port Arthur, Tasmania. He used an AR-15 rifle and a semi-automatic rifle which were both legally bought. The then police minister of Tasmania said: 'It wasn't a politically motivated thing, it wasn't a terrorist. This was just a psychopath killing people with guns.' The Port Arthur shooting took place six weeks after the Dunblane massacre in Scotland.

Twelve days later Australian Prime Minister John Howard made a decisive move to use the national tragedy and grief to take concrete action on gun control. It wasn't an easy political battle, given that guns were seen as a right and part of 'living in the bush' in Australia. Howard said: 'I decided this was big enough and important enough to use the authority I clearly had. At that time I'd only been prime minister for six weeks, I had a majority of 45 in a house of 150 . . . and I thought, "For heaven's sake, what's the point of being in office when you can't do something significant in relation to something that affects community safety?"'

Howard introduced a set of measures for each state and territory: a firearm licensing and registration system under which people would need to show a reason for having a weapon, like sport shooting, farming or hunting. Personal protection was not a valid reason. Automatic and semi-automatic long guns were banned. The government also introduced a national gun buyback scheme. After Port Arthur in 1996, and the introduction of gun control legislation banning automatic and semi-automatic weapons, there were no public mass shootings for roughly two decades. Reflecting on his political legacy in 2021, Howard said, 'We took hundreds of thousands of guns out of the community and the evidence . . . is that there have been no mass shootings since then.'

Howard was told, along with other senior politicians supporting gun control, that introducing these measures would cost them the next general election and their seats. It played out differently: the public supported these measures, and the politicians' popularity increased. Other political parties stood together to introduce the necessary legislation reform, and did it unanimously. As one political leader said, 'No one really attempted to make any political gains out of this even though there was a lot of pressure on individual members of parliament, particularly those in rural areas.'

It's not a happily-ever-after story. There are continued efforts to lighten the gun control restrictions, such as suggestions to reduce the cooling-off period for buying further guns, and making it easier to purchase firearms. But this pushback to gun control seems to be a small set of voices rather than general public opinion.

There's still considerable fight left in those who survived the 1996 shooting, but whose loved ones died. Carolyn Loughton lost her daughter Sarah in the shooting, and launched a public campaign against the importation of Adler A110 rapid-fire guns to Australia. Supporting her efforts, Police Constable Pat Allen, who responded to the Port Arthur shootings, said: 'We can't let these weapons be let back into the country because some would-be bloody army person . . . decides that, "I need an automatic shotgun because I want to go and kill five ducks at once instead of one duck." Government can't be tricked so we end up with another Port Arthur, we end up with another lunatic wandering around just killing all those people.'

When Never Again Means Never Again

New Zealand also has a history of gun ownership and 'freedom'. Until recently, there was approximately one gun for every four people, largely due to their use in farming and hunting. Any attempt to act on gun control resulted in attacks on those speaking up, including members of Parliament and academics. Philip Alpers, an early gun safety advocate, took a public stand on gun control in 1992. He received bullets and faeces in the mail and continual harassment. Reflecting on the abuse from the gun lobby in silencing gun control advocates, Alpers concluded: 'They are tiny but energetic – tiny, but effective.'

After the 1996 Port Arthur shooting in Australia, the New Zealand government commissioned a report into tightened gun control. The resulting Thorp Report in 1997 made sixty recommendations including a ban on military-style semi-automatic weapons, controls on handguns, registration of all firearms, and improved background checks.

The gun lobby pushed back to ensure these policies weren't implemented. They argued that compliance would be hard to enforce, would infringe individual freedom, and would be a massive task to implement. In addition, police minister Jack Elder announced that he wanted to keep gun owners 'on board' rather than 'waving a big stick' by threatening harsher measures.

This all changed in March 2019 when a white supremacist walked into two mosques in Christchurch and shot dead fifty-one people. He used at least two assault rifles in the attacks, which he had bought legally with a standard firearms licence. These weapons allow the shooter to fire continuously. You might remember the images of then Prime Minister Jacinda Ardern wearing a headscarf and showing solidarity with the Muslim community. Shortly afterwards, Ardern said in a press briefing: 'Every semi-automatic weapon used in the terror attack on Friday will be banned in this country.'

The first core policy was that gun owners had six months to sell back their weapons to the government, at a total cost of 100 million New Zealand dollars. Those who illegally kept their weapons faced a penalty of three years in prison and a fine of 4,000 dollars. Shortly after, in June 2020, a new set of policies was introduced, including a new firearms registry to track the buying and selling of weapons, shorter licences for first-time gun holders, and a ban on a wider range of guns.

The year 2019 was late for New Zealand to have acted on tighter restrictions on the use and type of guns, and even after the massacre it wasn't an easy battle. Simon Mount, who worked on the 1997 Thorp Report, reflected: 'The gun lobby strongly opposed even this weak form of regulation, and ultimately the bill did not proceed. Tragically, I believe if the Thorp recommendations had been implemented in 1997, the Christchurch attacker would not have been able to obtain the semi-automatic weapons he used in this country. The reality is these are the weapon of choice for mass killings, and have extremely high lethality.'

In October 2018, Sir Thomas Thorp, author of the report, died without seeing any meaningful change in gun legislation. He might have thought his 1997 report was in vain. But Ardern made it clear that she would act: 'When we saw something like that happen, everyone said never again, and so it was incumbent on us as politicians to respond to that.' And she did. Many of those recommendations are now law in New Zealand, although it took twenty-seven years and multiple deaths. Since the Christchurch massacre, there have been no mass shootings in New Zealand. Ardern's policy action changed the trajectory of the country, and the safety of those living there.

When People Are Sick of Violence and Want Peace

The policy stories from Britain, New Zealand and Australia are largely the same: a major gun massacre spurred politicians, supported by the public, to say 'never again' and to draft and implement strict gun control legislation. But as I mentioned earlier, most of the gun deaths in the world are of young men in Latin America. Almost 36 per cent of all gun-related deaths in the world take place in five Latin American countries: Brazil, Mexico, Colombia, Venezuela and Guatemala. What's happening in this part of the world?

Colombia has the fifth-highest number of gun-related deaths in the world (after Brazil, the US, India and Mexico). In November 2016, the Colombian government and the Revolutionary Armed Forces of Colombia signed a peace agreement which led to a reduction in conflict-related gun deaths. But gun deaths continued to stay high, especially in urban areas. The Colombian government introduced various temporary restrictions on carrying guns, such as on specific dates, or in specific neighbourhoods, and these are estimated to have reduced deaths by about 14 per cent.

Gustavo Petro served eighteen months in prison for illegally carrying a firearm as a member of the M-19 guerrilla group in the 1980s. The M-19 signed a peace pact with the government in 1990 under which he was granted amnesty, and he was soon after elected a representative in Congress.

Years later, in 2012, Petro was elected mayor of the Colombian capital of Bogotá and started his term by focusing on gun control. In his first speech in office, he said: 'More important than prohibiting people from drinking or dancing at night, or stores from opening, is prohibiting the instruments that allow people to kill other people. And of these instruments, in first place are firearms, which the law allows based on norms that I do not share . . . Bogotá will shout to the world that this is a space free of weapons.'

At the time, this was seen as one of the largest experiments in gun control ever attempted. Petro's chief of staff explained the logic behind the ban: 'People who own guns legally can still keep them at their homes or at their offices. But they can no longer bring them to public places, carry them while on the streets, have them in their cars. By doing so we will be protecting them from two things: from becoming a target for criminals who might want to take their weapons, and from using their guns in a moment of madness.'

Petro took this bold step as part of a larger movement towards peace, and to change Colombian attitudes to guns. 'It's not just about stopping people who own guns walking around with them. It's part of a policy of laying down weapons and generating a culture of tolerance and love. Carrying a gun isn't a defence mechanism, it's a risk.'

Residents were sceptical that it would make any difference to the gun-related death rate, given the difficulties in implementation and in regulating illegal guns. As a doorman in central Bogotá said: 'There should be limits to walking around with weapons but most crimes are committed with illegal ones so I doubt we'll see much difference.'

Soon after, the city of Medellín copied the permanent city-wide restriction on carrying guns. What was the impact? A study comparing deaths linked to guns before and after the ban found a reduction in mortality rates in both cities by a fifth, roughly thirty deaths a month in both cities. The researchers conducting the study noted that despite public perceptions that carrying guns is about personal protection and safety, they increase gun-related injuries and deaths at a community level. On the flip side, banning the carrying of guns reduced firearm deaths and injuries. The evidence is clear, even in the context of high ownership of illegal weapons and gang violence.

Medellín itself is a case study in reducing rates of violence through reducing the widespread visibility and use of guns. Medellín was once known as the murder capital of the world, and 40 per cent of Colombia's armed groups have a presence in the city. But a push for total peace among armed groups has led to discussions over how best to reduce violence and lives lost. Leadership on this issue comes from none other than Gustavo Petro, who was elected Colombian President in June 2022.

In February 2023, the government suggested offering money, even to criminals and gang members, for handing in their weapons as a part of a larger 'disarmament campaign', the goal being to reduce the number of guns in the country, estimated at 4.9 million in 2017 (in a country of 50 million), with about 4.2 million of them illegally acquired.

No one thinks it will be easy to achieve peace after decades of conflict and violence, but as Camilo González Posso, who runs a Bogotá-based think-tank tracking war and peace, said: 'The people don't want war, they don't want arms, or politics as we know it. They want change that will give this society a future. That's what we want with this project of "total peace": a future.'

From Widespread Gun Ownership to Mass Disarmament

Another country with a history of violence and gun ownership is Serbia. Until recently, it had the third-highest rate of civilian gun ownership per capita, roughly thirty-nine firearms per 100 people, largely a legacy from the Balkan wars of the 1990s. Almost 95 per cent of gun owners are middle-aged men who use them for self-protection and hunting.

On the 3rd of May 2023, a thirteen-year-old boy opened fire in a school in Belgrade, the Serbian capital, killing eight children and a school security guard, and injuring seven more, one of whom died later in hospital. The attack was carefully planned, with the boy using two of his father's guns and sketching out who he planned to kill and where. The head of Belgrade police said: 'The sketch looked like something from a video game or a horror movie, which indicates that he planned in detail, by classes, whom to liquidate.'

Two days later President Aleksandar Vučić said he would take steps towards an 'almost total disarmament of Serbia' to ensure this kind of mass shooting would never happen again. Vučić said: 'We must make a decision to confront this evil.'

The first step was to announce a gun amnesty, which ran for a month starting on the 8th of May 2023 and allowed any weapons to be turned in without explanation or consequences. The aim was to reduce gun ownership by 90 per cent. Follow-up steps included: a review of all existing weapons permits, a two-year moratorium on new permits for small firearms and hunting weapons, tighter conditions for keeping and carrying small guns, and regular checks on those holding weapon permits, including medical, psychiatric and drug tests. Penalties for the illegal production, possession and carrying of weapons were also increased. In short, the government made it easier for people to give up guns, increased the penalties if they didn't, and restricted guns through permits, background checks and banning the most dangerous weapons.

Serbia was following a successful recipe used in Australia, Britain, New Zealand and other countries to reduce the number of guns, and linked to that, reduce the risk of mass shootings and deaths by guns. Within three days of the amnesty starting, almost 6,000 unregistered weapons, 300,000 rounds of ammunition and 470 pieces of mines and explosive devices were turned in to the government. Public support was behind politicians, who used the combination of shock, sadness and anger about the massacre to push through strict gun legislation to prevent another tragedy happening.

Serbia and Colombia illustrate that even in the most heavily armed countries, where a history of violence and conflict means that ownership of guns is 'normal', political leadership and public support for peace can result in policies to limit the damage guns cause, especially in young people. Regardless of the culture, history or geography, there are certain policies that have a proven impact on reducing injuries, deaths and mass shootings. There's an elephant in the room, though: the United States. What is happening in this outlier of the world?

The Land Where Guns Are the Leading Cause of Death in Children

The countries I've talked about so far follow a pattern: governments, with the support of their citizens, saying 'never again', 'no more', either in relation to a specific gun massacre or to a generally high level of violence from firearms. The consequence has been the strict regulation of guns, whether in high- or middle-income settings, regardless of geography and culture, and even in places with a history of carrying arms for personal protection, through being 'out in the bush' like in Australia or because of gang warfare as in Colombia. There's generally international consensus about the damage that guns cause to human health and wellbeing, and the need for public policy measures to limit the harm they cause.

Except in my home country, the US, where gun violence numbers are eye-wateringly high. Here are just a few. In 2021, the most recent year for which complete data is available, almost 49,000 people died from gun-related injuries. This figure is a mix of murders, suicides, accidental death, and those involving law enforcement. Suicides account for more than half of US gun deaths: 54 per cent, while 43 per cent were murders. With only 4 per cent of the world's population, the US has about 44 per cent of the world's gun suicides. Around 80 per cent of murders in the US involve a gun, while 55 per cent of suicides are linked to firearms.

In 2020, gun injuries overtook car crashes as the leading cause of death in those aged one to nineteen. A meta-analysis of more than 150 studies noted that preventing children from accessing firearms is effective at reducing firearm deaths. Reducing easy access through, for example, restricting sales in shops, a minimum purchasing age, and ensuring that guns are kept unloaded and separate from ammunition, reduces suicides and homicides among young people. Elinore Kaufman, a trauma surgeon at the University of Pennsylvania, said: 'Reducing access to lethal means is an important form of suicide prevention . . . Actual suicidal impulses are very short-lived, but firearm suicides don't give second chances.'

The problem is getting worse: from 2019 to 2021, there was a 23 per cent increase in gun deaths, while gun deaths among children and teens rose 50 per cent in the same period. Handguns are used in 59 per cent of gun murders: these are the most dangerous weapon because they are usually concealed, lightly regulated, and ubiquitous. Compare these numbers to the thirty-one gun homicides in England and Wales in 2019. Per 100,000 people, the US in that year had roughly 100 times as many gun homicides as Britain. Japan and South Korea have close to zero gun-related deaths each year.

Mass shootings are also on the rise in the US. By the 26th of May 2023, there had been more than 200 mass shootings since the start of the year. By July there had been 345, and by December, 627. In each of the last three years, America has averaged almost two mass shootings a day.

School shootings are a constant threat and happen on an almost weekly basis. Getting shot at school is one of the most likely ways for a child to die in America. As Grant Rivera, a school supervisor from Georgia, said: 'You send your child to school every day with the expectation that they're going to come home . . . and I think moments like these tragic school shootings challenge that for all of us.' Using the emotive issue of children dying while in a place of safety and learning, US presidents have tried to make policy change.

After the prayer vigil held to commemorate the school shooting at Sandy Hook in 2012, in which twenty children and six adults were killed, then President Obama said: 'Can we honestly say that we're doing enough to keep our children – all of them – safe from harm? Can we claim, as a nation, that we're all together there, letting them know that they are loved, and teaching them to love in return? Can we say that we're truly doing enough to give all the children of this country the chance they deserve to live out their lives in happiness and with purpose? I've been reflecting on this the last few days, and if we're honest with ourselves, the answer is no. We're not doing enough. And we will have to change.'

In this speech, Obama didn't mention the words 'guns' or 'firearms' even once. He instead asked everyone to reflect on how to better care for children. However, less than a month later, he put forward a proposal to overhaul the gun laws to include universal background checks and other concrete measures to prevent mass shootings. Yet in 2013, this was rejected by Congress. Obama called this 'a shameful day', pointing out that those states and countries with gun control policies have far fewer gun deaths. He promised that each time there was another mass shooting, he would talk about gun control: 'Each time this happens, I'm going to bring this up. Each time this happens, I'm going to say we can actually do something about it.'

Similarly, after the Uvalde shooting in 2022 (where nineteen children and two teachers were killed), President Biden renewed his call for a ban on assault rifles, establishing universal background checks and firearm storage requirements, and basic gun control policies. He said: 'It's time to act. It's time to make our voices heard. Not as Democrats or Republicans. But as friends, as neighbors, as parents, as fellow Americans.' He also called out the gun manufacturing industry as the only major corporate entity legally shielded from prosecution over mass death.

But again legislation got stuck in the Senate, and faced fierce opposition from Republican members of Congress. Gun control is a highly partisan issue in the US: 91 per cent of Democrats support stricter gun laws, while only 24 per cent of Republicans agree with them. In contrast, in Australia, New Zealand and the UK, gun control had unanimous cross-party support.

I've been trying to get my head around why the US is unique in this regard: why the country is unable to develop effective policy solutions, despite the high death toll linked to guns and clear leadership from certain recent US presidents. Is it really that different to most other places on the planet? It's a complex issue (like most public health challenges) and hundreds of books and PhDs have been written on this topic. I'm going to try to simplify it to the three main obstacles, based on comparing the US experience to that of other countries.

First, the US has a relatively high level of home gun ownership. The US is the only high-income country where the number of civilian-owned guns exceeds the total number of people. Americans generally see owning a gun at home as a right. 'America is unique in that guns have always been present, there is wide civilian ownership and the government hasn't claimed more of a monopoly on them,' said Professor David Yamane at Wake Forest University. The US has an estimated 120.5 firearms per 100 residents, compared to 39.1 in Serbia, 34.7 in Canada and 31.7 in Iceland. The numbers continue to grow: 7.5 million US adults became new gun owners between 2019 and 2021.

States that have the highest percentage of gun ownership, like Alaska, Wyoming and Arkansas, have the highest gun-related death rates, while in contrast those with the lowest rates of gun ownership have the lowest gun-related death rates: New York, New Jersey, Connecticut and Rhode Island. Making it harder to buy guns lowers the gun-related death rate, while making it easier raises it.

Second, effective messaging and lobbying by the National Rifle Association (NRA) has conveyed that owning a gun is about self-defence and personal self-protection. Their solution to a large death toll by guns is to buy more guns. This has been referred to as the 'good guy with a gun theory'. We've seen this already in proposed solutions to Florida school shootings: simply buy guns to arm teachers.

It's completely opposite to the logic in Serbia, Colombia and other countries in which people turned in their weapons and agreed to gun control restrictions for the higher societal goal of community peace and safety. Community peace and safety in the US is equated with more guns. Which means more shooting, which in turn leads to more people wanting to own guns. A vicious and violent cycle of false logic, but one in which gun manufacturers win through increased sales.

Professor Jeffrey Swanson of Duke University has studied this issue for years and notes: 'The idea that the solution to mass shootings is that we need more guns in the hands of more people in more places so that we'll be able to protect ourselves – there's no evidence that that's true.' In fact, a 2021 study found that the rate of deaths in 133 school mass shootings between 1980 and 2019 was 2.83 times greater in cases where there was an armed guard present. Swanson continued: 'Other countries look at this problem and say, "People walking around in the community with handguns is just way too dangerous, so we're going to broadly limit legal access to that and make exceptions." Here we do just the opposite . . . everybody has the right to a gun for personal protection, and then we tried to make exceptions for really dangerous people, but we can't figure out who they are.'

Third, gun ownership has become tightly linked to the Constitution, especially since 2008 when the Supreme Court ruled that the Second Amendment protects an individual right to possess a firearm. The Second Amendment to the US Constitution (ratified in 1791) states: 'A well regulated Militia, being necessary to the security of a free State, the right of the people to keep and bear Arms, shall not be infringed.'

In June 2008 (in a 5–4 decision), in *District of Columbia vs Heller*, Justice Antonin Scalia said: 'an inherent right of self-defence has been central to the Second Amendment right.' Scalia specifically referred to handguns (the deadliest weapon), saying that lawmakers are not allowed to ban what he described as 'the most preferred firearm in the nation to keep and use for protection of one's home and family'.

Justices who dissented from this majority opinion noted that the Second Amendment linked a well-regulated militia to the right to bear arms, not to allow individuals to use weapons for personal self-defence. The Second Amendment dates back to the birth of the United States in the eighteenth century when different considerations were at play. As Supreme Court Justice John Paul Stevens said: 'The reasons that motivated the framers to protect the ability of militiamen to keep muskets, or that motivated the Reconstruction Congress to extend full citizenship to freedmen in the wake of the Civil War, have only a limited bearing on the question that confronts the homeowner in a crime-infested metropolis today.'

Regardless of the interpretation of the Second Amendment and who may be right or wrong, the Supreme Court decision in 2008 created an individual right to gun ownership, which made it easier to buy, own and carry guns. Since 2021, Texas has allowed residents to carry handguns with no licence or training. Soon after, Georgia eliminated the need for a permit to conceal or openly carry a firearm. I could go on listing the relaxed approach to guns across US states, and the constant rolling back of any efforts to restrict their sale, even minimum purchase age.

Making progress on gun violence in the US requires tackling the obstacles of home gun ownership, Second Amendment interpretation and the linking of guns to personal protection. All three can be overcome when enough Americans make gun control an electoral issue and vote for leaders who are willing to put in place policies for peace. I believe that political resistance would vanish if daily gun violence happened in affluent areas where politicians and their children live. Instead, firearm deaths largely happen in Black and Hispanic communities in poor areas; communities that are powerless (and largely voiceless) within the halls of power.

How to Stop People Killing Themselves and Others

Here are some simple take-aways from studying gun control policies across the world. First, individuals with severe mental issues and suicidal or homicidal intentions are found in all countries, cultures and communities. Yet whether this translates from an idea into reality – from thinking about killing children in a school or church into doing it – depends on the tools that are easily available.

Pesticides are easily available in rural India, which is why they're the most common way people try to commit suicide or poison others. Knives are easier to get in Britain than guns, which is why gang violence is largely through knives and stabbing. People generally harm themselves and others with what's easily accessible. Making these tools less accessible is a central public policy objective to prevent harm.

While it's of course necessary to recognize those struggling and needing mental health support, it's equally important for governments to limit the harm that one individual can inflict. It is largely impossible to kill thirty people within minutes with a cricket bat, a tennis racket, or even a knife. It is easy to do this with a semi-automatic weapon. Governments that have managed to regulate guns have managed to reduce mass shootings. It's not luck that Britain hasn't had a school shooting since Dunblane, and it's not because mental illness has been eradicated from the country: it's because it's extremely difficult to buy a gun now.

Second, culture isn't static, nor is historical consequence. Just because Colombia and Serbia have a history of firearms and violence doesn't mean that it was impossible for their leaders to push change towards peace. It requires an elected leader to use a window of opportunity following a massacre and public outrage, to say 'never again' and take on the gun lobby. The gun lobby is a small minority who resist any change because it impinges on their profits. It's money over lives.

Related to the politics, in those places where gun control was passed, various political parties, whether right- or left-wing, came together to agree that stricter gun control measures were necessary. This was true in Australia, New Zealand, Britain, and other countries as well. Gun control was seen as a public health and population safety issue, not a divisive issue to fight over. The main exception here is the US, where it continues to be a partisan issue tied to whether one is a Republican or a Democrat, as we have seen.

The role of parent groups in change is vital. Much of the change in gun control after school shootings was pushed forward by parents who lost children and didn't want their sons and daughters to have died for nothing. They wanted to ensure this doesn't happen to other parents and to channel their grief and anger into a greater purpose. They did this through showing politicians that public shock over massacres meant that public opinion was shifting to more restrictions on guns, and through offering concrete legislative plans on how to change policies. This is similar to the parent movements around safer roads that happened in the Netherlands.

Is the US too culturally different for policies that worked in other countries to work there? I would argue: no, it isn't. While there's a sense of hopelessness and complacency that, as shooting after shooting happens, nothing will change, this kind of thinking becomes self-fulfilling. If you think nothing will change, then nothing will change.

Most countries have recognized gun violence as a priority and a matter for state intervention: not just Britain but also New Zealand, Australia, Norway, Japan, Colombia, Serbia, India – the list goes on. How have these governments implemented public policy measures to limit the damage of guns? Solutions include: banning automatic and semi-automatic weapons from shops and retail; restrictions on the carrying of guns in public places; requiring safe and secure storage for guns in the home; requiring background checks for anyone purchasing a gun, with a cooling-off period; and having a 'buy-back' scheme for anyone wishing to give up their gun and be compensated. These have worked incredibly effectively.

Hopefully you live in a country with strict gun control laws so that they're not something you have to think about each day. Or if you live in a country with limited regulation, that your home city or state has adopted policies to keep you safe. If not, use your voice and power as an individual citizen to push for change. Dying from firearm violence is preventable, and too many people, especially children, die too soon due to lax gun control regulation.

It's not why I moved abroad to Britain, but yes, living in Scotland and under UK gun control legislation has increased my chances of getting to 100. It's also reduced my risk of dying another way: road traffic accidents.

7. Vision Zero

I regret getting into the back seat of the car. My grandfather (Nana) sits in the passenger seat next to his good friend Karthik, who is driving up the steep hill at 30 miles per hour. While Karthik is relaxed and laughing, I can see worry in Nana's face as he makes intermittent pleas to slow down.

I'm sixteen and wonder if I'm going to die in the middle of Andhra Pradesh, while heading to Tirupati temple with my family to seek the blessings of the Hindu gods. The road has sharp bends on a steep incline and the swerving is making me nauseous.

Tirupati is one of the most popular temples in India dedicated to Lord Venkateshwara, and sits at the top of the hills of Tirumala at 3,200 feet. Karthik races around another bend, narrowly avoiding the edge, and says, 'I've enjoyed Lord Vishnu's grace [the preserver and protector of the universe] for years due to my frequent visits to Tirupati. I can drive this road with my eyes closed because I know he's protecting me.' He makes a show of closing his eyes while turning through another hairpin bend.

I'm screaming inside, but don't make a sound in case I disturb whatever conversation he's having with Vishnu. I start one of my own. Prayer is the only control I have in this situation. I ask all the gods to get me off this hill alive. I'll give them whatever they want. Maybe it's not coincidental that the temple was built at the end of a risky journey that makes you feel like you're going to fall off the cliff and die at any moment. It makes a Formula 1 track seem straight.

Turn after turn. I count over fifty bends. We reach the top in less than twenty minutes, and as I step out of the car I thank the gods for still being alive.

Years later, while in Oxford, a friend asked if I wanted to go see this great temple in India that she had seen online. Tirupati, I asked? I googled to learn more and wasn't surprised to see it listed as one of the 10 Deadliest Roads in India. I didn't need the internet to tell me that. I almost died too soon there in 2000.

In 2013, officials had had enough of reporting 'accident' after 'accident' of vehicles falling off the hill and into the gorge. In one month that year, there were sixteen crashes resulting in fifty-two deaths and severe injuries. On the 27th of May, a driver of a speeding jeep lost control at the twenty-sixth turn, resulting in four people dead and nine severely injured.

The local police and road officials held a brainstorming meeting to solve this ongoing problem. They introduced speed restrictions through a minimum travel time. Vehicles going up the hill should take a minimum twenty-eight minutes from start to finish (roughly 11 mph), and those going down should take forty minutes minimum. They also set up speed blocks in the one-mile straight stretch of the journey to stop drivers crashing into a side wall. After just a month, accidents were reduced by half on the road, and none were fatal.

While Tirupati is a unique example of a risky road up to a temple on a hill, India altogether has some of the most dangerous roads in the world. I remember going to Chennai as a child and being overwhelmed by the traffic on the roads: women walking with buckets of water on their heads, men dodging through traffic on motorbikes, elephants and cows roaming the streets, buses with people holding on to the outside.

It was surprising that more accidents didn't happen, as there seemed to be no rules on the road beyond jungle law: stay out of the way of the larger vehicle and honk as much as you can. Sidewalks were non-existent, which made walking perilous, and near misses seemed to happen in whichever direction I turned.

But I wouldn't fully understand the extent of death linked to unsafe roads until I was asked by a colleague, Kevin Watkins, to help with the First Global Ministerial Conference on Road Safety in Moscow, in November 2009. As I put together the background research for the report, which documented the scale of injuries and death to road traffic disasters, it became clear there was a huge gulf between high-income and low- and middle-income countries.

A ten-year-old boy on his first trip alone crushed to death by a reversing bus in Delhi, by a bus company that already had killed 100 people in crashes that year. Fifty-four people killed in Guatemala when a bus carrying seventy-seven passengers skidded into a ravine. The stories went on and on.

When the actual episodes were reported, the general theme was 'what bad luck'. While those killed did indeed have tragic bad luck that day, there's a general pattern that certain countries have more dangerous roads, certain roads have more accidents, and certain types of road users are more likely to die. These kinds of accidents weren't happening in Sweden, Japan or Britain.

Road traffic deaths are an issue where it is hard to gain traction with policy-makers in low- and middle-income countries: somehow an undernourished child, or an infectious disease like malaria, captures hearts and minds. There is the impetus in those cases that something needs to be done, and an injustice is at the heart of it. But no one seems to care that children are dying walking to school, and perhaps the problem is in the word 'accident'.

Accident implies no one is to blame – just bad luck, being in the wrong place at the wrong time – and often at first glance it can seem like that. Until a pattern emerges that these aren't accidents. This is intentional disregard by government officials of the fact that there are solutions to this problem, that it isn't predetermined, and that intervention can make a difference. Certain prominent foundations have tried to convey this message to leaders.

Michael Bloomberg set up Bloomberg Philanthropies to give away most of his wealth, estimated at more than $54 billion. In 2007, their Initiative for Global Road Safety was launched to help implement a comprehensive package of interventions which have been proven to save lives. The goal has been to partner with governments and the WHO to strengthen national legislation, improve data collection, change road user behaviour, improve road infrastructure, and upgrade vehicle safety.

The initiative has spent hundreds of millions of dollars across the world towards these objectives. Have they worked? A study evaluating the impact of the initiative, undertaken with funding from Bloomberg Philanthropies, estimated that 311,000 lives had been saved between 2007 and 2020 because of various interventions, versus the status quo of 'doing nothing'.

My research for the Moscow Ministerial in 2009 was funded by the FIA (Fédération Internationale de l'Automobile) Foundation, which is an international charity working towards safe and healthy journeys for all, through safer vehicles and highways, clean air and electric cars, safe motor sports and low-speed streets.

Ironically, the FIA Foundation is the independent charitable arm of (and gets its funding from) the FIA, which is the sporting association that puts on Formula 1 races. It was established in 2001 with a $300 million donation made by the FIA. It might seem bizarre that the organization in charge of super-fast motor racing in Formula 1 also founded a charity aimed at slow speeds and safe driving. But heigh-ho, that's the world we live in.

Road Deaths Are Going Up

Road traffic injuries are the leading cause of death for people aged between five and twenty-nine globally. Roughly 93 per cent of traffic fatalities happen in low- and middle-income countries, with the death rates highest in Africa and lowest in Europe. It's the eighth-leading cause of death worldwide. Each year 1.3 million people die in a road traffic accident, while 20–50 million suffer injuries. Seventy-three per cent of all road traffic deaths are in men under the age of twenty-five, who are almost three times more likely to be killed in a crash than a young woman.

Between 2013 and 2016, no reductions in the number of road traffic deaths were observed in any low-income country, while some reductions were observed in forty-eight middle- and high-income countries. Overall, the number of deaths increased in 104 countries during this period. Knowing the true scale of deaths is also tricky, given that many countries don't have comprehensive traffic data. To assess the scale of the problem, researchers look at small-scale surveys on crashes, or data from hospitals and police reports, and then extrapolate to national level.

Extrapolation is a fancy term for using what limited data we have to make an educated guess about what the data we don't have is most likely to be. It's like having half the puzzle pieces for a picture, and having to use those to guess what the other pieces are likely to be. It's far from perfect, but it's how health metrics are estimated in low- and middle-income contexts.

Why are so many people dying in road traffic accidents in low- and middle-income countries? It's pretty obvious. First, speeding. An increase in average speed is directly linked to the likelihood of a crash and to the severity of a crash. For example, every 1 per cent increase in average speed translates to a 4 per cent increase in fatal crash risk, and a 3 per cent increase in serious crash risk. A 5 per cent cut in average speed can result in a reduction in the number of fatal crashes. Data on speeding has also been used to argue for 20 mph limits in built-up areas.

Other key components are driving under the influence of alcohol or drugs, and equally dangerous is distracted driving: not paying attention to the road, most likely because of a mobile phone or fellow passengers. Other factors are not wearing seatbelts in cars, or helmets on bikes and motorbikes, and not putting children into car seats.

While much emphasis is often put on driver behaviour – whether it's speeding, driving under the influence of alcohol, or texting or talking on the phone while driving – an equally important factor is the design of roads and how they influence the neighbourhood around them. Ensuring that roads are built with footpaths, cycle lanes, safe crossing points and traffic management measures can significantly reduce accidents and injuries for all users, including pedestrians, cyclists and motorcyclists.

We know a lot about how to prevent road traffic deaths and injuries, which is why they're incredibly low in certain countries like Sweden. In October 2017, the WHO released evidence-based guidelines of the key public health interventions to support government planning around driving. They called this 'Save LIVES' and recommended six strategies and twenty-two interventions, drawing heavily on Sweden's 'Vision Zero' strategy. I'll talk more about Sweden below but, in short, the government has the long-term objective of achieving no fatal or serious injuries within the transport system.

The WHO puts forward four central guiding principles to help design safer roads. First, people make mistakes that can lead to road traffic crashes. One estimate is that road user error causes over 90 per cent of all road accidents. To mess up is human. The WHO says that human error should be a built-in assumption into any policy discussions around reducing harm.

The second is that the human body has a known, limited physical ability to tolerate crash forces before harm occurs. This knowledge can help figure out a balanced approach to various speed limits: fast enough so people can get where they want to go quickly, while slow enough to ensure that accidents don't equate to fatal accidents. For example, on highways, driving at 80 mph if other cars are going 70 mph increases the risk of a crash by 31 per cent, raises the probability of a collision with injuries by 49 per cent, and increases the potential for a fatality by 71 per cent. Having these facts at hand can help policy-makers decide on optimal speed versus health risk.

Third, there's a joint responsibility between those who participate in the road traffic system (whether as drivers or cyclists) to follow the law and comply for the safety of everyone, and for those who design the system to make it as safe as possible for all users.

For example, if a bus crashes on a notorious highway where many accidents have happened in the past, it's not only the fault of the driver, it's equally the fault of those overseeing the highways. They should have identified it as a danger and taken steps to make it safer.

The final principle is that road users should be protected within a complex system, even if one safety part fails. For example, if someone chooses to disregard the speed limit signs, there should be speed bumps or other measures in place to slow the vehicle down. The same goes for separated cycle lanes, so that if a driver is distracted by texting on their phone, cyclists are protected from them swerving out of their lane. There has to be the assumption that parts of the system might fail, but it shouldn't result in injuries, especially to vulnerable users like pedestrians and cyclists.

The WHO Save LIVES package combines the practical interventions that governments can implement, and these have been chosen because of the strong evidence base that they work in saving lives:

1. **Speed management**: establishing and enforcing speed limits, including using speed bumps, narrow lanes and pedestrian crossings.
2. **Leadership** through ensuring there is one agency responsible for road safety, funding a road safety strategy and collecting data on road traffic accidents, injuries and deaths.
3. **Infrastructure** design and improvement, which means ensuring there are enough sidewalks, safe crossings, cycle lanes, safer intersections, and vehicle-free zones. It also means restricting traffic near schools and homes as well as offering better public transport as an alternative to private cars.
4. **Vehicle safety standards**: cars must have seatbelts and other safety mechanisms, as well as room for child car seats and fixed insertions such as Isofix.
5. **Enforcement of traffic laws**, which means there are consequences for drinking and driving, or not using motorcycle helmets, seatbelts and child restraints. It's not enough to have legislation if it's not followed because it's not enforced or checked on. Drivers need to know they will face a serious punishment for drinking and driving; there has to be a deterrent to reckless behaviours.
6. **Post-crash Survival**: having a health care ambulance system that responds quickly to crashes. Research indicates that reducing the time between the crash and the arrival of emergency medical services from twenty-five to fifteen minutes could reduce deaths by a third. About 50 per cent of deaths from accidents occur within minutes at the scene or in transit to the hospital. For those patients who make it to hospital, 15 per cent of deaths occur within four hours after the crash. The basic message is that the shorter the time between a collision and emergency services arriving, the higher likelihood of survival for those injured.

Governments have been given clear advice from the WHO on steps they can take to reduce deaths in road traffic accidents. We know what to do. However, the number of road traffic deaths has been constant for the past fifteen years, and is going up in a number of countries, as we saw earlier. No significant decline has occurred, despite the evidence base being robust on what to do. It's clearly not about knowledge, but about implementation.

Yet it's important to recognize that not all countries are going backwards. Fortunately, some have recognized road safety as a priority: not just the Netherlands, as I talked about earlier, but also Sweden and Japan. How have these governments implemented public policy measures to protect cyclists and pedestrians in road traffic design and construction? What can other countries learn from their experience? Are the lessons only applicable to high-income settings, or could more be done in low- and middle-income countries? Let's take a look first at Sweden, which probably has the 'gold standard' for road traffic safety, and compare it to what's happening in other parts of the world.

Accidents Are Unavoidable, but Fatal Accidents Are Preventable

Sweden has one of the lowest traffic fatality rates in the world (three deaths per 100,000 people each year) and it's also the country that designed the mainstream approach to road safety, known as Vision Zero, adopted in 1997. Vision Zero has been used across the world and is arguably one of Sweden's most successful international exports.

The overarching vision is that no one should be killed or seriously injured because of traffic accidents in the road transport system. Maria Krafft, head of traffic safety at the Swedish Transport Administration, put it this way: 'People will always make mistakes. You can't count on that never happening. But just like at a nuclear power plant, human errors on the roads need not have devastating consequences and so we focus on building systems that counteract such consequences.'

One core component is road design to limit the likelihood that an accident results in serious injury or death: 'For instance, if you need to have an intersection on a road where the speed limit is 80 kilometres per hour, then you design the road in a way that ensures you bring down the speed of cars successively so as to prevent fatal accidents at that intersection. You may add a roundabout ahead of it, for instance.'

Sweden's approach was radical at the time, as it turned on its head the idea that bad driver behaviour was the single cause of accidents. Vision Zero accepted that humans are imperfect and make mistakes. Instead, it was a shift within safety research from a view of accidents as the main problem to one of kinetic energy and the tolerance of the human body to impact as the real cause of deaths and serious injuries. For example, 98 per cent of pedestrians survive if hit by a car going 20 mph, while only 60 per cent survive if the car is going 40 mph.

Sweden's approach was unique: instead of traditional cost–benefit calculations, where the cost of improving roads or enforcement is set against the benefit in terms of lives saved, or in reduced health care costs from treating injuries, the logic of Vision Zero has been focused on ethics and total elimination of deaths and serious injuries. The Swedish government's Vision Zero Bill says, 'No one shall be killed or seriously injured due to road traffic accidents within the road transport system', with the added principle that 'life and health can never be exchanged for other benefits within the society'.

Once the Vision Zero strategy was agreed by government, planning and design were orientated around limiting harm, especially to vulnerable road users. The measures introduced included low urban speed limits, pedestrian zones, separated cycle lanes, and '2+1' roads where each lane of traffic takes turns using a middle lane for overtaking. In addition, 12,600 safer crossings, including pedestrian bridges, zebra marks with lights, and speed bumps, were estimated to have halved the number of pedestrian deaths between 2009 and 2014 in Sweden.

Sweden's proactive approach to preventing serious injury and death works. Annual road traffic deaths declined from 541 in 1997 to 192 in 2021. Road deaths in children under seven have fallen from fifty-eight killed in 1970 to only one in 2012. During this same period, the number of cars on the roads increased. This shows that it's possible to increase traffic levels without a rise in harmful accidents. The Swedish approach to road safety has been adopted by the European

Union, the UN, more than half of US states, and several European countries. It's also inspired the Dominican Republic, which I'll talk about soon.

As an aside, it seems ironic that the country which immediately went for a 'living with COVID-19' approach prior to a vaccine, and had a much higher death toll in 2020 compared to its Scandinavian neighbours, was also the one that adopted public health legislation in 1997 that 'life and health can never be exchanged for other benefits within the society'. As I discussed in my last book, *Preventable*, Sweden's laissez-faire approach during the pandemic was based on wanting to balance life and health with other benefits in society, including the personal freedom to live as one wants to.

How does one reconcile the fact that in Sweden, deaths in the first wave of COVID were seen as acceptable, due to 'other benefits' and 'freedom' being treated as more important than life and health, while when it comes to road traffic accidents, no level of injury or death is acceptable, regardless of the cost or infringements of personal freedoms? Driving legislation that has harsh penalties (including prison time for drinking and driving or speeding) could be seen as infringing someone's liberty to do what they like with their time and car. Legislation that asks those with COVID to isolate could be seen to infringe someone's liberty to decide where they'd like to go, whether to restaurants or a workplace.

Public health has always been about the balance between the freedoms of people, at a population level, to live their life protected from risks that might harm their health and longevity, and the freedoms of individuals to make choices about how they live their own life. This balance seemed to get lost in the debates during the pandemic: the risk appetite for road traffic deaths versus COVID deaths is the complete reverse in Thailand compared to Sweden, as we'll see later on.

Provide Cheaper, Faster Alternatives to Cars

Another country that has managed to go against the tide and reduce road traffic deaths is Japan. In Japan, fewer than 3,000 people died in road crashes in 2021, compared to almost 43,000 in the US. On a per capita basis per 100,000 people, this works out to a rate of 2.24 in Japan and 12.7 in the US. In 2021, the country saw the fewest road fatalities of any year since 1948.

It's not because the Japanese have always been this way. In the 1960s, annual fatality figures were six times higher than they are today. The annual roadway deaths exceeded those from the First Sino-Japanese War, leading some to refer to the high level of road deaths as the 'Traffic War'. How did Japan manage to bring down its road fatality rate?

The first element was providing public transport alternatives to taking a car, especially within cities. On a per capita basis, Japan's average resident drives a third as much per year as an average American, and taking the car is an option rather than a necessity. An engineering professor at the University of Tokyo said: 'Available land in Japan is very limited and people tend to live in large cities like Tokyo, Osaka and Nagoya. They don't drive, because a well-established public transport system supports their mobility.' Within Tokyo, the metro has twice as many daily passengers as New York's subway, and it's faster to get around the city by using one of its 285 metro stations than by driving.

Travelling around the country also doesn't mean having to drive on motorways at high speeds. In 1964, Japan launched the world's first bullet train, the Shinkansen, and it's continued to build up an efficient and affordable railway system. For example, the trip from Tokyo to Osaka is under two and a half hours by train, while it takes at least six hours by car. The same professor at the University of Tokyo said: 'If you travel with your family for a long distance by Shinkansen, the cost is higher than using a car. But even so, many Japanese choose to use the train because the system is so strong.' It's incredibly safe: the Shinkansen has never had a fatal crash since being built.

Overall, public transport is safer than being in an individual car, whether in Japan or anywhere else: a study in the US looking at data from 2011 to 2021 found that passenger death rates in cars were twenty times higher than on buses, seventeen times higher than on trains and 595 times higher than on commercial airplanes. Basically, you're seventeen times more likely to die travelling the same distance in a car than on a train. Being in a car is the second most deadly form of transport, with only motorcycles resulting in more fatalities per kilometre or mile.

If you want to save lives, the first clear policy intervention is giving people an alternative way to get around that doesn't rely on a private car, whether that's within a city or across a country.

The second key component in Japan was an adopted policy to limit on-street parking. Car owners must obtain a certificate, or *shako shomei sho*, which shows they have a secure place to store the vehicle overnight, either at their home or in a parking garage. Vehicles can't normally be left streetside overnight. The expense and hassle of having to park a car has been a deterrent to private car ownership. It also improved street safety by making them more pedestrian-friendly: for example, no parked cars increases children's ability to see oncoming traffic and to be seen by vehicles when going to cross the street.

The third key component has been the type of car being sold in Japan: the bestselling car in Japan weighs around 2,400 pounds and is 130 inches long, compared to the bestselling car in America, which is 6,400 pounds and 230 inches long. Japanese mini-cars, referred to as *kei* cars, have been designed for navigating narrow streets and tight parking spots in urban environments. They're also affordable (costing between $10,000 and $20,000), and even cheaper with government subsidies. And they're popular, making up a third of new cars sold in Japan. From a safety perspective, kei cars have less force in collisions, have reduced driver blind spots and are less likely to kill someone upon impact. Occupants inside the vehicle are equally as safe as those in full-sized cars, and those outside are much safer.

We don't have enough public discussion in most countries about the type of cars being driven, and their impact on road safety. For example, a study in the *Journal of Safety Research* notes that children are eight times more likely to be killed in a collision with an SUV or pick-up truck than they are in a crash with a standard car. The researchers looked at collision and hospital admission data in Illinois, from 2016 to 2019, and concluded that SUVs and large motor vehicles result in more fatal accidents. They point to factors such as the size and weight of these cars, as well as their drivers' highly restricted vision, especially towards children.

While Japan recognized this early on, other places are starting to replicate policies to help shift away from SUVs. For example, Paris has seen an increase in SUVs by 60 per cent over the past four years, and they now make up 15 per cent of the 1.15 million private vehicles parked in the city. The deputy mayor reflected on the absurdity of driving an SUV in Paris: 'There are no dirt paths, no mountain roads . . . SUVs are absolutely useless in Paris. Worse, they are dangerous, cumbersome and use too many resources to manufacture.'

In a unanimous vote in May 2023, Paris councillors approved a measure to change the price of paid parking to make it progressive according to the weight and size of the vehicle. The bigger the car, the higher the parking fee. It doesn't simply have a road safety benefit, but improves air quality too, which I'll talk about in the next chapter.

Improving Roads When 30 Per Cent of People Live in Poverty

Improvements are also being made in certain low-income countries. The Dominican Republic sits on the island of Hispaniola with a population of over 10 million people. Despite a growing economy, more than 30 per cent of Dominicans still live in poverty. It's also quite a deadly country for road traffic accidents, ranking fifth for road deaths worldwide with almost 3,000 deaths in 2021, largely in the capital city Santo Domingo. The twenty to twenty-four age group is the worst affected, with 480 deaths in 2021. Speeding is behind more than half of road deaths.

With economic development aimed at lifting people out of poverty, there's been an associated steep increase in the number of cars on the road, from 2.2 million in 2003 to 3.6 million 2015. This means more vehicles on the existing road networks, and a move towards prioritizing cars over attention to safety and ease of movement by cyclists and pedestrians. When people get wealthier, they tend to shift from walking and cycling towards car ownership: it's a step up the ladder in a low- to middle-income country context.

In March 2023, the mayor of Santo Domingo, Carolina Mejía, announced the introduction of a 35 kph speed limit on the Malecon (a busy coastal road) after studies showed that it could reduce fatal child injuries by 70 per cent. She also introduced a traffic diversion scheme to cut the number of trucks and heavier vehicles using this road. Within the city, she's planning to reduce the speed limit from 60 kph to 50 kph and to introduce safe routes across the city so that children can reach parks, cycle paths and play areas without being hit. The Vision Zero approach adopted by the WHO is explicitly mentioned as guiding the policy changes.

These are all small steps in the right direction, and as Mejía says, 'What we're trying to do . . . is to find all those small action items that we can start on right away. With all the difficulties we have, we cannot afford to wait until we have everything worked out.'

Children: The Most Vulnerable Road Users

High-income countries could do even more in this area, but the real challenge is in poorer countries. Poor countries account for just under half of the cars on the world's roads, but nine in every ten fatalities. A person in a poor country is at least twice as likely to die on a road as a citizen of a high-income country. A person living in Kenya is twenty-nine times more likely to die from a road accident than a person living in Monaco, and ten times more likely to die than a person living in Sweden. This is despite Sweden having thirteen times as many vehicles per 1,000 people (601) as Kenya (forty-five).

Kenya has one of the highest road fatality rates in relation to vehicle ownership in the world, with road traffic accidents the third-leading cause of death after malaria and HIV/AIDS. Three thousand people die each year in road crashes, which is a rate thirty to forty times greater than in high-income countries. Since 2015, the country's fatality rate has increased by 26 per cent and the injury rate by 46.5 per cent. Accidents involving vulnerable road users have increased over 300 per cent in the same period. In Kenya, it's getting worse over time, not better.

Roughly 55 per cent of road deaths in Kenya are pedestrian deaths: that is, people who aren't in cars or motorized transport. This is a general pattern found in low- and middle-income countries: typically around half of those who die in road traffic accidents are pedestrians or cyclists. In short, those who are too poor to own a car face the highest level of risk. These road users are referred to in public health as 'vulnerable road users' because they're most vulnerable to death from poor road design and safety.

Road traffic injuries are a top-five cause of death for Kenyans aged five to seventy, and the leading killer of boys aged fifteen to nineteen. A fifth of deaths are in those younger than twenty, and more than 75 per cent of road traffic casualties are economically productive adults. While those causing the accidents are most likely to be in a car, the fatalities are concentrated in those using the roads while walking or cycling – and more often than not, they're children.

Children are probably the most vulnerable road users, especially when going to school. They're shorter, which makes it difficult for them to see their surroundings in traffic, and for other road users to see them. They're also more likely to be hit on the chest and head, resulting in serious injury, compared to adults who are more likely to be hit on the legs.

Children also have a less developed perception of depth, so they struggle to assess the trajectory and speed of cars, which is essential to crossing roads safely. As anyone who's been around kids will recognize, they're often easily distracted and impulsive, which can lead to them suddenly running into the road without realizing the consequences.

No one would think to blame children in this situation. Children are precisely that: children. They need protection and guidance. The onus on keeping them safe falls on governments and communities to ensure that they are supported to use roads without severe injury. It's not an impossible task, as policy experiments within Kenya itself have demonstrated.

In 2011, awareness increased about the large number of children who were being fatally hit by motor vehicles while going to and from school in the Naivasha and Thika sub-counties of Kenya. A baseline study between January 2008 and July 2011 identified 266 injuries near schools in this area, which resulted in thirty-eight deaths. However, not all schools had the same level of road traffic injuries and deaths. These were much higher in schools around busy highways and roads.

Based on this data, twenty primary schools were selected to be part of a pilot project from 2011 to 2014 to see whether road safety interventions could improve the situation for children travelling to and from school. These included speed controls around schools, making road crossings more visible and ensuring they were supervised, and other measures to reduce speed, increase safe pedestrian routes and raise awareness. These interventions targeted over 20,000 children getting to school on foot.

Four years later, the number of crashes had dropped by 37 per cent in Thika and 49 per cent in Naivasha from the baseline figures, and the number of deaths declined by 83 per cent in Naivasha and 60 per cent in Thika. The take-away is that small, inexpensive changes can lead to huge gains in road safety. If these are implemented around schools, they prevent children dying.

While these sub-national pilots show promising results in certain intervention areas, the picture throughout Kenya isn't improving. Analysis has shown an increase of more than 9 per cent from 2021 to 2022 in weekly traffic fatalities. Just this week, while I was editing this chapter, Kenyan world-record marathon runner Kelvin Kiptum died in a car crash aged twenty-four. He was close to being the first person to finish a marathon in under two hours. One headline read: 'The life of the extraordinary marathon world record holder that ended too soon.'

The Kenyan transport minister pointed to human error for the high road fatality rates, such as drinking and driving, speeding, fatigue and dangerous overtaking. Dr Duncan Kibogong, the deputy director of safety strategies, said: 'We tend to view road crashes as an act of God, yet accidents are within the control of human capacity. When someone drinks and drives or drives at a speed of 220 kph then crashes, is that not predictable?'

The question then becomes how to limit the damage that human error can have on others. Mistakes are universal. Yet high-income countries have found a way to contain the negative impact of human error through policies and infrastructure design.

Where Fatal Road Accidents Cause a Third of All Deaths

At least Kenya is trying to take steps to improve the roads. Thailand, in contrast, is clearly in the red category. At least 20,000 people die on its roads each year, making it the ninth most dangerous place in the world for road safety. The UK has a similar-sized population to Thailand, but only has about 1,800 road deaths per year, according to the WHO.

In 2021, the WHO said that traffic-related incidents were resulting in nearly 33 per cent of total deaths in Thailand. Most of those deaths are in young people aged fifteen to twenty-nine, and 75 per cent are users of two and three wheels, on bikes and motorbikes. This is a remarkable number. In Thailand, children are most likely to die due to being hit by a motor vehicle (60 per cent of injury deaths) and then by drowning (35 per cent of injuries). Injuries cause 50 per cent of all child deaths, while 25 per cent are from infectious disease.

Why are the death rates so high in Thailand? It comes down to a few risk factors: people drinking and driving, speeding, and motorcyclists not wearing helmets. If people would wear a helmet when on a motorcycle, and they didn't drink and drive, over 60 per cent of the lives currently lost on the roads would be saved. That's 12,000 people saved and living longer. Drinking and driving causes 28 per cent of all traffic deaths: almost 6,000 people dying on the roads each year because of alcohol.

But enforcement is a real problem. As the *New York Times* reported, a Thai woman was riding on her motorcycle to work when a truck, driven by an off-duty police officer, hit her. He'd been drinking. She was killed almost instantly. The consequence? He kept his job and his driver's licence, and court deliberations resulted in no prison sentence or punishment. Examples like this show that those in positions of power, or the super-rich, know that they can do what they like without facing consequences. This results in low compliance with legislation on drinking and driving and speeding.

Another problem is inequality, with Thailand being named the most unequal country of the forty major economies surveyed by Credit Suisse. This results in fancy cars driven by the rich at high speed on well-paved roads, alongside the many poor who can only afford a scooter or motorcycle, and for whom a high-quality helmet is a luxury. The result is few usable sidewalks, because the rich (and their children) don't use them. Why would the powerful invest in solving a problem that doesn't affect them personally, and where the solutions are to the benefit of the poorest? It's only the poor who get hit and die.

It's a political problem at its core. Dr Tairjing Siripanich, secretary general of the Don't Drive Drunk Foundation, said: 'No political party has made this an issue. No leader wants to do anything. They just make promises to halve the number of road deaths even though they know it's impossible. Maybe they think we'll forget about the promises they made.'

No single agency seems to take responsibility for road traffic deaths. The department of disaster prevention and mitigation at the Ministry of the Interior, and the Office of Transport and Traffic Policy and Planning, point to the police as the problem, and the lack of enforcement. But the head of police has refused to accept this, saying: 'As police, there are many things we cannot do. We cannot build more roads and public transportation. We cannot change the number of cars on the road. We cannot change the attitudes of people so they have discipline.'

Yet Thailand was one of the most successful countries when it came to managing the pandemic: the government managed to keep COVID-19 deaths to fewer than sixty in 2020. Compare this to the almost 94,000 lives lost to the virus in Britain in that year. This contrast indicates how countries must continue to learn from each other: Thailand can learn from Britain's approach to road safety, and Britain has much to learn from how Thailand managed the pandemic in 2020.

How do locals explain the difference between a proactive and effective response to an infectious disease, and the lack of progress on a key cause of preventable death? Dr Siripanich gives his take: 'Everybody took COVID-19 so seriously. The authorities and the people, so we could control it. But with road accidents, we do not take them seriously.' He thinks it's about politics: 'Corruption, patronage, lifestyle – it always comes back to these three big problems. People use corruption to get away from what they did wrong . . . it's like they buy a licence for doing wrong.'

Perhaps that's the core difference between Thailand's responses to COVID-19 and to road safety. Infectious diseases bind us: the pandemic put a fear into the powerful and wealthy that they could also get COVID and die from it. It wasn't a problem restricted to the poor. Once the leadership decided this was a collective problem, solutions were found. The Ministry of Health took leadership and responsibility to develop a well-funded strategy, and implemented it.

The capacity, resources and policy interventions are available: the political will is absent. Does anyone care that children from poor backgrounds are dying on the streets while they walk to school? Which politician will take on the issue of road traffic injuries being the number one cause of child death? So far, in Thailand at least, no one has decided to push the agenda forward.

If We Know What Works, Why Isn't It Being Done?

Disappointingly, little has changed in many countries over the past twenty years, and while the Sustainable Development Goals called for a 50 per cent reduction of road traffic injuries by 2030, most countries won't reach this target and are going the other way. It's largely children and young people who are being killed, whether walking to school or work, or on two- or three-wheel vehicles. These are chiefly the poor in society who can't afford a safer way to go about daily life.

We know what works in saving lives, and we know that implementing these policies works, whether in remote Kenya or the urban Dominican Republic, and in cultures as different as Japan and Sweden. We know that the WHO package Save LIVES lists the interventions that governments must adopt to reduce deaths to close to zero. A *Lancet* analysis estimated that even a few interventions – like curbing speeding and drink driving, and the use of helmets, seatbelts and child restraints – could avoid 25–40 per cent of fatal road injuries.

What are the solutions? It starts with having a clear plan of action and implementing evidence-based policies. It's a pretty straightforward list, and one which should be uncontroversial: Speed limits (supported by speed bumps and other measures) that are enforced. Legislation banning drinking and driving, which is enforced. Continuous footpaths and pavements, wide enough to support pedestrian traffic, on both sides of the road. Physically separate cycle lanes. Effective lighting next to roads to increase pedestrian and cyclist visibility. Zebra crossings with stop lines and flashing lights in areas where many pedestrians need to cross. Providing pedestrian holding areas at the roadside at each intersection, where pedestrians can wait together before crossing the road. Pedestrian bridges across highways and freeways, and near areas of increased pedestrian activity. Providing adequate public transport to give people an affordable and accessible alternative to cars. Traffic calming measures and patrols near schools to keep children safe. Helmet laws for motorcyclists. Mandatory seatbelts and child car seats. Incentivizing people to use smaller cars, which are safer than SUVs and trucks.

But as is clear from the statistics on road traffic deaths, this 'obvious' list isn't being implemented. How to explain the gap between the non-existent, or even backwards, progress on reducing deaths to road traffic accidents in low- and middle-income countries, and the growing evidence base that we know what works?

It's politics and economics. It affects the poor, and the wealthy and powerful are protected. It costs money to invest in solutions. It falls under the remit of police and law enforcement, urban planners, transport designers and engineers. No one profession or sector has overall responsibility for road traffic injuries, and so no single profession is sufficiently accountable.

Don't forget the massive automobile lobby, which has tried to present the solution to road traffic injuries, for example in the US, as buying an even bigger car to protect yourself from the high death rate of road traffic accidents. This results in people who can afford to, buying a bigger car to feel safer, and in doing so, making everyone else less safe.

This circular logic is quite similar to the guns story. Buy more of the thing killing others to protect yourself from it. The outcome is that the entire community is more at risk. The point is, there's a private lobby working for profit, not in the interests of general population health. That's the job of government.

The story of how to prevent people dying from road traffic accidents is a pretty simple one. Injuries and deaths are preventable, especially in children. If governments are led by politicians willing to make road safety a priority and implement the proven interventions, tens of thousands of people would live longer.

If you've read this chapter and you live in Britain or a European country, you might think it all looks obvious, low-cost and already implemented to various degrees. But it could be implemented even better (especially in relation to pedestrians and cyclists) and this would bring down road traffic injuries and deaths even further.

Edinburgh, where I live now, has done a decent job of bringing in a 20 mph speed limit, has strict enforceable laws on drinking and driving, invests in affordable public transport networks, and prioritizes pedestrians. Cyclists still have major safety issues, but the general direction of travel (excuse the pun) is the right one.

Don't even ask me about the roads in Miami, where public transport options are super-limited, pedestrians and cyclists must navigate busy intersections, and vehicles drive at high speeds on highways, weaving between lanes. It's better than my Tirupati near-death experience, but that's a low bar. My risk of dying in a road traffic incident is significantly lower having moved to Scotland. Unlike eating a more balanced diet or exercising more, this isn't an issue that can be solved easily at an individual level: it's about oversight of the entire road safety system by the government, and the policies they put in place to prevent people dying too soon.

8. The Water Fountain

It takes three days to die of thirst. I think about this each time I fill up my water bottle. I haven't taken living in a country with clean running water for granted since I watched the roof of my house blow off in South Miami during Hurricane Andrew in 1992. At that time, Andrew was the costliest hurricane in US history: a powerful category 5 storm that ripped through the city, destroying more than 63,000 houses and causing billions of dollars in damage.

I was eight, and two things stuck with me: first, all the animals that escaped, including 1,000 monkeys from damaged zoo facilities, who roamed around the city. Three baboons decided to make a federal prison their new home, until they were caught by marshals. Not the brightest idea to move from one prison to another. Over 3,800 exotic animals were on the loose, including boa constrictors, parrots, iguanas, capybaras, wallabies, water deer and huge lizards. Most of these animals were never recovered and either died (not being able to survive in urban Miami) or became absorbed by the local ecosystem (i.e. the Everglades).

Four years later our school 'Outward Bound' residential was to the Everglades, where we paddled in kayaks throughout the swamp. If we made it to dry land, we pitched up a tent and could zip away the outside world of spiders, raccoons and snakes. If our navigation failed, we tied the kayaks together, pulled out long boards from the bottom of the boats and placed them on top, so we had a makeshift ground to sleep on until sunrise.

The boys pushed to the middle of the platform and the girls made a circle at the edges. I couldn't sleep those nights, nervous that I would roll into the water and be eaten by an alligator or python. Or any of the other exotic animals that escaped the zoo and found a new comfortable home in the Everglades. It sounds surreal but, yes, this was my childhood in Florida. I was happy to learn upon moving to Scotland that the country has no apex predators.

The second thing I remember about the hurricane was how hard it was to get clean water. My youngest brother Arun had been born just a few weeks before the storm hit, while my youngest sister Priya was just over a year old. My mum needed clean water to make formula for the newborn, and to wash the bottles and utensils for feeding. The tap water was contaminated from the storm, and bottled water was almost impossible to find, and priced extortionately. Boiling water was a short-term solution but required electricity which the city didn't have. Fortunately, the military arrived and provided free bottled water, and my parents were lucky enough to find a generator to help sterilize bottles.

Not having clean water is especially risky for babies and young children. Diarrhoeal diseases (linked to dirty water) are one of the leading causes of death in children under the age of five worldwide. They kill largely through dehydration and malnutrition. Over days of diarrhoea, a child loses water and electrolytes such as sodium, chloride, potassium and bicarbonate which are essential to bodily function. If these aren't replaced quickly, a child will die of organ failure as the brain, heart, kidneys and liver begin to shut down.

As a teenager, it was already hard for me to understand my father getting ill and dying of cancer, something that I thought we should have better tools to treat. But to have kids dying from lack of something as simple as clean water stuck with me. I decided in Oxford to focus my Masters and PhD research on preventable child deaths.

During my studies, I met an Irish doctor based in Malawi called Dr Bernie O'Hare. She was soft-spoken, highly intelligent, and wanting to collaborate. After working in the NHS, she moved to Blantyre (the second-largest city in Malawi) as a paediatrician, which saw her looking after poorly children. Her frustration mounted as she saw preventable health conditions day after day. She felt she was simply putting a Band-Aid on wider problems: unclean water sources, poor diet, and poverty. She argued that much could be done to help children at a population level if basic public health policies would be implemented.

But this required money and investment in the health sector. So, Bernie's focus shifted towards government revenue generation, health financing, and good governance. She saw these as essential towards delivering better health to children. Bernie wondered: why keep trying to treat patients when there's a way to prevent them becoming ill in the first place?

I decided to tackle a similar question in my first book, *The Battle Against Hunger*. I wanted to understand how India, a food-producing country that has enough grain to reach to the Moon and back, has the largest number of undernourished children in the world and a high child death rate.

Two of the surprises over the course of my research were that the answer didn't lie in food storage, or production. It lay in clean water and in girls' education. Malnutrition in the places I was studying in India was largely linked to being afflicted with diarrhoeal disease. A child can lose 2–3 per cent of their body weight each day while sick. There's no point offering a child food supplements if they just get repeatedly ill from the dirty water they're drinking.

When I was interviewed by *Grazia* Pakistan in 2022, I was asked if there was anything I would change in the world. My answer was that I would love to see more girls staying in school – being supported by their families, communities and teachers to get an education. Research shows clearly that when girls are educated, child survival improves, domestic violence goes down, societies are more equal, and there's a greater sense of community and wellbeing.

After observing the world for four decades, I think most of its problems could be solved if more girls were able to stay in school, if they were able to go on to higher education, and if we had more female leaders across the world in government, the private sector, the arts and other areas. I'm not alone in thinking this. Melinda Gates, co-founder of the Bill & Melinda Gates Foundation, wrote an entire book, *The Moment of Lift*, about how empowering women changes the world. She said: 'If you want to lift up humanity, empower women. It is the most comprehensive, pervasive, high-leverage investment you can make in human beings.'

What Would You Like to Be When You Grow Up? Alive

About a third of diarrhoeal deaths in children are due to rotavirus. People who are infected with rotavirus shed the virus in their faeces. If these particles are ingested by someone else, either through unwashed hands or a contaminated surface or food, they'll become sick with the virus as well. This is why handwashing is important in avoiding diseases that come from human excrement getting into our mouths and digestive systems. Once infected, vomiting and watery diarrhoea can last for days.

To prevent children dying, they need to stay hydrated with fluids and minerals. Prior to the 1960s, diarrhoea was treated with expensive intravenous rehydration therapy, providing a saline solution in a hospital setting. This is highly effective, with immediate impact. Treating diarrhoea in hospital was possible in high-income settings but unrealistic for the millions of children living in low-income and rural contexts, or during an epidemic of, let's say, cholera, because of limited hospital capacity to treat an influx of patients in a short time period.

During the Indo-Pakistani War in 1971, cholera spread through refugee camps, and in these desperate circumstances almost 30 per cent of patients were dying because they couldn't get access to hospital IV fluids. Dr Dilip Mahalanabis, a local doctor, decided to take matters into his own hands and started providing bags of oral rehydration salts (or ORS) to people in the camps. These bags were a simple solution of salt and sugar dissolved in water.

In just a few months, the case fatality rate from cholera fell below 4 per cent for those receiving ORS, compared to 30 per cent before. This was crucial data in showing the effectiveness of ORS as a cheap, accessible treatment for diarrhoea. The *Lancet* called it the 'most important medical advance of the 20th century'. In 1978, the WHO created the diarrhoeal disease programme, with ORS a key plank within it.

In 1982, UNICEF launched the Child Survival and Development Revolution to save the lives of millions of children each year through four low-cost measures, referred to as GOBI. G was for growth monitoring: tracking the growth of newborns and children to recognize malnutrition early. O was for ORS: access to rehydration treatment at a community level. B was for breastfeeding, which provided sufficient and hygienic nutrition for newborns, especially those living without clean water. I was for immunization against the common childhood killers. The campaign tagline was: 'What would you like to be when you grow up? Alive!'

Through the efforts of governments, supported by UN agencies, global child deaths fell significantly. One in eleven children died before reaching the age of five in 1990. It was one in twenty-seven in 2019. The number of under-five deaths globally fell from 12.6 million in 1990 to 5.2 million in 2019. Since 1990, the global under-five mortality rate has dropped by 59 per cent, from ninety-three deaths per 1,000 live births to thirty-eight in 2019. These positive trends were pre-COVID pandemic.

Since 2020, these gains have stalled due to paused vaccination campaigns, limited reach of health care workers (meaning children not getting ORS when ill), school closures, and backwards progress on clean water and clean air in several low-income contexts. Progress is not always linear and continuous. It depends on conducive public policies and a stable situation, which obviously wasn't the case during the pandemic.

In 2015, Chelsea Clinton and I wrote an article for CNN highlighting the fact that 'Helping babies survive the first day, the first week and the first month of life remains the greatest challenge in global health.' We argued that infectious disease outbreaks like Ebola and MERS become black holes, sucking the necessary ingredients from health systems that could be allocated towards saving babies.

When looking at the toll of a major outbreak, or pandemic in the case of COVID, it's not enough to look at the lives lost directly to the disease. It's important to also measure the indirect toll on the lives of infants and children, who because of the strain on already fragile health systems, die from easily treatable conditions. UNICEF has referred to these as the 'uncounted dead' in relation to the Ebola outbreak in West Africa in 2014, with estimates of additional deaths linked to disruption in vaccine schedules and suspension of health care works. The same analysis is being conducted for the children and infants affected by the COVID pandemic.

John Snow: The King of ~~the North~~ Public Health

Within global health circles, there is a clever acronym relating to safe water: WASH (water, sanitation and hygiene). Dirty water is responsible for over 1 million deaths a year globally and is implicated in several diseases, not only diarrhoeal diseases, but also typhoid fever, dysentery, hepatitis A, polio, hookworm, other parasitic worms, guinea worm disease, trachoma, schistosomiasis, and Buruli ulcer. The list goes on, but the basic point is that infectious diseases thrive when there's unsafe drinking water and poor sanitation.

John Snow – no, not the King of the North or the Channel 4 news presenter – discovered that unclean water is the transmission mechanism for certain pathogens. Let's head to London in the mid-nineteenth century, when it looked not too dissimilar to the poorest parts of the world today, in that public water supplies and waste disposal systems were largely non-existent. The introduction of rudimentary sanitation systems was a step forward, but these drained directly into the River Thames, which became an open, stinking sewer. People were reliant on the water of the Thames for bathing, drinking and washing. The consequence was multiple diseases running rampant, such as cholera, dysentery, typhoid, and a range of diarrhoeal diseases.

But people back then didn't know that these illnesses were linked to the water they were drinking. Cholera was linked to 'miasma', which meant bad smells or poisonous vapours entering the human body. The theory was originally advanced by Hippocrates in the fourth century BC, and it was only in the nineteenth century that the germ theory of disease replaced it. Germ theory is simply the idea that pathogens or 'germs' cause disease, even when these are invisible to the human eye and often microscopic. It sounds obvious now but as we saw in the COVID pandemic, there are still thousands of people who question whether viruses even exist. I received hundreds of letters asking for proof that SARS-CoV-2 existed. They simply wanted me to mail back samples of the virus that could be seen.

Let's head back to August 1854 when an outbreak of cholera in Soho, London, killed 127 people in three days, and 616 within the month. In September that year, a local medic called John Snow sent a letter to the *Medical Times and Gazette* about the outbreak. He wrote: 'The most terrible outbreak of cholera which ever occurred in this kingdom, is probably that which took place in Broad Street, Golden Square and the adjoining streets, a few weeks ago. Within two hundred and fifty yards of the spot where Cambridge Street joins Broad Street, there were upwards of five hundred fatal attacks of cholera in ten days ... The mortality would have undoubtedly been much greater had it not been for the flight of the population ... in less than six days ... the most afflicted streets were deserted by more than three-quarters of their inhabitants.'

Snow created a map showing where cases of cholera were located, and where they weren't, and found positive cases clustered around a water pump on Broad Street. He didn't know what exactly was causing people to get sick, the exact pathogen, but he took a step back to look at the larger environment in which people lived and how the disease could be linked to something within that community.

In his letter, Snow pointed to 'contamination of the water of the much-frequented street-pump in Broad Street'. He looked at a workhouse and brewery nearby and found that they hadn't been affected by cholera. They had their own water source and didn't rely on the Broad Street pump. He concluded: 'The result of the inquiry then was that there has been no particular outbreak or increase of cholera, in this part of London, except among the persons who were in the habit of drinking water of the above-mentioned pump-well.'

Snow then met with the parish Board of Guardians, who agreed to disable the Broad Street pump. He noted: 'Two to three days after the use of water was discontinued the number of fresh attacks became very few.' Soon after, London overhauled its water and sanitation systems, which rendered cholera largely non-existent within the city. City officials didn't know what the pathogen was – and the cholera bacterium wouldn't be identified by scientists until 1883 – but they knew that faeces-contaminated water could cause disease, and the importance of addressing this.

For his cholera research and population-level health efforts, John Snow is often regarded as the father of public health and epidemiology. You can find a small memorial to him on Broadwick Street in London, along with a replica pump and a namesake pub.

Snow's findings on water-borne diseases were a major turning point in government leadership on building and maintaining safe water and sanitation systems across the industrializing world. The major increases in life expectancy across the Western world in the nineteenth and first half of the twentieth century are linked not just to modern medicine, but to public health interventions like clean water and sanitation systems. While the challenge of water-borne diseases might seem solved in Britain or the United States, dirty water is still a major cause of disease and death across the world, especially in young children.

How to Build a Water System

The 'rich world' and 'poor world' are divided on this problem. Death rates from dirty water in low-income countries, especially in sub-Saharan Africa and Asia, are often greater than fifty deaths per 100,000, and largely in children. Compare this to death rates across Europe, which are below 0.1 per 100,000. That's a 500-fold difference in deaths: completely preventable deaths.

High-income countries started this journey in the nineteenth century. For example, Stockholm had an annual death rate of fifty-nine per 1,000 in 1878, which was reduced to two per 1,000 by 1925. A study from Lund University notes that water-borne diseases were virtually eradicated by the construction of piped water and sewerage services between 1876 and 1930. The study points out that while this came at a substantial cost and resistance to investment, the system was ultimately built, with a large impact on saving lives.

What do water and sanitation systems require? Clean water sources are about appropriately treating raw source water, protecting sources from contamination, and ensuring safe distribution of treated water to people. Water treatment plants use a number of steps to ensure water is safe for drinking: coagulation (chemicals added to the water), flocculation (mixing), sedimentation (allowing large, insoluble particles to settle to the bottom of the tank), filtration (eliminates particles and parasitic protozoa), and disinfection/chlorination (which kills bacteria and viruses).

Sanitation systems need to ensure that wastewater – which contains human waste, food scraps, oils, soaps, chemicals from homes and factories – is treated before being released back into nature. This involves a piping system to remove wastewater from buildings, screening the wastewater for large items, carrying out primary treatment (to remove solids), secondary treatment (pumping air into the water to remove harmful bacteria) and a final treatment (filtering water through a bed of sand to catch any remaining particles). The wastewater is then safely returned to local rivers and streams in a form that means it doesn't make people sick who later use it. Treatment plants can reduce specific pollutants within water, but business and industry need to also ensure their wastewater runoff is to an acceptable standard.

Access to clean water is linked to population income: there is a positive correlation between average GDP per capita and access to improved water sources (meaning piped water in taps). Countries with the least access to clean water tend to be poorer: places like the DRC, Burundi, Mozambique, Kenya, Uganda; while those with the highest access tend to be richer: Germany, Italy, Britain, the United States, Japan.

The WHO/UNICEF assess the quality of drinking water from the worst: surface water (water directly from a river or lake or outside source), to unimproved (water from an unprotected dug well/spring), to limited (over thirty minutes to collect from a public tap with treated water), to basic (under thirty minutes to collect from a public tap with treated water), to safely managed (located on the premises and available when needed).

The Lucrative Market of Bottled Water

In 2023, the UN estimated that 2.2 billion people did not have access to safe drinking water. The bottled water industry has grown to fill this need. Low- and middle-income countries depend on it to bring this essential good to their populations. Bottled water is the main form of water for an estimated 600 million households.

It's a lucrative market. The bottled water market saw 73 per cent growth from 2010 to 2020, and consumption is on track to increase from about 350 billion litres in 2021 to 460 billion litres by 2030. The largest bottled water company in the world is Nestlé Waters, with gross annual sales of $104.11 billion. This is out of a total market size of $342.4 billion in 2023. It's becoming an easy solution for governments which abdicate responsibility to provide clean water. While a short-term fix, relying on bottled water has major problems.

First, a natural resource is extracted that negatively affects groundwater levels. Nestlé Waters extracted 3 million litres each day from Florida Springs in 2020 (that's just over an Olympic-sized swimming pool a day), while in France, water company Danone extracted up to 10 million litres each day (three huge swimming pools) from Évian-les-Bains in the French Alps. There is little regulation or management of groundwater extraction and the impact this could have on local water resources and people relying on groundwater for their drinking needs.

Second, seeing bottled water as the solution takes pressure off government to invest and build up a public water supply system. For example, Egypt, which faces water scarcity from public sources, had the fastest-growing market for treated bottled water from 2018 to 2021. As water expert Vladimir Smakhtin said: 'To a somewhat surprising extent, bottled water grew immensely over the last few decades while in the conventional and more reliable public and domestic drinking water supply, progress was slow paced.'

It becomes a vicious cycle: without public provision of clean water through taps, people rely on bottled water and give their money to private companies. These companies then further push bottled water and expand their operations and market, no investment goes into public sector provision of water, and groundwater is depleted.

Third, bottled water has an enormous environmental toll in several ways. Producing plastics requires fossil fuels and increases greenhouse gas emissions, and 85 per cent of the 600 billion plastic bottles used each year (that's 1.1 million bottles used every minute) end up in landfills. These plastic bottles also end up in the ocean and are a major cause of plastic pollution.

Plastic bottles can take up to 1,000 years to degrade fully, and while degrading they leach toxic chemicals, which make their way into the animal and human food chain. Plastic bottles also break down into microplastics (pieces smaller than 5 millimetres) in the ocean. A 2020 study found 1.9 million microplastic pieces in an area of about 11 square feet in the Mediterranean Sea. These are ingested by fish and other sea creatures, with real risk to human health. A 2021 study found more than 10,000 unique chemicals in plastic, of which 2,400 were concerning for health reasons. In laboratory tests, microplastics caused damage to human cells.

Despite these concerns, global sales of bottled water are expected to double between 2023 and 2030 in a booming market. The industry is growing, with a clear incentive to increase sales and expand markets, taking advantage of limited clean drinking water from taps. If governments provide free drinking water refilling stations, this cuts into bottled water company profits. It reduces their market.

Singapore and Australia were the biggest per capita consumers of bottled water per year in 2020, and more than a third of Americans report using bottled water as their main water source. It's not because they don't have access to clean tap water. As a researcher at the UN Institute noted, 'Campaigns run by corporations have a bigger influence on perceptions that bottled water is a better option.' It's marketing through using global brand ambassadors: just think of tennis stars Emma Raducanu, Maria Sharapova and Frances Tiafoe, or pop star Dua Lipa, promoting bottles of Evian on social media.

While bottled water provides a Band-Aid solution, governments are ultimately accountable for providing clean water to their populations. Living in Edinburgh, I find the widespread reliance on bottled water surprising. Here, the water coming from taps is clean and the city is installing an increasing number of public water stations to refill water bottles. The Top Up Tap programme is part of the publicly owned Scottish Water's Your Water Your Life campaign, and offers free drinking water to people on the go. In 2022, this was the equivalent of 2 million bottles of water across the country. If you head to Rome, Paris or Brussels you can get free sparkling water at kiosks throughout these major cities.

But these cities are not the norm. Providing clean water is an ongoing challenge for governments across the world. I'll take a look at four different situations: when no water system exists at all, when the existing one is broken, when the existing one isn't regulated properly, and when there are underlying water shortages.

When No Water System Exists

Port-au-Prince's streets are littered with plastic rubbish, largely empty *sachés dlo*, nine-ounce water bags that are sold throughout the country. Without a central water system bringing clean water into homes and workplaces, people are reliant on water bags to survive. These are sold by street vendors, mostly women, at an affordable price, providing employment and livelihood. While some of these packages come from companies abroad (based in Alaska, for example), any individual with a packing machine can start producing and selling water bags. There's no formal quality control or law over the water being packaged and sold.

Once emptied, these plastic bags are thrown directly into the city's streets and rivers. There's no formal sewerage system to manage the reuse, recycling or even the proper disposal of dirty, used bags. Port-au-Prince is one of the largest cities in the world without a central sewerage system. This means a functional piped system that brings sewage waste from toilets in homes and other buildings out and away to be treated and managed. This is something we don't even notice when we're in Britain or travelling across most of the world, because it feels normal to have access to some kind of toilet without worrying about where the stuff coming out of our bottoms ends up.

It's a different story on this Caribbean island of 11.6 million people. In Haiti, it's estimated that more than half the population lack access to safe drinking water and only one third of people have access to basic sanitation like a toilet. This is far below the 90 per cent average in Latin America and the Caribbean, and access to drinking water in Haiti is going down decade after decade, instead of up. Those who can afford it, buy drinking water from street sellers in plastic bags or canisters. Those who can't, drink from the rivers which are full of sewage: the result is that 80 per cent of the disease burden in Haiti is because of dirty water.

From a global health perspective, Haiti is one of the countries worst afflicted by preventable diseases, and death, due to failed policy and governance. When I started a large Wellcome Trust grant to study governance in global health, one of my post-docs, Dr Felix Stein, said he wanted to choose Haiti as his case study. This meant fieldwork: going to live in the country for at least a year, and in the true anthropological sense, becoming part of the community to observe, study, do interviews and then analyse this data to understand the public health challenges of providing clean water.

We kept in touch via calls and emails over the year, and Felix's observations about governance and public health in the country were fascinating. In April 2019 he was back in Edinburgh and gave a talk at our team's public outreach event on Healthy and Sustainable Futures on 'Water and Cholera in Haiti'. His main observations were that drinking water was a private market in Haiti, meaning that private vendors were the main supply for those living in the city, as we have seen.

Any attempts to build a public central water system were curtailed either by corruption at high levels (officials taking large amounts of development assistance and not using it for the intended objective), or by smaller-scale resistance from water vendors who were afraid that public water provision meant the end of their livelihoods. There was also societal hesitation towards the quality and drinkability of something not coming from a bag or canister. Haitian people have experience of getting extremely sick from dirty water. They're careful with where they get their water, and they trust the water bags.

Felix's main concern during his fieldwork was personal safety. He described groups of young men roaming the streets with military-style weapons, arbitrarily enforcing their own laws; gun violence was the top concern for those living in the city. State police are basically non-existent, and are generally poorly equipped against the heavily armed and larger gangs.

Gang violence has only increased in Haiti since Felix left. In 2021, the assassination of President Jovenel Moïse led to much of the country's territory falling out of government control. In 2023, almost 5,000 Haitians were killed and over 2,490 kidnapped in extreme brutality and violence. In August 2023, the UN Secretary General António Guterres told the Security Council that a 'robust use of force' by a multinational deployment was needed to disarm the gangs and restore order and peace to the country.

What does gang violence have to do with clean water? Everything. In the absence of a functioning government that can keep peace and enforce law and order, it's basically impossible to build and maintain large public sector projects such as water and sanitation systems. This is despite millions flowing into Haiti for development from organizations like the World Bank and the US government. The World Bank has launched several clean water projects but these are small-scale and trying to support a particular community of, for example, 20,000 people through building water kiosks and the like, and the struggle is for these to be maintained and functional after the initial start.

Haiti has also been unlucky with natural disasters. On the 12th of January 2010, a magnitude 7 earthquake struck the country, affecting an estimated 3 million people. Roughly 250,000 homes and 30,000 office buildings collapsed, and death tolls range from 100,000 to 250,000. To assist the country, the UN sent in peacekeepers from different nations, including Nepal. Nine months later, in October 2010, cholera became endemic across the country, infecting nearly 800,000 Haitians and killing more than 9,000. This was the first outbreak of cholera in Haiti in over 100 years. Obviously, it led to questions about where the disease had come from.

Cholera is caused by a bacterium that, when ingested through contaminated food or water, leads to diarrhoea and vomiting, and it can be fatal without proper treatment: in short, it comes from contaminated poo finding its way into drinking water. The suspected source of the bacteria was the Artibonite River, where tens of thousands of Haitians bathe, get drinking water, swim and wash their dishes and clothes. Scientific research traced the source of the cholera bacteria to a UN base, home to Nepalese peacekeepers, positioned near the river. The authors of a study looking at DNA sequence data concluded that: 'The Haitian epidemic is probably the result of the introduction, through human activity, of a *V. cholerae* strain from a distant geographic source.' You can only imagine the international furore and blame that followed on from these findings.

Cholera could spread in Haiti because of the mixing of human waste and drinking water, called the faecal–oral transmission route in public health. It is not a disease that spreads through human-to-human breathing like COVID. It usually spreads through a contaminated source of water or food that somehow contains the faeces of an infected person.

Cholera is straightforward enough to eliminate within a region or country if there are functional water and sanitation systems. All it requires is keeping what we drink and eat away from where someone infected defecates. It seems simple enough from a public health perspective, compared to stopping diseases like malaria from mosquitoes, or COVID from other humans. But within the context of Haiti it has proved an elusive goal, and is linked to Haiti being ranked worst, of all countries in the world, for its clean water reach. This shows that disease linked to contaminated water is linked to water and sanitation systems, which are linked to a functional state and governance, which is linked to being able to enforce law and order.

Broken, Neglected Systems

Schools moved to virtual learning in Jackson, Mississippi, in August 2022. No, this wasn't linked to COVID disruption. It was a long-standing problem faced by the city because of water issues. On the 29th of August 2022, the largest water treatment plant in the city broke down, leaving 160,000 people – and hospitals, schools and fire stations – without safe drinking water.

Erica Jones, president of the Mississippi Association of Educators, said that 20,000 students were moving to virtual learning because of disruption to the water system into schools. The district sent out a brief statement to parents: 'We will continue to closely monitor the water conditions on a day-by-day basis at our schools while conferring with city officials to determine when scholars and staff can safely return for in-person learning.'

School closures due to clean water supply issues were not a new problem in Jackson. When Jones was an elementary school teacher between 2010 and 2014, schools would be 'days, weeks, without water'. She continued: 'The learning experience of Jackson students at every level is being disrupted without notice and with lasting harm due to lack of water, low water pressure and dependence on bottled water.'

Almost fifteen years ago, in 2010, a storm caused hundreds of water mains to burst, leaving local residents without water for weeks. In 2013, a Jackson master water plan was updated, noting that more than 112 miles of water pipes were of unlined cast iron and most were more than 100 years old. It noted problems in the system but almost nothing was done to rectify these. In 2014, a winter storm resulted in water shortages, which happened again in 2018. Years and years going by with the same problems, and nothing done to fix them.

In 2019, more than 3 billion gallons of sewage were released into the Pearl River, used by locals for swimming and fishing. In 2020, the city's sewage overflowed and nearly 5.7 billion gallons of minimally treated sewage were dumped into the river, along with half a billion gallons of raw sewage. To give you a sense of how much sewage this is, visualize over 9,000 Olympic-sized swimming pools being dumped into one river. Again no action. In February 2021, Jackson residents had no drinking water for a month due to a storm. In August 2022, as I described above, the entire system collapsed.

On the 20th of August 2022, President Joe Biden declared a ninety-day state of emergency in the state, authorizing federal funds to cover 75 per cent of the costs of the emergency, and pushing the state of Mississippi to fix the ongoing water and sanitation problems. Yet into 2024, few improvements have been made because of fighting between federal and state officials over who should pay for the repairs. The tap water still isn't clean enough to drink. The result is frequent school closures, dependence on bottled water, advice not to rinse toothbrushes in tap water and not to get water in your mouth during showers, and daily planning to rethink cooking options and to allocate time and money for travel to water stations.

Why isn't more being done to address this issue? It only takes a closer look at the demographics of who is affected: 80 per cent of residents in Jackson are Black, and about 25 per cent live in poverty. Mississippi is the state with the lowest life expectancy and highest rate of infant mortality, both robust indicators of the 'health' of a community.

Perhaps more would be done if the people affected were powerful, or white, or had close links to politicians. Instead they're marginalized, and even within one of the wealthiest countries in the world, clean water is proving a challenge and schools are shutting down because of this. A local resident said that it feels like a Third World country. Professor Richard Mizelle from the University of Houston said: 'The water is a window into that neglect that many people have experienced for much of their lives.'

'Profit Over Human Health' Systems

In 1985, Feargal Sharkey's solo single 'A Good Heart' went to the top of the charts in several countries including the UK. Sharkey, from Derry, Northern Ireland, had already had several hits with his band The Undertones, including 'Teenage Kicks' and 'Here Comes the Summer'. He continued to make waves within the music industry in the decades to come, and received an OBE in the 2019 Birthday Honours for services to music.

But instead of a recording studio, he's more likely to be found on the water these days – or at an environmental protest. Sharkey, a lifelong fly fisherman, is furious about the increase in untreated sewage being dumped into UK waterways and along its coasts. In an interview with the *Observer* in 2018, he talked passionately about the lack of investment in clean water infrastructure in England, and the lack of responsible behaviour from private water companies.

He said: 'We can't continue this decimation of 85% of the world's chalk streams. They're our Amazon rainforest. If it was some other country doing this, the UK would be at the bloody UN shouting and screaming.' Chalk streams are lowland rivers that provide a home for an exceptionally high number of species to breed and thrive. These types of rivers are rare, with only 260 in the world, and are sensitive to pollution due to their very clear and alkaline water. The sewage flowing into them is causing irreversible damage to the creatures living within them, and destroying a unique environmental resource.

Sharkey points to water companies drawing supplies from already shallow rivers, leading to drying riverbeds, which are then dumped with excess sewage. He also points to 5 per cent of homes in London having their waste going directly into rivers rather than the sewage system, and one school in north London which he claims dumps 100,000 litres of untreated waste each day into the local river.

The consequence is that people using those rivers are getting sick. In August 2023, at least fifty-seven people fell ill with diarrhoea after competing at the World Triathlon Championship Series in Sunderland at Roker beach. Samples from the beach showed 3,900 *E. coli* colonies per 100 ml (*E. coli* is a bacterium that can cause bloody diarrhoea), more than thirty-nine times higher than the previous month. The beach is near a stretch of coastline where untreated sewage is discharged.

As an Australian triathlete at the event said, 'Have been feeling pretty rubbish since the race, but I guess that's what happens when you swim in shit. The swim should have been cancelled.' Another competitor from Leeds said: 'I like to swim outdoors but don't have any confidence in the cleanliness of seas, rivers, lakes etc. because of the dumping of sewage or other effluents.'

I talked earlier about how the Thames was seen in the nineteenth century as a large sewer, and due to concerns about cholera and other diseases, efforts were then made to create safe water and sanitation systems. A basic principle is to keep untreated sewage away from the water that people come into contact with. Yet this has been eroded in modern Britain today, and the lessons forgotten about the importance of clean water to good health.

Sewage normally should go to treatment plants to be made safe and then released into seas and rivers to re-enter the water cycle. In extreme cases of flooding, water companies can release it before being treated to avoid sewage flooding streets. However, in recent years, water companies have been releasing untreated sewage even during dry periods, or when there's no environmental trigger.

For example, in 2022, sewage was dumped into waters near England's beaches for nearly 8,500 hours. A separate review found that there were 1,504 discharges that year on beaches supposed to be free from pollution. Recent data has shown that water companies collectively dumped sewage 372,533 times in 2021 and 301,091 times in 2022.

The problem goes back three decades, when water companies were privatized in England and sold off by then Prime Minister Margaret Thatcher, in 1989. The consequence has been that water companies operate to make profits for their shareholders rather than to provide affordable water for people living in England and to ensure that waste is handled appropriately. For example, the payouts in dividends to shareholders of parent companies between 1991 and 2019 was £57 billion, which is more than £2 billion per year on average. Many of these private parent companies are in fact foreign-owned, so the profits aren't even kept in Britain.

In addition, the earnings of the nine water companies' directors continue to rise, with salary packages such as £2.4 million and £2.3 million (Severn Trent and United Utilities respectively). In contrast, the CEO of the publicly owned Scottish Water earned £295,000 in 2023. Scottish Water has also invested nearly 35 per cent more per household in infrastructure than the privatized water companies since 2002, it charges users 14 per cent less, and it doesn't pay dividends. Professor Dieter Helm of Oxford University isn't surprised: 'The water companies behaved exactly how we believe a commercial company does behave... What we have seen is a complete regulatory failure to control the companies.'

This situation has resulted in the Liberal Democrat Party calling for a sewage tax on annual profits and a ban on water company bonuses until this problem is sorted. In July 2023, Tim Farron, the Lib Dems' environment spokesperson, said: 'Coastal communities are at the mercy of water companies who unapologetically discharge raw sewage into popular swimming spots. This Conservative government needs to stop letting water companies off the hook and finally ban these disgusting sewage discharges.'

Health officials are concerned too with people getting sick from dirty water, and the lack of accountability of water companies. England's Chief Medical Officer Chris Whitty wrote a piece titled 'Sewage in water: a growing public health problem', where he notes: 'the principal public health responsibility for ensuring human faeces and viable human faecal bacteria do not get into waterways... rests squarely with the water companies and their directors.' Aside from the shit in our rivers and oceans, at least Britain has safe tap water for almost 100 per cent of its population.

Clean Water Shortages

I bring up the case of water shortages, because some see water wars in our future. As climate change gets worse, droughts and floodings more common and clean water more limited, fights for water, the most precious resource of all, become more likely. In 1995, former World Bank vice president Dr Ismail Serageldin said: 'If the wars of this century were fought over oil, the wars of the next century will be fought over water – unless we change our approach to managing this precious and vital resource.'

By 2025, the UN predicts two thirds of all people on the planet will live in water-stressed areas. There's no ambiguity with water compared to other goods: humans, animals and plants cannot live without water. Find fresh water or die.

Let's head south to Cape Town, a city of 4.6 million that's struggled with providing clean water to its residents. Between 2015 and 2018, Cape Town experienced a drought, leading the South African government to count down to 'day zero': the day the city would run out of water and taps would be turned off. This seems the stuff of sci-fi: the idea that an international city, on the coast, would simply no longer have the most basic thing that humans need to sustain life.

The 'day zero' messaging by government shocked the residents into becoming more economical in their use of clean water: water use was restricted to 50 litres per person per day, which meant bucket showers, toilet flushes once a day, and recycling of water within the home. One resident explained: 'The day zero campaign made us all think twice about water. We'll never, ever, ever take water for granted again.'

While day zero was averted in 2019, the looming threat of limited fresh water remains a challenge, especially with more climate change-induced drought periods. Ideas being floated in South Africa include harvesting water from the air, and even towing a 100-million-tonne iceberg from Antarctica.

One expert suggested wrapping the iceberg (half a mile in length, 500 yards across and 250 yards deep) carefully so it doesn't melt, then using a supertanker to drag it 1,200 miles to Cape Town. Once there, melted water would be gathered, producing 40 million gallons of clean water each day for a year. The expert estimates it would take three months at a cost of $100 million to move the iceberg, and another $50–$60 million to produce clean water from it for a year. This hasn't been implemented yet in Cape Town. Indeed, no country anywhere in the world has tried towing icebergs to supply drinking water. But, with only 2.5 per cent of the world's water being fresh, drinkable water, perhaps more governments will see it as not such a crazy idea.

'Água': Cristiano Ronaldo's Message to the World

At a Euro 2020 press conference, football star Cristiano Ronaldo moved the Coke bottles placed in front of him (Coca-Cola was an official sponsor of the tournament) and instead picked up an unbranded bottle of water, saying in Portuguese, '*água*' (water). A simple action to say that people should drink water instead of unhealthy soft drinks. The clip went viral on social media and knocked $2 billion off Coca-Cola's market value.

A few years later, two social media influencers, Logan Paul and KSI, created a product called Prime Hydration, which they cleverly marketed with video content on their YouTube channels. Through creating scarcity, they made Prime a product that teens and young people wanted, but couldn't buy easily. The result was people hunting for it, talking about Prime, and paying up to £100 for a bottle. The drink itself is a caffeinated energy drink (which isn't even recommended for under-eighteens) in colourful bottles. It's nothing special, yet the marketing strategy was highly effective.

What a strange world we live in, where people ignore the most precious resource being offered for free at the water fountain, to spend money instead on packaging and products that aren't even good for health. A success of the marketing industry and a failure of public health messaging.

We have the knowledge on how to protect people from illness related to a lack of clean water. Water and sanitation systems have been built in most countries in the world, although it has proved challenging in fragile states and rural areas. These systems are coming under stress because of more frequent extreme climate events. This could be heavy rain and flooding, resulting in untreated sewage overflowing and mixing with clean water, or it could be drought – the absence of enough water to nourish crops and feed a population. Both are challenges for governments and another consequence of global warming. Can you imagine a world in which there is no fresh water to drink?

As with most things in health, lack of progress to make clean water accessible hits the poorest the hardest, whether it's forgotten Black communities in the US, coastal communities in England, or those living in rural India or South Africa. Not having access to clean water is making people sick: we are already seeing this across Britain in swimmers and those using the water for recreation, but it's also true in Jackson, Mississippi, where a range of health challenges have been linked to the water shortages. In low-income contexts like Port-au-Prince and New Delhi, the cost of dirty water is paid in children's lives, especially in those under the age of five.

Why are we going backwards in Britain on separating our water from our poo? Why do hundreds of thousands of people in the US lack clean water, with schools shut down because of this? Why do millions of children still die from something utterly preventable?

It's politics and economics. It comes down to leaders willing to make political choices, including financial allocations and planning projects, to invest in public health rather than take for granted the gains that have been made in reducing water-borne infectious diseases. It takes public policy choices to regulate private water companies to ensure they're investing in the necessary maintenance and infrastructure and not to see bottled water (and lobbying from bottled water companies like Nestlé Water) as the solution.

It shouldn't take a resurgence of cholera or *E. coli* infections to bring this to leaders' attention, and Feargal Sharkey should be free to fish and make music rather than holding an incompetent government to account on our behalf. It should be self-evident from our history, and from looking at places like Haiti which show the dangers of leaving water to purely market forces and not building basic water and sanitation systems.

Hopefully, having access to safe water isn't something you worry about each day. It's an issue that we're highly dependent on our governments for. If there is clean tap water, drink that for free using a reusable water bottle, avoid buying single-use plastic water bottles, wash your hands often, especially after going to the bathroom, and whenever you can, advocate for clean lakes, rivers and oceans. Clean water is essential for all of us to live to 100, and it's a collective endeavour which must be led by government.

9. Just Breathe

I struggle with anxiety. I worry about tomorrow, about what-ifs, and with uncertainty. I read the last chapter of crime novels so I know the ending before I start the story. I check flight times repeatedly to make sure I don't miss my departure. I read episode summaries of TV series so that I know what happens before I watch them. I purposely arrive ten minutes early for appointments in case of unexpected delays making me late. I don't like the idea of not knowing what's ahead in the future, and I like to plan and make lists and organize. I know rationally that I can't control everything, but a large part of my brain is spent trying to control the future. Sometimes that ongoing worry is manageable and sometimes it's debilitating.

While pharmaceutical companies are quick to offer medical solutions such as anti-anxiety pills or sleep aid medications, especially in the wild west of the US free-market medical system, my work in public health and personal training has turned me towards more holistic solutions. This isn't hocus pocus kind of stuff. There is an emerging evidence base on the health benefits of yoga and breath exercises for anxiety management, mood stability and better sleep.

Scientific research shows that mindful breathing – paying attention to your breath and trying to slow it down – is one of the most effective ways to reduce stress and improve overall mental and physical health. The autonomic nervous systems control the body's sympathetic (fight or flight) and parasympathetic (rest and restore) response, which links to heart rate, breath rate and digestion. Fast breathing triggers the sympathetic nervous system, increasing stress hormones, heart rate, blood pressure and anxiety, while breathing slowly triggers the parasympathetic response to calm down.

Chronic stress, and over-exposure to the stress hormone cortisol, has a negative impact on health: it results in headaches, upset stomach, high blood pressure, chest pains, heart attacks, panic attacks, depression and difficulty sleeping. Chronic stress also suppresses the body's immune system, making it harder to recover from disease. It's well known that stress is bad for health, and can trigger alcoholism, over-eating or drug use as coping ('self-medicating') mechanisms.

Breathing is one of the most fascinating things that we do as humans. It's one of the few muscular processes that is both voluntary (we can control it with our mind) and involuntary (it happens without us having to think about it). Breath control, or *pranayama* in Sanskrit, is one of the key parts of yogic practice. *Prana* means 'vital life force' and *yama* means to gain control.

In yoga, the three-part breath is supposed to symbolize: inhaling pure, fresh outside air; retaining it inside as oxygen spreads through our cells; and then exhaling carbon dioxide and visualizing exhaling the stress. It's usually done to a four-count inhale, retaining for four counts, and exhaling for four counts. When I struggle to sleep or feel anxiety rising in my chest, I come back to this breath sequence. There are many other variations of pranayama, but the basic idea is control over breath, slowing of the heartbeat, and seeing breath as a vital tool in control of the mind, including stressful thoughts.

In Sanskrit this is called *Chitta Vritti*, which literally translates as the whirling of the mind stuff or mind chatter. It's often referred to in yoga practice as 'monkey brain', which is when thoughts and worries run through your brain and you can't make them stop. They can become paralysing when trying to focus during the day, or cause insomnia at night when any attempt to rest is thwarted by a mind running through to-do lists or jumping between regret over the past and worry about the future.

In its most severe state, monkey brain leads to panic attacks. Breath control, through deep inhalation, retention and exhalation, is one of the best ways to deal with monkey brain. It's simply mindful meditation.

Yoga has become trendy in the past decade, but the origins lie in ancient India over 5,000 years ago, where it was created as a spiritual practice linking mind, body and breath. Some of this essence has been lost with the rise of social media and influencers posting backbends on tropical beaches while marketing clothing brands, linking yoga to a high-status lifestyle. But the core of yoga isn't about certain poses, whether you're good or bad at it, or how you look. It's about how you feel. It's about finding stillness in our minds through control of our body and breath.

Near my grandmother's home in Chennai, a local park offers daily 5 a.m. yoga practice. She attended regularly for years as part of her morning routine, but recently it's been cancelled at times because of poor air quality. The inhaled air is toxic, instead of cleansing. Unfortunately, outside activities are becoming more limited in India with increased air pollution. In 2017, a Sri Lanka–India cricket test match was the first recorded instance of an international sports event being halted due to air pollution. It was a worrying sign of a future when just breathing air outside, a necessary function to live, is akin to being poisoned.

Vomiting Cricket Players

During a test match in New Delhi on the 3rd of December 2017, several players started continuously vomiting. No, this wasn't norovirus or a stomach bug. It was air pollution. Toxic smog covered the pitch as pollution levels reached fifteen times the WHO limit on 'healthy air'. Sri Lankan coach Nic Pothas said: 'We had players coming off the field and vomiting. There were oxygen cylinders in the change room. It's not normal for players to suffer in that way while playing the game.'

He pointed to the player Suranga Lakmal being repeatedly sick in the changing room: 'I think that's the first time that everybody has come across that situation. There aren't too many rules regarding pollution. What we are going to do tomorrow is in the hands of the match referee. They will have meetings tonight to put in some sort of precedent if it happens like this tomorrow.'

Delhi officials tried to play down the seriousness of the situation. One said: 'If 20,000 people in the stands did not have problems, and the Indian team did not face any issue, I wonder why the Sri Lankan team made a big fuss?' Some Indian fans accused the Sri Lankan players of being melodramatic. The Sri Lankans tried to continue playing with face masks but struggled with respiratory issues.

Fast forward four years. On Tuesday the 16th of November 2021, New Delhi went into lockdown, shutting schools, imposing 'work from home' orders and asking people to stay indoors. No, not over COVID or an infectious disease, but over another deadly health challenge. The city was facing another wave of severe pollution, with thick brown smog blocking any view of the sky.

It wasn't hard for officials to enforce the air pollution lockdown and ensure people stayed at home. Who would want to go outside when it was difficult to breathe? People who ventured out reported stinging eyes, nausea, and breathing difficulties. Hospitals reported a steep rise in admissions related to respiratory and cardiac problems. A survey of families in Delhi reported that 86 per cent had someone suffering from toxic air-related illness such as sore throat, headaches, breathing difficulties and chronic cough.

The state government had been warned about this problem for years, and it was becoming a seasonal occurrence. As winter approaches, pollution becomes trapped over the city, resulting in air pollution levels twenty times higher than those deemed healthy by the WHO. Already in November 2019, the Supreme Court had highlighted this problem, noting that 'Delhi has become worse than *narak* [hell],' with Justice Arun Mishra saying, 'The world is laughing at us. You are reducing the lifespan of people. Why are people being forced to live in gas chambers? Better to get explosives and kill them all in one go.'

In 2021, the Supreme Court called on the authorities to shut down the city for two days. A seventeen-year-old student filed a plea, as the air quality index in Delhi hit 400–500. Keep in mind that anything above 50 is harmful to health. In response, Chief Justice N. V. Ramana said: 'Take immediate control measures. Tell us how immediately we can reduce the air quality index by 200 points. If required, think of a two-day lockdown or something . . . How will people live?' Justice D. Y. Chandrachud added: 'You have opened all schools and now you are exposing little children and their lungs to the hazardous air at seven in the morning.'

By 2022, Delhi was the world's capital of pollution. A WHO survey of 1,650 world cities and a think-tank survey of 7,000 cities put Delhi's air quality as the worst in the world. Local researchers estimated that breathing Delhi's air was equivalent to smoking ten to fifteen cigarettes every single day in terms of the damage to the lungs. Fifty per cent of children in the city already have irreversible damage in their lungs. India has the world's highest death rate from chronic respiratory diseases and asthma too.

The main difference from cigarettes is that air pollution is beyond an individual's control: it's often the result of excessive vehicle emissions and industrial pollution. In short, those who are causing the dirty air don't bear the cost of it – instead it falls on those most innocent: children from poor families walking to school, outdoor labourers working on construction sites, and street vendors selling their goods along busy highways.

The 'Pay to Breathe' Industry

Air pollution has real consequences for health: Delhi's air is so toxic that it cuts the average life expectancy of those living there by almost seventeen years. The mortality rate in Delhi from air pollution is 134 per 100,000 people, double the global average of sixty-four. One third of deaths per annum in India – more than 2.5 million people – are a result of air pollution.

In 2019, the government launched a National Clean Air Programme. At the time, 102 cities failed to meet the federal air pollution standards. By 2023, this had grown to 132 failing cities. India is going backwards in reducing air pollution as it continues to be neglected as a top priority for government, and the cost is being paid in too many people dying too soon.

Professor Suryakant Waghmore of IIT Bombay said: 'We are normalizing a world that hardly values nature and natural rights – basic necessities like clean drinking water, fresh and unpolluted air, space to walk for pedestrians is neither part of urban planning nor [do they] concern our collective conscience. The public is left to decay and degrade.'

Medical associations and those on the frontline of seeing patients are frustrated at the lack of progress on an issue with clear health implications. Mumbai-based pulmonologist Revathy K. said: 'If you don't get something as basic as fresh air, then what's the point of living in our country?'

While you'd think air was something that affects everyone equally within a city, wealth does offer a way around this problem. A new 'pay to breathe' industry has taken hold. Those with money in Delhi try to insulate their children from pollution: luxury private schools offer built-in, industrial-grade air-filtration systems. These classrooms have the cleanest air in the city. Portable purifiers are used in cars, while air-filtering masks are used to move around outdoors.

The cheapest air purifier model starts at 6,000 rupees (roughly $72): this is in the context of a population where 60 per cent of people live on less than $3.10 per day, and almost 50 per cent of the population work outdoors. It's an out-of-reach expensive solution, but one that wealthier residents are using as they move from air-purified flats to air-purified shops to air-purified malls, all in air-purified cars. Wealth has created a bubble where being able to breathe clean air is a luxury product instead of a human right. The market for air purifiers is forecast to grow by 35 per cent to $597 million by 2027.

But as one parent noted, 'What if the kids forget to close the classroom door? How about crossing the grounds to lunch, the sports hall, the auditorium? You start obsessing about every breath, and soon you find yourself imprisoning your children at home while praying for a good, strong wind.' Similar to the toddlers throwing tantrums about wearing masks during the pandemic, Megan Stack, an expat parent in Delhi, noted in an article for the *New Yorker* in 2018 that her son protests against wearing one for air pollution: 'I don't want to wear the mask! I hate the mask!'

Dirty Air Kills

Air pollution isn't unique to India. It's a truly global problem in which 4.2 million people die too early each year from breathing dirty air, with 89 per cent of deaths in low- and middle-income countries. In 2019, the WHO estimated that 37 per cent of premature deaths were due to heart disease and stroke, 18 per cent due to chronic obstructive pulmonary disease (a group of lung conditions that cause breathing difficulties), 23 per cent to acute lower respiratory tract infections, and 11 per cent due to cancer within the respiratory tract.

Air pollution affects people throughout their lifetimes. Exposure to dirty air affects babies even before they're born. Breathing dirty air while pregnant is associated with low birth weight and premature birth. For the pregnant mum, air pollution is associated with high blood pressure (pre-eclampsia), oxidative stress and inflammation. Certain components of air pollution can enter the blood and cross the placental barrier to interact with the developing foetus. One theory for slowed or delayed foetal growth is that air pollution alters blood flow between the umbilical cord and the placenta, lowering oxygen levels.

It's not only a concern for women. A meta-analysis with over 4,500 men found that exposure to air pollution was associated with significant decreases in semen volume, concentration of sperm, motility (ability of sperm to move efficiently) and normal sperm shape and size. Basically, high pollution results in fewer, abnormally sized sperm, which tend to swim slower through the female reproductive tract to reach and fertilize an egg. The consequence is an increase in the number of men who are infertile.

Exposure to air pollution during childhood is linked to asthma, slower development of lung function, developmental problems, more wheezing and coughs, and even changes in the heart. Reduced lung volumes have been found in primary-aged schoolchildren growing up in inner-city London. Researchers tested the lung function of over 2,000 children between the ages of eight and nine, and found that on average 5 per cent of expected lung volume was lost due to air pollution. This was most clearly linked to nitrogen dioxide (from traffic).

Dozens of studies have found a significant association between development of asthma in children and exposure to traffic-related air pollution. The particles and gases cause inflammation in the lung, increase airway hypersensitivity and make breathing more difficult. In children, studies have shown changes in biomarkers of cardiovascular function, such as blood pressure and pulmonary arterial pressure, after exposure to air pollution.

Given its impact on the lungs and heart, it's not surprising that traffic-related air pollution negatively impacts the development of the brain. In Barcelona, a large research project looked at levels of air pollutants in the school environment and the impact on brain development. It found that an increase of 70 micrograms per cubic metre in indoor and outdoor levels of air pollutants, specifically benzo[a]-pyrene, was associated with a reduction of almost 2 per cent in caudate nucleus volume. The caudate nucleus is part of the basal ganglia that's responsible for movement, learning, memory, reward, motivation and emotion. In other words, being exposed to air pollution at a high level was linked to smaller-sized brains in children. Another study found that hyperactivity and inattention increased in children aged seven to eleven with higher levels of exposure to traffic-related air pollution.

In 1993, the US 'Six Cities Study' found that those adults living in more polluted places lived shorter lives, even after controlling for smoking, work history, poverty and socioeconomic factors. In adults, air pollution is linked to asthma, coronary heart disease, stroke, lung cancer, chronic obstructive pulmonary disease and diabetes. All result in early death. In addition, a large UK study of 360,000 people aged forty to sixty-nine found that those living in polluted areas were more likely to be living with more than one long-term illness. This isn't surprising, given all the evidence of the negative impact of air pollution on the body.

In the elderly, air pollution is linked to asthma, accelerated decline in lung function, lung cancer, diabetes, dementia, heart attack, heart failure and strokes. The more you look into what air pollution does to our bodies, from its effects on a developing foetus to preventing healthy ageing, the more bad stuff comes up. Air is ubiquitous, invisible and vital. We tend to go about our lives ignoring it and not knowing enough about how bad air pollution is for our bodies and minds. But the damage is being done day by day, and we're paying for it in more illness and shorter life expectancy.

Why Is Air Pollution Bad for Our Health?

Why exactly is air pollution bad for us? Air pollution is a complex mix of particles and gases of both natural and human origin. Particulate matter and nitrogen dioxide are both key components of urban air pollution, and there is no clear evidence of a 'safe level of exposure'. Particulate matter is a generic term used to describe the range of solid and liquid particles in a range of sizes that come into our bodies. Larger ones are mainly deposited in the nose and throat, while smaller ones end up deep in the lungs. Long-term exposure to these particles increases diseases in the heart and lungs. In addition, they have been classified as carcinogenic to humans and a cause of lung cancer.

Nitrogen dioxide is a gas produced by combustion, such as by diesel cars, power generators, industrial processes and domestic heating. It's closely linked to road traffic. Short-term exposure to this gas causes inflammation of the airways leading to coughing, shortness of breath and production of mucus. Studies have shown that it has a range of negative impacts on health including reduced lung development, respiratory infections, and shorter life expectancy.

There are other dangerous gases such as sulphur dioxide, which is produced when sulphur-containing fuels like coal are burned, or from domestic sources like boilers and stoves. Sulphur dioxide irritates the lining of the nose, throat and airways.

Mortality from air pollution is linked to exposure to fine particulate matter, which causes acute and chronic health conditions such as coronary heart disease, strokes, asthma and lung cancer. The air we breathe affects our daily health.

How does someone living in a city know the quality of the air they're breathing, and how bad it could be for their health? To calculate and communicate how polluted the air is, air quality indices have been developed by the WHO and government agencies. Different countries have their own index based on their own national air quality standards, although the WHO has been trying to standardize these. For example, the European Air Quality Index adopted in 2017 informs the public about air pollution. Low is 0–25, while very high is over 100. In India, the National Air Quality Index was launched in 2014 and has six categories from good (0–50: minimal impact) to hazardous (401–500: may cause respiratory impact even on healthy people, and serious health impacts on people with lung/heart disease).

While the level of air pollution is important information for governments, the problem is in the translation of this data for people living in a particular city. What are you supposed to do about knowing that the air quality is hazardous, or very poor? If air pollution is bad, does this mean indoor confinement with an air purifier? Does it mean wearing a mask outside? And that's for people who have a choice about their daily routine, which isn't true for daily labourers or the 50 per cent of people who work outside in India, for example.

The challenge is that the data is important to know, but the real action must come from governments to regulate air quality at a macro level. It's beyond any individual to control what they breathe when going outside.

The Lucrative Industry of 'Bottled Air'

Clean air might feel like the great equalizer, given its collective nature. Dr Maria Neira of the WHO said: 'The problem is that when you're a citizen, you can't choose the air you're breathing. You breathe whatever is available.' Compared to other issues like the food you eat, the amount of exercise you do, or whether you choose to smoke or vape, environmental issues such as clean air are a communal problem. But, as we've already seen in Delhi, the rich are finding ways to create a personal 'clean air' bubble to live within, using air purifiers, and the private sector has found a way to make money from this problem too.

Take the company Swissbreeze, which was founded by Moritz Krähenmann to literally sell 'clean air' in bottles to consumers living in places with high levels of air pollution. Using a small compressor, he collects hundreds of thousands of litres of fresh air each month from the Swiss Alps. He ensures the air quality is good that day using publicly available government data, and travels to Davos, Lucerne, Interlaken or St Moritz. He then filters and purifies the air collected, and sells an eight-litre canister of Swiss air for £17.60. The slogan for the company reads, '100% Swiss air/100% power to live', while their Instagram tagline is: 'providing pure and clean air, gathered in the most beautiful regions of Switzerland'. Swissbreeze isn't alone in this growing market.

In early 2015, Moses Lam and Troy Paquette, two friends living in Canada, filled a Ziploc bag with fresh air and sold it on eBay for 60p. They then posted another bag and this went for £99 after media coverage drew public interest. Almost overnight, Lam and his friend saw this as an easy way to get rich, and decided to model their bottled air business on the bottled water industry. Vitality Air was born, and they found growing demand not only in Los Angeles, but also in Beijing, New Delhi, Vietnam, South Korea, Iran, Greece and Mexico. Their target market became people living in the world's most polluted places.

Vitality Air sells an eight-litre canister for £19, which isn't a lot of air: we breathe six litres a minute. £19 for one minute of clean air from a can. Lam described their strategy as 'We're literally taking clean, pristine air and moving it from one part of the world to another . . . I want to be known as the king of air. I want to be known as the first person in the world to sell people air.'

There's not much evidence that breathing a can of clean air for one minute has positive health effects. This kind of individually tailored strategy also neglects the larger issue. As Dr Neira said: 'It's like accepting what should be unacceptable. When you are in a city where the air is totally polluted, and you try to solve it by breathing with your own device, it's like you are accepting that breathing polluted air is something normal. And it shouldn't be.'

But those selling 'bottled air' see an expanding future market of products. For example, an air pack that people can wear like a backpack that provides clean air lasting eight hours. The private sector is rushing to provide individualized solutions for those desperate and wealthy enough to spend money just to be able to breathe clean air for a small part of their day. Even if it's just for a minute or two. Somehow this is seen as a solution, instead of focusing on the emerging environmental and health challenge.

We Know What Causes Dirty Air

It's not just in Delhi that air pollution levels are rising to alarming levels. As urbanization takes off across the globe, an increasing percentage of the world's population is living in cities, and often these cities are built without consideration of the air we all breathe. What's causing this air pollution? It comes down to road transport (especially diesel cars, trucks and buses), along with coal-burning power plants, industrial incineration, industrial production and household energy use through, for example, gas boilers or wood fires. We know why air gets dirty and what causes it.

The question then becomes not which is the most polluted city in the world, but are there places that are managing to have better air quality? There were only thirteen countries, territories and regions globally that met the WHO's guidelines on healthy air quality in 2022, according to a report from Swiss air quality tech company IQAir. The report examined data from more than 30,000 stations and sensors that monitor air quality in over 7,000 cities across 131 countries. The only places that met WHO standards were: Australia, Estonia, Finland, Grenada, Iceland, New Zealand and seven territories in the Pacific and Caribbean such as Guam and Puerto Rico. Chad had the worst air quality, followed by Iraq, Pakistan, Bahrain, Bangladesh, Burkina Faso, Kuwait and India.

You'll notice that the places with the cleanest air tend to have less industrialization and urbanization. They're also largely islands, so they have geography on their side. But what about cities that are densely populated, in the middle of land blocks or affected by neighbouring countries' air quality, and that have populations able to afford private ownership of cars, heating and other emissions-producing assets? What are their governments trying to do?

Does Any Major City Have Clean Air?

Ahead of the 2020 Tokyo Olympics and Paralympic Games, air quality became a major focus for the Japanese government. Takao Nishimura, a lawyer working with a group fighting for patients affected by diseases caused by air pollution, told the *Japan Times*: 'Air pollution causes respiratory diseases such as asthma and chronic bronchitis, and I believe this is a public health hazard. Although there has been some improvement in recent years, air pollution in central Tokyo is still at worrisome levels . . . there are also concerns about the health and condition of athletes due to air pollution.'

In December 2019, in preparation for hosting the Olympics, the city published the Zero Emission Tokyo Strategy. Within this plan, the city defined seventeen major targets to be achieved by 2030. One key element was the expansion of zero-emission buildings, so that by 2030, energy consumption would be reduced by 38 per cent compared to 2000, and greenhouse gas emissions reduced by 30 per cent, compared to 2000. This was to be done by relying on renewable energies such as solar power and hydrogen energy.

Another key element was to promote the spread of zero-emission vehicles so that by 2030, 50 per cent of new passenger car sales are aimed to be zero-emission vehicles, and by 2050 all cars driven in Tokyo are to be zero-emission. These include electric vehicles that don't emit gases during driving. To put this in perspective, Norway has the even more ambitious goal for all new vehicles sold to be zero-emissions by 2025; and the same in the Netherlands by 2030. It's a lofty goal, given that zero-emission vehicles made up only 1.6 per cent of all new passenger car sales in 2018 in Japan.

The Japanese government recognizes the barriers for people to make this switch: in a 2018 public opinion poll, 45.2 per cent expressed concerns about too few places for charging or refuelling, 24 per cent on the long times to charge or refuel, 22.7 per cent on the limited distance capabilities, and 17.8 per cent on the few vehicle models available. These are all reasonable concerns, and the government made a targeted plan, including the installation of thousands of public fast chargers. Another concern was higher vehicle purchase price, because electric vehicles tend to be more expensive. In response, the government has developed initiatives such as subsidies to reduce the purchase price, tax incentives, and ensuring that public vehicles such as buses are zero-emissions.

Tokyo's efforts to keep its air quality within 'healthy human' limits is working. Overall, considering its population density and location, the air quality is pretty good. It's one of the most crowded cities in the world, yet it rarely features in the top ten or even twenty for air pollution. Beijing, for example, is fifteen times more polluted than Tokyo, and Tokyo has better air quality than Los Angeles, New York, London and Berlin.

A similar story could be told about Zurich, the least polluted city in the world in 2024. Back in 2010, air pollution was quite high, largely caused by road traffic and wood burning in the winter. The city committed to lower the overall air pollution from traffic, which required a dual strategy of fewer cars and less polluting vehicles. The core of the strategy has been replacing driving with cycling, walking and 'clean' public transport options like trains, buses and subways. To reduce polluting vehicles, limits were introduced in terms of where they can go in the city, often referred to as 'low emission zones'. I'll talk more about low emission zones soon.

It's naive to look at Tokyo or Zurich's air quality and say, 'They've always been this way,' or 'It's their culture.' It's been a deliberate choice by their government to plan ahead and set ambitious targets, and to create public policy that addresses people's concerns. It's been recognition by city officials that air quality matters to healthy city life, and that there are steps, especially with new technology, that can be taken to address the problem. It's recognition that a large part of city design is figuring out how to get people to where they need to be, without the only option being owning a car.

If alternatives are available, which are cheap and easy to use, then the incentives are strong to rely on 'cleaner' methods of transport that have the additional benefit of breathing clean air. It's not unique to the Japanese or Swiss, by the way. The Swedes, Norwegians, Finns and Dutch are all moving in the same direction. But efforts to reduce air pollution are not without backlash, as the experience of London shows.

Creating Ultra-Low Emission Zones

In London in 2020, Ella Adoo-Kissi-Debrah became the first person in the world to have air pollution listed as a cause of death on her death certificate. Ella was extremely healthy until being diagnosed with asthma at age seven. Two years later she had a fatal asthma attack after being exposed to a toxic level of air pollution at her home in south-east London, which was near one of the city's busiest roads. Her mother Rosamund warned: 'Children are dying unnecessarily because the government is not doing enough to combat air pollution.'

Ella's mother expressed regret that she did not have clear information that air pollution was life-threatening to children suffering from asthma. She said: 'We need action and we need it now. The coroner was very clear: unless the government takes this matter seriously, more children like my daughter are going to continue to die.'

Ella's mother also said that there needed to be clear public information about the daily levels of air pollution and the health risks associated with these. Air pollution is not just an environmental issue but also a public health emergency. Just because, as Rosamund said, 'you can't see particulate matter with the naked eye', doesn't mean it is harmless.

She co-founded the Ella Roberta Foundation in 2015 to promote clean air goals more widely and raise awareness about the health dangers of air pollution. These efforts to ensure that lessons were learned from the death of her daughter made the front page of newspapers across the country, which helped the London mayor, Sadiq Khan, build the public support to tackle air pollution.

As he describes in his book *Breathe: Tackling the Climate Emergency*, Sadiq Khan's awareness about the dangers of air pollution goes back to 2014, when he was training for the London Marathon. Daily running in the streets of London damaged his lungs, resulting in an asthma diagnosis at the age of forty-three. He also met with Ella's mother to talk about her death and made a clear public commitment to cleaning up London's air.

The main problem in London is road transport and congestion, with dangerous gas emissions from diesel vehicles. As a Policy Exchange report said: 'There needs to be recognition at European, UK and London level that diesel has been the primary cause of the current air pollution crisis.' The steps that Mayor Khan outlined to clean up London's air were straightforward: restrict the most polluting vehicles from entering London, promote electric vehicles and car clubs, promote electric taxis and buses, incentivize a shift away from diesel cars through taxes on new purchases and having a diesel exchange scheme, and finally, tackle emissions from gas boilers.

In April 2019, Khan launched the Ultra-Low Emission Zone, which involves a charge on older diesel and petrol cars of £12.50 per day. A poll by YouGov showed that 72 per cent of those living in the city supported this approach to tackle air pollution and traffic congestion. A study of sixteen school streets in London showed that nitrogen dioxide (a major pollutant from traffic) was reduced by 23 per cent when traffic was restricted on the street, and the number of children walking or cycling to school increased by 18 per cent.

Plans for an ultra-low emission zone were first announced by a Conservative mayor, Boris Johnson, in 2014. Johnson was building on the previous Labour mayor Ken Livingstone's London-wide Low Emission Zone. Johnson said: 'The world's first Ultra Low Emission Zone is an essential measure to help improve air quality in our city, protect the health of Londoners, and lengthen our lead as the greatest city on Earth.' What started as a Conservative policy was championed soon after as a Labour policy under Khan. Improved air quality was framed as a cross-party public health objective, not a partisan issue to bicker over. As evidence came out on the impact low emission zones were having on reducing polluting vehicles and improving air quality, the zone was extended to a larger area.

Ella's mum Rosamund had a clear list of asks from city officials to keep the air clean: an expanded scrappage scheme that encourages people to trade in polluting cars for cleaner alternatives, improved and cheaper public transport, safer walking and cycling with separate lanes, car-free zones around schools with awareness campaigns around the dangers of exhaust fumes, and enshrining the human right to clean air in UK law.

This clean air legislation has been referred to as 'Ella's Law', and it establishes a right to clean air along with a commission to oversee government policy and progress. It has enjoyed cross-party support, from the Green Party to the Conservatives, after a UK Ministry of Health report was shared with MPs. This clearly laid out the toll being taken: 4,000 Londoners die from breathing polluted air each year, with 28,000 to 36,000 deaths across the country linked to air pollution. At the time of writing, the bill has passed in the House of Lords and is now in the Commons.

Whether or not progress happens is in the hands of politicians, and unfortunately, since 2022 onwards, there's been a backlash against 'clean air' measures. For example, in September 2023, then Prime Minister Rishi Sunak held a press briefing to say he wouldn't be moving the UK towards net zero emissions, and made a public shift away from low emission zones and measures to improve air quality. Clean air measures have been depicted by the right-wing media as a luxury, green, middle-class hobby, and 'anti-car'. After Sunak's briefing, Conservative politicians did TV interviews linking the green agenda to meat being taxed, having to use seven recycling bins, and losing the freedom to drive a car.

Returning to Ella, during his tenure as prime minister, Sunak never replied to Rosamund's letters about clean air, and declined an invitation to meet to discuss Ella's Law. Ella's mum said, 'We think the government wrongly feels this is something people don't care about. When I talk to people, yes, they care about the cost of living, but they also care about the air that they are breathing. I feel like the British public has been hoodwinked into thinking, this is a little green issue some middle-class people are concerned about. No, this is something that impacts all of us.'

The backlash against clean air measures is baffling: we all live longer with cleaner air, and the issue should have widespread appeal. It's never been a Labour or Conservative core issue until the past few years. It's been a UK-wide public health issue, and that's why London was able to make the progress it did until 2023.

Those Who Create Pollution Should Clean It Up

I've just covered three high-income contexts: Tokyo, Zurich and London, probably all seen as leading 'healthy' cities in the world in terms of air quality policies. Are these transferable to a lower-income context? I turn now to Cape Town in South Africa.

While we often point to South Asia, China and the Middle East for poor air quality, the African region has seen rising air pollution, tied to the move towards economic development and growth. With wealth creation came a shift to increased reliance on cars and vehicles to get around, and more industrial manufacturing. The debate used to be 'green or growth', which sadly meant that developing countries followed a path like Britain, France and others without learning from our mistakes. But Cape Town shows that it's possible to grow and be green too, if the policy foresight is there.

The city of Cape Town's main focus has been on poverty alleviation, given the high percentage of residents who live in the poorest communities. In 2019, more than 45.9 per cent of people lived on less than R1,227 (£64) per month. It makes sense that employment and financial security should be the city government's main focus, but it has also been concerned by air pollution for two decades.

Each winter a brown haze envelops the city, resulting in dangerous levels of air pollution. This hits the poorest, who live in shacks and can't create an indoor bubble of air purifiers and masks. This cloud of smog has become worse with time, and often features in the background of holiday photos of the city.

In 2005, the city committed to developing and implementing an Air Quality Management Plan, with the goal of making Cape Town the city with the cleanest air in Africa. This was in response to data in 2003 from air quality monitoring stations which revealed 162 days of poor air quality, with levels exceeding what was deemed 'acceptable' to health. One of the key principles of the plan was that any person or institution that generates air pollution is accountable for managing their footprint and for the full costs associated with the pollution (including monitoring, management, clean-up and supervision).

The causes of the brown haze smog are similar to those in high-income countries: the bulk of bad air quality is caused by emissions from vehicles, with diesel vehicles the main culprit; other sources being industrial growth and energy generation and consumption. The government has tried to reduce the emissions from each of these sources, starting with vehicles. But it's been a challenge for the country to manage the increased use of private cars with air quality and environmental concerns.

One solution has been to provide and invest in public transport options, such as buses. While there has been investment in alternative options to private cars, crime is an obstacle to widespread usage, including by tourists. Cape Town is ranked as the eleventh most dangerous city in the world, with a high murder rate and hundreds of deaths a year in mass shootings. Gang violence is at the core of this, as well as high drug use and low trust in the police to do anything about it. In this context, public transport isn't seen as safe enough, and Cape Town remains a beautiful but deadly city.

How does Cape Town's air look today after almost twenty years of targeted efforts at the main causes of emissions? The air quality data is clear on the city's success. It's in the top ten of least polluted regional capitals out of 116 cities in the world. It's one of the least polluted cities across Africa, and air quality generally ranks as good outside of the brown haze winter months. Cape Town is testament to the fact that certain policies work at reducing pollution and improving air, and that these can be implemented in the context of a low-income country.

Unfortunately, this isn't how the rest of South Africa looks: the country is among the biggest polluters in the world. Eleven out of the fifteen most polluted African cities are in South Africa, including Sebokeng, Soshanguve, Sasolburg, Pretoria, Springs, Midstream and Ga-Rankuwa. As the 2020 World Air Quality report notes: 'In 2020, only 4.9% of South African cities met WHO targets for annual pollution exposure. South Africa's heavy reliance on coal-based energy and other fossil fuels, comprising 91% of the country's energy mix, is a major source of ambient particle pollution.' There's nothing inherently 'cleaner' about Cape Town, or accidental about its cleaner air: it's been a deliberate move by city government officials within a difficult national context.

Cape Town is far from a policy oasis, though: crime, gun violence, ultra-processed foods, road traffic injuries ... it struggles with many of the issues I've been tackling throughout this book. It also has a major problem related to clean water, which I covered earlier. But even just taking the step for clean air has contributed to the city having the longest life expectancy in South Africa: 71 years for women and 65.6 for men. Contrast this with Mangaung, where on average women live until 61.2 and men to 54.5. Clean air. Ten more years of life.

When Breath Becomes Poisonous

Breath, which should be a powerful tool for health and wellbeing, has becomes poisonous to most of the world's urban population. The tragedy with air pollution is that each breath pollutes the body with toxic gases and tiny particles that go into our lungs, blood and bodies, causing harm.

Yet we can't stop breathing to avoid this health harm, like we can avoid cigarettes or sedentary behaviour. Breathing is an essential function of living, and we don't get a choice over the air we let into our bodies. As individuals, we are at the mercy of our governments and public policy to regulate this larger issue. We are dependent on collective action, led by government, to ensure that breath is a positive life force, not a negative one.

Clean air is important, not just for climate change and future generations, but for those of us living and breathing today. Yet it feels like most people don't know how bad it is for their own health and for their loved ones. I didn't realize how detrimental diesel vehicles were for years, in terms of the gases (nitrogen dioxide) produced, and the negative impact on the health of those near the vehicle, including the actual driver and their families.

We might spend our time exercising, eating well and not smoking. Making healthier decisions to live healthy, longer lives. Yet we neglect the one thing we're exposed to twenty-four hours a day, seven days a week, because it's invisible and feels out of our personal control. Perhaps there's also a cynical fatalism at play: we can't imagine environmental issues being any better, or we have politicians telling us that the air is what it is, and so we accept a sub-optimal situation.

But we know the solutions to reduce air pollution. It's a messaging battle over why these measures are important and in line with the best public health evidence, and how everyone wins with clean air and alternative travel options. It's about more freedom, not less.

I say everyone wins, but that's not completely true. Certain stakeholders lose. Those car manufacturers that aren't shifting to electric or hybrid vehicles, those selling bottles of clean air to the dirtiest cities in the world, the air-purifying industry, and industries wanting to dump pollutants into the air without paying the cost or being responsible for the clean-up – they are the ones that lose out. There are stakeholders fighting to maintain the status quo, because they make a profit from it.

Who are the groups fighting for clean air? Similar to the other issues of road safety and guns, it's parents and citizens. Ella's mum Rosamund wants no other parent to feel the loss of a child from a preventable problem. She is using her grief to spur change in London and beyond, and using her platform to push for awareness, legislative change and policy implementation. Unfortunately, those most affected by toxic air, the poorest and those in outdoors labour, are least able to lobby ministers and effect change.

I'm fortunate to live in Edinburgh where the air quality is generally good, and which has been shown to have the cleanest air in a study of UK cities and towns. However, compared to European cities, it ranks low and could do much more to reduce pollution. Even saying this feels like a political statement in the context of Britain in 2024. Efforts to manage air pollution are seen as 'lefty' and radical here, but these measures are just seen as the norm in other European capitals, regardless of political leaning.

Are policies that European governments have adopted realistic in rapidly growing economies like Bangladesh, Pakistan, China and India? Well, it's up to governments to implement these, in the face of major pushback from the car and manufacturing industries, which are powerful political stakeholders. But short-term bending to these stakeholders means creating a longer-term health problem: one in which children are literally fighting to breathe and growing up to be adults at greater risk of dying too soon.

10. I Need a Doctor

Let's go back to the day that I got the phone call from the nurse about my smear results. I was on my way to work and got off the bus at the stop near the main university campus. I went directly to knock on Jocelyn's door, which is down the hall from mine. She's my New York Puerto Rican best friend in Edinburgh, and a cancer researcher.

She opened the door with a big smile: 'What's up babe?' Deep breath. 'So, I got the results back from my smear, and it's bad news. Looks like my gut was right and they found something.' I made a nervous laugh and then silence, unusual for us. Jocelyn reassured me. 'This is totally normal – lots of women get this result, and it's treatable. When are you seeing a specialist for a colposcopy?'

There's the question that's haunted me since the phone call. I know the NHS has major waitlists. I've seen the headlines about delays in care. I've written *Guardian* articles about delayed diagnosis and treatment, and how difficult timely care is with a backlog.

I felt like screaming at the nurse when she said she had no idea how long an appointment would take, but that would be pointless. She's not responsible for creating more doctors, nurses or appointments. She's just conveying the message that the system can't cope. I'm just a data point on those 'look at how long waitlists are' graphs, and already my lab results had taken two months to be returned, compared to the US where I know results are back within days, if not hours. My thoughts were consumed with, 'What's been growing invisibly in my body while I've been blissfully continuing through life like I'm totally fine?'

Early diagnosis is important because it means better survival. In England, more than 90 per cent of people survive bowel, breast and ovarian cancer for at least five years if diagnosed at the earliest stage. This allows treatment to start earlier, before the cancer has spread through the body. Yet even with a cancer diagnosis, the NHS has struggled to provide treatment within the current sixty-two-day target time: in 2022, 36 per cent of patients waited longer than sixty-two days in England, 21 per cent in Scotland, and 43 per cent in Wales.

Jocelyn asked me again: 'When are you seeing someone? Get it treated and you'll be fine. Don't freak out. And at least you won't be bankrupted by cancer, like back home.' In the States, more than 40 per cent of cancer patients spend their entire life savings in the first two years of treatment, while almost a third of Americans with cancer history have problems paying medical bills, going into debt or filing for bankruptcy because of the treatment costs. The National Cancer Institute estimates the average cost of medical care and drugs to be over $42,000 per year following diagnosis, while some treatments can reach $1 million.

True, thank god for the NHS, where every time I've shown up with loved ones in the minor injuries clinic, GP practice or hospital, the anxious question, 'Can I afford to see someone?' just hasn't been on my mind. In contrast, cancer patients in the US pay $16 billion out of their own pocket annually for treatment.

Going Broke Paying for Medical Care

Having to pay for medical care at the point of receiving it is referred to as 'out-of-pocket' payments, and it's the main way health care is paid for in certain countries, from India to Venezuela. Nigeria is at the high end, with out-of-pocket expenditures roughly 77 per cent of total health spending, compared with 37 per cent for other African countries and 18 per cent as the world average. Government health spending, in contrast, is roughly 5 per cent of total health spending in Nigeria, in contrast to 7.2 per cent in Africa as a whole and 10.3 per cent as the global average.

Paying user fees to access health care, or having to pay the full cost of medical care at the point of treatment, is a major cause of families falling into medical debt and poverty. Eight hundred million people spend at least 10 per cent of their household budgets on health expenses for themselves, a sick child or other family member. For almost 100 million people, these expenses are high enough to push them into extreme poverty, forcing them to survive on just $1.90 or less a day.

The result is families trying to find ways to avoid routine medical care, given the costs involved. This was also largely true in the United States until former President Obama introduced a universal package of health care: it's still a problem there, but now a much smaller one. In Nigeria, which I'll come to soon, this has led to a higher death rate for women giving birth, as they rely on free or low-cost care from families, friends and traditional healers instead of trained medical professionals.

The consequences of not being able to access care when needed, either in emergency or chronic situations, are dire for health outcomes. There are multiple examples beyond maternal death in Nigeria, even from countries like the US and Britain. The factors behind why care isn't available are mixed, from concern about individual medical debt, to entire systems not having adequate funding, to household survival strategies. The common theme across all of these is individuals or systems not having enough money, although it manifests in different ways.

Insanely High Medical Costs: United States

For example, in the United States, medical costs are insanely high. In 2017, Lindsay Clark, a thirty-six-year-old from Texas, fell down a friend's stairs, resulting in a $1,200 bill. She still hadn't paid this off when, two years later, her two-year-old broke the child-lock seal and took an unknown number of pills of the drug Dramamine. Clark had no idea how many pills her daughter had consumed, and called a poison control hotline. The advice was to go straight to an emergency room, because Dramamine overdoses can lead to seizures and be life-threatening. She asked the hotline what doctors would do to intervene, and they said they would give activated charcoal, monitor for seizures, and possibly pump her stomach.

Clark and her husband drove to the emergency room, but stayed in the car parked outside. They bought some charcoal to administer themselves and after their daughter seemed fine, they drove home without seeking medical assistance. Clark recounts: 'I was sitting there thinking, am I a bad person? I'm weighing my daughter's life against how much the bill would cost.'

Medical bills can vary from $629 for a Band-Aid, to $1,200 for an X-ray, and upwards of $20,000 for cycle and car crash injuries. The result is that those who have insurance, or can cover their health care costs comfortably, get care, and those who worry about how they'll pay for support, end up avoiding it. They have no idea what kind of bill will be on the other end.

As I noted in my last book, *Preventable*, avoiding going to hospital was exactly what happened during the COVID pandemic in the US. In April 2020, those who were hospitalized could expect to pay between $42,000 and $72,000 for an average six-day hospital stay. The result was many uninsured individuals (largely from minority African-American and Hispanic communities) getting sicker and sicker at home, and trying to decide between going into hospital and taking on debt, or having their family and friends try to help them at home. In a survey in 2020, 69 per cent of uninsured adults reported delaying or avoiding care due to cost, compared to 16 per cent with insurance.

What became clear with COVID is that early intervention was a major factor in improved survival: this is how South Korea kept its case fatality rate quite low in 2020, before vaccines and formal treatments arrived in 2021. The government health system monitored COVID patients, moved them into supported medical facilities at an early stage, and then quickly admitted them into hospital if they deteriorated. Having adults (and children) sitting outside hospitals hoping they get better and avoiding medical care just means that the health problem becomes harder for doctors to fix if someone does go into a critical state.

Going Blind on a Waitlist: Britain

Contrast this with the NHS in the UK, which, while far from perfect and struggling with volume and quality of care, still holds true to the principle of free treatment. No one is asked for payment when arriving at hospital, giving birth, or having a heart attack. The NHS was born out of the idea that health care should be free at the point of care, a right to all regardless of ability to pay, and a core part of a government's responsibility to its people. But just because it's free and cost isn't a concern for individuals, doesn't automatically mean that care is available. Waitlists and delays in diagnosis and treatments mean that avoidable chronic illness and mortality are high in Britain. This is a real concern if you're waiting on care for potential cervical cancer (like I was), or other treatable diseases.

I was back in Miami seeing my family in 2023 when my brother Jay, who works as an ophthalmologist in the US, asked: 'Why are so many people going blind in Britain when treatment is available?' He pointed to an article circulating among his professional colleagues about the hundreds of people losing sight because of treatment delays within the NHS. Waitlists are long in almost all areas, but especially for ophthalmology, which has the second-largest backlog.

There are treatments for common blindness-causing conditions such as macular degeneration, but to get them patients must be able to access the service. As I explained to Jay, the NHS just doesn't have the capacity to deliver them in a timely way. Those who can afford it, move into the lucrative and growing private sector. Those who can't pay for private care risk going blind while waiting for treatment.

Having lived in Britain for over twenty years and studied various health care systems, I can see the importance of the NHS (and its core values of being free and universal) to the British public. The problem has been in its delivery, and in choices made by the government in charge.

Before 2010, real efforts were made, including with financial allocation, to reduce waitlist times for what's called 'elective care'. Elective care doesn't mean that the care isn't important: it just means it's planned in advance, in contrast to emergency care.

But since then, years of austerity and public-sector neglect – and the shifting of resources and wealthy patients into the private sector – has meant that the NHS has been narrowed from a robust, preventive health care service into an acute one. Its basic offering seems to be: 'If you're dying, we will save you.'

However, if you go inside a hospital and talk to staff, it's even more dire than that. The NHS has become neither an acute health care service nor one able to deal with more chronic issues. Now, its offering is, as described by an Accident & Emergency consultant friend: 'Even if you're dying, we're not sure we can get an ambulance to you, or have you seen quickly enough in A&E.' The main bottleneck is staff shortages and underinvestment, which Brexit and the pandemic made more acute. Systems don't fail overnight. It happens over the course of years, and often deliberately.

You only have to look at the NHS budget compared with other countries. The UK spends far less on health care, resulting in fewer doctors and fewer hospital beds per person than the EU-14 countries. The UK would need to spend 21 per cent more to match the per-person spend in France, and 39 per cent more to match the spending in Germany. Even within its current envelope, the UK spends too much on people in acute care and hospital (care for a brief and time-limited serious illness or injury) and not enough on keeping people out of hospital (preventive and community care). It's an inefficient way to run a health care system.

Instead of preventing someone becoming sick in the first place through primary and community-based care, the NHS steps in when someone is already ill, suffering and needing more costly care. For example, the UK ranks the highest for rates of hospital admission for asthma compared to European countries, a condition that would be treatable if primary care were available, and preventable with public health interventions such as clean air and insulated housing.

When the public sector is failing, wealthy people simply exit and find another way to use their resources. This likely means paying privately for health care services in Britain, or flying to other countries that offer this type of care.

With this thought in mind, I admit to googling 'private colposcopy Edinburgh' to investigate potential options if the NHS was too slow to provide an appointment. Immediately a private hospital popped up: they offered next-day appointments for around £2,000. That's just to see a doctor to make a diagnosis. If further steps are needed, such as freezing of cancerous cells, or referral for surgery or chemotherapy, that could run into the tens of thousands of pounds. This just wasn't an option for me, plus I have uneasy feelings of supporting private health care in the UK instead of staying in the public sector system, so it was back to waiting on that NHS letter.

Imprisonment Until Payment: Nigeria

What happens when emergency health care isn't free or covered by insurance? In Nigeria, if you can't cover medical bills, the consequence has been hospital detention. An activist from the country said: 'Typically the women would be kept in a separate ward. In some instances, they couldn't see sunlight, they would be forced to sleep on the floor, and they wouldn't be given any food. It was a condition of detention that amounted to torture, in many instances.'

Women face a higher risk of medical detention due to the need for emergency medical intervention while giving birth, for example a c-section, or a longer-term stay in hospital owing to birth complications. It's a major reason why Nigeria has the second-highest rate of maternal mortality in the world. The lifetime risk of a Nigerian woman dying during pregnancy, childbirth, or post-abortion is 1 in 22, compared to the lifetime risk in developed countries of 1 in 4,900. The maternal mortality rate of Nigeria is 814 (per 100,000 live births), in contrast to 11.6 in Britain and 4 in Japan.

These maternal deaths are directly linked to three factors: delays in seeking medical care, delays in finding somewhere to go, and delays in receiving care once at a health facility. Why would women not seek medical help if giving birth? If women are afraid of being imprisoned due to medical bills, they're likely to avoid seeking medical care even if they need it. They'd rather just try to give birth at home, which carries the risk of maternal and infant death.

Take the case of Folake Oduyoye. She was a busy fashion designer and already mum of three when she went in to give birth to her fourth child at a private hospital in Nigeria in August 2014. After developing post-delivery complications after a c-section, she was transferred to the Lagos University Teaching Hospital, a government medical facility. The charges for an extensive time in hospital, and in ICU, were high (1.5 million naira or about £7,100) and her husband couldn't pay. The average salary in Nigeria was roughly £500 per month in 2014.

The hospital said that until her husband settled the bill, either through producing the cash or a guarantor to underwrite the debt, they wouldn't provide further treatment, or let Oduyoye go home. They moved her to a guarded ward where she was literally imprisoned alongside others who couldn't pay their medical bills. Her husband recounted: 'At this point they policed me everywhere, saying I might smuggle my wife out of hospital. I slept beside her all 45 days in the hospital, watching other patients die on a daily basis.'

While there, Oduyoye developed other health issues including a chronic cough and her condition worsened. Despite being unwell, she received no further medical care, resulting in her dying from sepsis and pneumonia on the 13th of December 2014.

Her death through literal medical imprisonment triggered major protests at the hospital. One of the activists, Dr Abiola Akiode, said: 'Since they no longer would provide her care, why detain her from getting help elsewhere?' Akiode pointed to how Nigeria makes up more than 10 per cent of the world's maternal deaths, the main problem being inaccessible or poor care for women during and after birth. Oduyoye's situation wasn't unique. Other protestors noted: 'We are invoking the Freedom of Information law and have demanded that the hospital publish the statistics of women still being held in detention over bills. We are aware that some have been held there since over a year.'

Be Born a Boy, or You're on Your Own: India

In India, out-of-pocket expenditure makes up 62.6 per cent of total health expenditure – meaning the bulk of health care costs are paid by individuals. This is in the context where almost 13 per cent of the population is below the poverty line, with large health care costs one of the key factors driving families into debt and poverty. To cope with large, unexpected costs, households will often sell assets and borrow money. Think of someone giving birth and unexpectedly needing a few more days of medical care due to complications, or a child getting hit by a car while crossing the road, or a father having a heart attack and going into hospital.

Knowing how expensive going to a health facility or hospital can be means that families make decisions over accessing medical care. In the US the choice might be to wait outside an emergency room to see whether a condition is life-threatening. 'Will my child's breathing stabilize or is it worth paying thousands to get them oxygen and steroids?'

In India, the choice is often between multiple children with health needs within the context of poverty and limited resources. During childhood, which is a risky time for disease and death, families in most of India are more likely to pay for medical care for a boy. This is seen as an economic investment in the future, given that boys become men who have paid employment and contribute to the household income. In contrast, the perception is that girls become women with unpaid and unvalued housework, such as cooking and cleaning.

Adding to this, traditionally, girls get married and join their husband's family. They no longer contribute to their parents, which has led to the Indian colloquial phrase: 'Raising a daughter is like watering your neighbour's garden.' In contrast, boys get married and bring a wife into their familial home, and they are the social security net for ageing parents, who rely on their eldest son to take care of them until death.

In India, lack of access to health care is reflected in high mortality rates for girl children. Nobel Prize-winner Amartya Sen raised these issues in the 1980s and 90s, referring to the phenomenon of 'missing women'. Writing in the *New York Review of Books*, he said: 'More than 100 million women are missing.' He started with the premise that in Western countries, women outnumber men after birth in all age groups due to certain biological advantages that women have over men in survival: the ratio of women to men in Europe, North

America and Japan is 1.03. Sen contrasts this with India where the ratio of women to men in states like Punjab and Haryana is 0.86.

Girls who should survive to become women were instead dying too soon. Sen calculated the number of 'missing women' by looking at the number of women who should exist in Indian society, if the country had the same ratio of women to men as places where girls and boys receive the same level of medical care.

The advice for 'How not to die' in many rural Indian villages would be to be born a boy. It's worth thinking about whether those 100 million women would be missing if health care were free at the point of care, or if families had enough extra cash. Would they also have received medical attention when necessary, and gone on to live life as an adult?

How Can Governments Provide Health Care?

Within global health, it's accepted that universal health care is essential to living a long and healthy life. That is, that all people have access to the full range of quality health services they need, when and where they need them. As we've seen above, not having access to timely care – whether because of waitlists, fear of going into debt or falling into poverty – is a major factor in dying too soon.

But organizing health care is easier said than done. The WHO has agreed certain principles that should guide health care systems. For example, one core component is that households are protected from financial risks due to unexpected health costs (referred to as 'Health for all with financial protection'). Another is that quality health care services are available at the community level, often referred to as primary health care. But how the system is organized is up for debate.

I've taught health care systems at the university for about two decades and have done my best to simplify it for students wanting to understand the nuts and bolts. In short, there are three different models of health care used across the world, and most countries have a variation of one of these three, or even a mix of these within the population.

If you're British and reading this, you'll immediately think about the NHS. The NHS is what is called the 'Beveridge model' and was introduced to the UK on the 5th of July 1948. It's financed through central and targeted taxes (National Insurance contributions), and these resources are pooled centrally. The government is heavily involved in the financing, organization and delivery of health care, and guarantees that those living within the country have access to health care free at the point of care. The NHS was the first health system in any Western country to offer free medical care to the entire population.

The core of the idea came from William Beveridge, who was asked by the government to chair a committee on social insurance in June 1941, in the depths of the Second World War. His report was widely read, a key component being his assertion that: 'The purpose of victory is to live in a better world than the old one.' Beveridge also made the case for 'the best possible medical, surgical and hospital treatment . . . available to everyone'. This led to the drafting of a white paper in 1944, entitled 'A National Health Service', and four years later the NHS was created.

The NHS was ambitious, world-leading at the time, and based on the core principles of equity, universality, protection from cost at the point of care, and the human right to health care. People loved it. In public opinion surveys, people often list the NHS as the institution they're most proud of in Britain. In 2012 when London hosted the Olympic Games, the opening ceremony featured the NHS. As Cal Flyn, a Scottish journalist studying the NHS, said: 'The fact that we don't need to pay for health insurance, and yet it is always there for us, especially at our lowest moments, makes it very morally unquestionable. It is seen as a force of pure good.'

However, as I discuss above, lack of resources for the health system, including providing adequate pay to those working within it, has resulted in the idea of the NHS not translating into accessible, timely care. The consequence is a growing economically inactive population (people who should be in work but aren't, due to waiting on medical intervention for health issues) and a relatively high avoidable mortality rate due to delays in seeing a doctor.

The second model is the Bismarck model, which is a social insurance system jointly financed by employers and employees through payroll deduction. It's how health insurance is offered in Germany, France, the Netherlands and Japan. But unlike the US insurance system, Bismarck-type insurances don't make a profit and must include all citizens. The government has tight regulation over different insurers to ensure there is cost control and that no one goes without any form of insurance.

The scheme is named after the Prussian Chancellor Otto von Bismarck, who pushed the model of the welfare state in the unification of Germany in the nineteenth century, and who created the first health insurance scheme in 1883. Several principles underlined the scheme, including: the principle of solidarity (the size of insurance contribution is based on ability to pay, and the benefits are according to need); compulsory participation, in which employers must pay part of the costs; and partnerships with 'sickness funds', which are private health care providers regulated by the state.

While the way resources are raised is different to the NHS, it is still a major undertaking of the state in partnership with employers and employees. The social security contributions for public health care insurance in Germany are 14.6 per cent of an employee's gross salary: 7.3 per cent from the employer and 7.3 per cent from the employee. This 'statutory public health insurance' covers 89 per cent of the population, while the other 11 per cent pay extra for completely private health insurance. Contrast this to the NHS in Scotland, where employee contributions are 12 per cent if you earn between £242 and £967 per week, and a further 2 per cent charge on any earnings above that limit.

The third model is 'out-of-pocket' health care, which I've covered before: it basically means that you have to pay directly for the services you use, and it is generally recognized as a terrible way of providing health care at a population level, whether it's in the US, Nigeria or India.

Given the ongoing challenge in providing universal health care in higher-income contexts like the United States and Britain, is this too ambitious a goal for low- and middle-income countries? It's worth heading south to countries that have attempted to provide health care to their people within extremely limited resources. The twin goals have often been to establish primary health care in all communities so that it is accessible and available, and to ensure that some form of insurance covers communities so that families don't fall into poverty or severe debt because of catastrophic health costs.

The Poster Child of Health Care

Thailand is the poster child of the health care movement. In a whirlwind trip to Bangkok in 2008, I sat in a hotel conference centre listening to the Minister of Health explain how they've managed to achieve universal health coverage in the country.

Thailand looked a lot like other countries in 2001: nearly one in four people were uninsured, those insured had partial coverage, and out-of-pocket spending on health pushed 20 per cent of struggling households into further poverty. In 2002, the government established universal health coverage for the entire Thai population of 66.3 million people. This meant that every Thai citizen was entitled to essential preventive, curative and palliative health services for their entire life – free at the point of care.

In the ten years after the health care programme was created, life expectancy at birth increased by three years and there was a reduction in the number of households falling into poverty due to catastrophic health costs. Between 1970 and 2017, infant deaths reduced from more than 100 per 1,000 live births to 9.5 per 1,000.

Seventy-two per cent of the population is covered by the universal health coverage programme from the public health ministry. The remaining 28 per cent is covered by social security schemes and civil servants' medical benefit schemes. The Ministry of Public Health determines which health services are offered by the programme; this is an evidence-based systematic process conducted by the Health Intervention and Technology Assessment Programme.

To finance universal health coverage, the government relies on general taxation. The cost of the policy was 17 per cent of total government expenditure in 2017, making it one of the highest percentages of government spending for health in the developing world. But in a country with limited GDP, it still presents challenges to funding the full needs of the health system, and this in the face of rising demands. Air pollution, road traffic accidents, rising chronic disease and an ageing population mean the strains on health care grow greater, while the resources to fund these often remain static or decline.

Aware of this, Thai policy-makers have brainstormed innovative ways to raise funds for health: for example, 'sin taxes' in which unhealthy products such as tobacco, alcohol and fizzy drinks are taxed, with the resulting funds earmarked for health. In addition, efforts have been made in prevention, such as clean water, improved sanitation and better housing infrastructure, to reduce the burden on health care services. Basically, investing in prevention to reduce costs for acute care. Thailand has been successful, making it one of only twenty-five countries to halve multi-dimensional poverty within fifteen years.

Returning to the question: why did Thailand take on health care? It was a political choice. In the lead-up to the 2001 national elections, the populist Thai Rak Thai party campaigned on a platform of 'free health care'. Their slogan was, 'Thirty baht treats all disease.' Initially, users paid a co-payment of 30 baht (around 50 pence) per medical visit. The party's landslide win in 2001 resulted in the National Health Security Act in 2002, which established universal health coverage and the financial base for it in general taxation. In 2006, the 30-baht fee was eliminated. The collection of co-payments had cost more than the revenue it generated.

Within global public health circles, Thailand has become the example of how quality, accessible health care can be achieved in a lower-middle-income country. It shows what's possible with political will, public support, technical guidance and a moral commitment to the right to health. Current Health Minister Anutin Charnvirakul expressed it well: 'With political strong commitment, multi-sector and people's participation and ownership, and accountable and careful management of limited resources and finance, we can achieve a "sustainable Universal Healthcare".'

In contrast to the view that health care is a luxury for the rich, former Minister of Health Piyasakol Sakolsatayadorn argued: 'Because we are poor, we cannot afford not to have universal health coverage.' Nearly a decade later, President Macky Sall in Senegal made similar arguments.

Making Universal Health Care a Key Election Promise

I hired Marlee by video call to join our team as a post-doc researcher studying the health system in Senegal in 2015. She was based in California but ready for a Scottish adventure. She stood out from the dozens of applications with her detailed fieldwork in Dakar on universal health coverage and malaria. When she walked into my office in Edinburgh, it was her tattoos that I noticed. I had been wanting to get one for a while.

I hadn't worked deeply in West Africa before, but I wanted to expand our team's research into the region. Senegal is a small-ish country at 16.9 million and known for its stable democracy, strong public health institutions and great surfing. Senegal was also one of the positive examples of a national COVID response, as I covered in *Preventable*. The government supported the rest of the region with testing and surveillance, and in its proactive public health actions to contain the disease, while also protecting the poorest households from the impact of any restrictions.

In 2013, the Senegalese government set up a universal health insurance policy called *Couverture maladie universelle*, with the goal of protecting people from catastrophic health costs and impoverishment while increasing access to health care services. This policy works with small health insurance community funds (called *mutuelles*) to provide cover: there are over 700 mutuelles in the country, and they vary in size from a few hundred participants to a few thousand.

To participate in a health fund, each person contributes a fixed cost, roughly £4.80 a year to enrol, and the government matches this amount. This is pooled by the fund to provide care when needed. Mutuelles cover 80 per cent of health centre and hospital costs and 50 per cent of the costs of speciality medicines, while the patient pays the rest. But there are limitations on what insurance will cover: for example, quite a few funds won't cover chronic illnesses, and hospital fees are often capped at seven days. This ensures that the mutuelles are able to pay out and don't go under.

Mutuelles are in a financially fragile position, depending on the health needs of their participants. Risk pooling is vital here: ensuring a diverse range of participants so that costs are balanced out between those who will require less health care (e.g. young adults) and those who might require more (e.g. young children or the elderly). In addition, they often rely on charitable donations – for example, voluntary contributions from local wealthy people, reflecting community, solidarity and charity, which goes directly to those who need it.

The universal health insurance scheme hasn't solved all of Senegal's problems. It's a country with a high level of poverty: 38 per cent of the population lives on less than $3.65 per day. This goes up to 74.4 per cent of the population if the poverty line is taken as $6.85 per day. Fifteen per cent of the population has no access to drinking water, 37.4 per cent no sanitation, and 26.6 per cent no electricity.

But it has brought down out-of-pocket health expenditure (as a percentage of total health expenditure) from almost 56 per cent pre-2013 to 42 per cent. In contrast, external health expenditure, from donors and international agencies, increased from 4 per cent in 2002 to almost 20 per cent in 2022. This likely reflects donors' trust that funding going into the country was supporting an established health scheme and plan.

Stepping back from those statistics, the basic message is that even in a country with limited resources and high poverty, universal health coverage is seen as a crucial goal, not only for the human right to health but also as a step towards poverty reduction, economic productivity, and human security. How did the country manage to achieve this? Again, it comes down to politics and leadership.

President Macky Sall is the person responsible for these changes. He has been at the forefront of advocating for investments in health internationally, trying to showcase his efforts to raise revenue in

Senegal for health purposes. According to Sall, 'Health for all, from baby to senior, is the first human security requirement.'

Sall was born to a modest family: his dad was a caretaker and his mum a peanut seller. He first trained as a geological engineer in Dakar, and was special advisor for energy and mines to President Abdoulaye Wade from 2000 to 2003, and director general of the Petroleum Company of Senegal from 2000 to 2001. He was then appointed Minister of Mines, Energy and Hydraulics, and later Minister of State for the Interior and Local Communities.

Years later in 2012, Sall ran for president with the slogan, 'The Path of Real Development', and a platform based on improving the country's economic and health position in the world. Once elected, he moved in 2013 to establishing universal health insurance – the scheme described above – as well as raising $7.5 billion for his economic development plan, called 'Emergent Senegal'. The goal was to boost the economy by 2035 with investments in agriculture, infrastructure, tourism and health.

In 2019, Sall won re-election, and soon after in 2022 became chairperson of the African Union. His goal, in his own words, was to unite African interests: 'It is time to overcome the reticence and to deconstruct the narratives that persist in confining Africa to the margins of decision-making circles.' With the country's strong performance in the pandemic and in expanding universal health coverage, he continues to assert that African leaders must be at the centre of the table in international discussions around economics, vaccine production and public health.

Framing Health Care as a Social Right Instead of a Commodity

Progress isn't always linear, though. I mentioned Julio Frenk earlier, in the chapter about smoking: he's the current chancellor of UCLA, former president of the University of Miami and former Minister of Health of Mexico. Julio was crucial in moving Mexico, a country of more than 100 million, towards universal health coverage in less than ten years. As another Mexican Minister of Health, Salomón

Chertorivski, said: 'Mexico devised and implemented a reform and then demonstrated, with evidence, how a large, middle-income country can transform its health system and successfully achieve universal health coverage in one decade.'

Prior to 2003 in Mexico, the population was not covered by any government social security, which meant that accessing state and federally run health services required paying a fee. Health insurance was available to those in salaried, stable employment, but 50 per cent of the population was left without access to any form of pre-paid health insurance, including those from the very poorest households. The consequence, highlighted in the 2000/2001 National Health Programme, was that these families were at high risk of falling into extreme poverty due to unexpected health costs. There was also patchy coverage of the population for basic health services.

In 2003, the Mexican Congress established the Sistema de Protección Social en Salud (System of Social Protection in Health), which laid the groundwork for government health insurance. Known as Seguro Popular, this scheme aimed to ensure that everyone, even the poorest, was covered by an adequate standard of care. By 2012, nine years later, 52.6 million Mexicans who were previously uninsured had coverage, and as Professor Felicia Knaul of the University of Miami says: 'Every Mexican, regardless of their socioeconomic situation, has access to the financial protection in health that shields them from facing the terrible choice between impoverishment and suffering or even death.'

How did the scheme raise funding? Seguro Popular had three pots to draw on: the federal government, a co-responsible contributor, and the beneficiary. The federal government part (called the social contribution) was a fixed allocation per family, funded entirely from general taxes at the federal level. The co-responsible contributor was usually an employer, but for those who had no employer, it became the local state responsibility. This was the same in all states, set as half the federal social contribution, and it came from state-level revenue.

The third part was the family contribution, based on a formula for ability to pay. Capacity to pay was based on disposable income, which was total household spending minus spending on food. Families in the lowest two income deciles did not contribute financially, but had to participate in other preventive health interventions, and for other income deciles the family contribution was a fixed, equal proportion of disposable income capped at 5 per cent.

The insurance scheme then worked with largely public providers to offer services to the population. This was through an essential package of covered services, which every provider offered within that insurance. The package was determined by cost-effectiveness (what was the best use of money) and public health benefit (what was the maximum health gain for a given level of money), and most importantly, it offered an entitlement to health care.

What are the lessons from Mexico's efforts to reach universal health coverage? First, that progress is possible if health care is framed as a social right, instead of a commodity to be bought in the marketplace or a luxury privilege for those with enough disposable income. Not having adequate health care means reduced economic productivity of the population as well.

This requires technical knowledge (a second lesson) on the exact package of interventions to have maximum benefit in terms of health and economic growth. In Mexico, this evidence empowered Julio Frenk and other Mexican policy-makers to convince the Ministry of Finance and Congress to put the necessary state and federal funds into health insurance. Third, health care is popular, and if politicians can be convinced that it will help them in future elections, they will vote towards some kind of universal health coverage.

From 2000 to 2015, the Ministry of Health budget increased four-fold, which translated into large-scale investments in health infrastructure and expansion of the package of guaranteed services. This resulted in better coverage, both in terms of who could access health services, and the services they could get under their insurance. This model was then used to design and reform health systems in India, China and Turkey.

Evaluating the Mexican experience, an eminent group of *Lancet* authors concluded that it 'offers a conceptual and practical model that aims to attain the elusive goal of universal coverage, so that every person has an equal opportunity to exercise the right to high-quality health care with social protection for all'.

But it has not been without its challenges, especially with the pressures that COVID brought, and with new political leadership. In December 2018, Andrés Manuel López Obrador was sworn in as Mexican President after campaigning for improvements to Seguro Popular and saying that major reorganization of the health system was required.

But soon after, he began dismantling the health system and in November 2019, Seguro Popular was eliminated and replaced by a system called the Instituto de Salud para el Bienestar (the Health Institute for Welfare). The new system didn't have a management plan, a package of interventions, operational rules, or sufficient funds to offer health care. The Ministry of Health's budget declined, and that meant financial viability was a problem for the scheme. A leadership change (to someone who wanted to differentiate his impact from older administrations) had significant repercussions for health care delivery. López Obrador eliminated one system before thinking through what a new system would look like.

The Mexican experience shows that progress is easily reversed with political changes. As Julio Frenk and colleagues reflected, Mexico was 'once a model for how to do health system reform, now a model of what not to do'. The country entered the pandemic with depleted capacity to deliver health services, longer waitlists, and a decreasing health budget. The consequence was that Mexico was hit badly in the pandemic, and is still struggling to rebuild.

As Frenk and his colleagues noted: 'The percentage of the population covered declined sharply between 2018 and 2020, by 16.8 per cent. Patients are waiting longer to see doctors, paying more out of pocket, and encountering shortage of medicines. Funding for certain types of specialized care – such as childhood cancers – has fallen. Improvements in key indicators such as maternal mortality have reversed. During the COVID-19 pandemic, the country had among the highest levels of mortality of any country.'

Medical Care: Whether You Live or Die

We know that living a long and healthy life also requires access to health care when needed. I think of my own health situation: treatment by trained medical personnel is a vital component in survival. It's the final line of defence in saving someone. I use the football-pitch analogy with students: medical care is the goalie.

What makes up the rest of the team? The defence is the equivalent of secondary prevention, which is identifying indications of potential disease and intervening earlier, for example high blood pressure, pre-diabetes and cancer screening. Moving forward on the pitch, the rest of the 'life expectancy' team is made up of all the issues I've focused on in this book. The entire team saves the most goals (i.e. prevents early disease and death) when it works together.

The changing demography in most countries of the world from young to old, and the linked rise in chronic disease, means that health care systems are under strain. Roughly twelve years back, I travelled to Abu Dhabi to the World Economic Forum 'ideas' meeting, where we discussed the health industry. My key take-away from that meeting was that all governments should be investing in public health prevention and healthy ageing to keep the burden off doctors and nurses.

Yet prevention is a tough sell to politicians who think in short-term political cycles to win votes, rather than long-term planning where the benefits of interventions, for example to reduce childhood obesity, come to light twenty to thirty years later when reductions in hypertension, diabetes and chronic disease occur.

Universal health care requires a societal contract in which everyone pays in based on their ability to pay, and everyone gets health care based on their health need. This means those who are healthy subsidize those who are ill, the young largely subsidize the old, and the rich subsidize the poor. This is at the core of what's called 'risk pooling' in insurance: some people get more out of the scheme, and some get less. But this is a political decision to bring society together and recognize that 'health for all with financial protection' is a basic responsibility of the state. The larger and more diverse the group, the better the risk pooling works, which means a national base like in Britain and Thailand is ideal.

Britain got there in 1948 and provided a model for the rest of the world of what was possible. But the NHS is struggling and falling apart, whether it's from long waiting lists, strikes among medical staff over unsafe working conditions and pay, medical staff emigrating to other countries for better conditions, or a heavy push towards privatization. Private insurance is big business in the US, with health care one of the most profitable markets. These companies are entering the UK because there's money to be made in private health care.

Private health care is attractive to those who can afford it: why not? But it's a dangerous system where pre-existing conditions, such as diabetes or asthma, mean that those individuals who most need medical care are often excluded by insurance schemes. In contrast, those who are least likely to need medical care are sought out by private insurers.

It makes sense: why would any private company want to have to cover the medical costs of someone who will need ongoing medical care? This is the danger of leaving health care to market forces, and health care isn't a luxury like a handbag or designer shoes. It's essential to not dying too soon.

I don't believe the UK needs a 'new' model of health care: some look to the US and say its approach would be better than the crumbling NHS. These are the usual non-expert commentators, or those knowing how much money is there to be made if the health care market is largely private. The US system is great if you're rich and terrible if you're poor, and it means people going without medical care because of the cost.

The UK's NHS is seen as a shining light across the world: universal quality health care, free at the point of care, regardless of the ability to pay. It's still highly trusted by the British public, as demonstrated by the highly efficient delivery and take-up of the COVID vaccine. The NHS did an exemplary job of getting the vaccine quickly into priority groups who needed it the most, and these groups trusted the NHS and its staff.

What the NHS needs is a government willing to put the investment in: into prevention and public health so Britain doesn't have an increasingly unhealthy population; into adequate financing and putting the money into the public sector instead of falling to lobbying interests and moving it into private company hands; and into its staff who are the backbone of the service offered. That leadership has been lacking for over a decade, which is a political choice.

These choices – over investing in the public system, ensuring that health care workers are compensated and feel safe at work, or determining how long people wait for appointments – have life and death consequences. Maybe not for those in the top 1 per cent, or the Cabinet and their family. But for normal people who have a normal job, who pay their taxes and National Insurance contribution each month from their salary, and who are reliant on the health care offer from the state.

I felt this acutely myself because I was completely reliant on the medical system to book me an appointment for timely treatment. I was fortunate to get this, but it had less to do with any individual behaviour on my part, and more to do with the country I live in, and the government's decision in 1948 to build the NHS.

11. How to Live

In 2023, when international travel opened fully after the pandemic, I went to visit my Nani, which is Hindi for maternal grandmother, in Chennai. Nani was celebrating her ninetieth birthday and laughed when I told her the title of this book. I asked her about living even longer – to 120 or 130 years old, escaping death for another few decades, but she's not interested. In her words, it's not about how not to die. It's about how to live.

My grandmother says that life is special because it is finite. When we face our mortality, we must think about how best to use our limited time on this planet. I think getting to 100 with full mental and physical abilities is an ambitious goal, given the risk factors we face each day affecting our health. As well as being lucky. My objective is to maintain functional health with each passing year: can my mind and body do the things that I want them to do, and can I avoid the health conditions such as type 2 diabetes and hypertension that tend to come with being older and South Asian?

I asked my grandmother for her approach to ageing. She wants to keep mentally active and stay socially connected in a community. She wants to keep independence in movement, such as being able to go to the bathroom and shower herself and move about her flat in Chennai. She talks quite a lot about diet: eating a simple, vegetable-based diet and limiting her caloric intake to what her body needs.

My Nani is also a spiritual person and talks about being kind and generous, and putting out good energy into the universe. She says you should carry on every day with a positive mindset to the best of your ability. We always have a chance to re-evaluate our life and think whether we'd like to go in a new direction. She says that changing your mind is not a sign of weakness, but of growth.

Things that increase happiness also relate to meaning in daily life through a job, vocation or role, being part of a community, having several close friends and family, and being healthy and free of pain. I haven't talked enough about the importance of family, friendships and relationships in living longer. Loneliness, especially for those aged fifty or older, has potential consequences, including a 50 per cent increased risk of dementia, 29 per cent increased risk of heart disease, 32 per cent increased risk of a stroke, and a significant increase in risk of premature death from all causes.

The Okinawans talk about living close to family, which is hard for people like me with family thousands of miles away, or for those with strained relations. Friends are the substitute family we build wherever we might be living. In the social media age, it's easy to fixate on the number of friends you have on Facebook, or the number of followers on Instagram. Virtual relationships can help connect us to others, but real-life interactions and a few close friendships bring more happiness and better quality of life.

I've talked extensively in this book about wealth and finances. While of course adequate income is important to happiness, it's far from sufficient. In fact, past a certain income threshold – once someone can meet their basic needs such as housing, safety, food, heating, and leisure pursuits such as holidays – additional income doesn't increase happiness. It plateaus.

In 2010, Nobel Prize laureates Daniel Kahneman and Angus Deaton published a paper showing that a rise in income increased people's wellbeing until roughly a ceiling of $75,000. This was based on analysing 450,000 responses to a wellbeing index which surveyed 1,000 US residents on a daily basis. Similarly, in 2023, Professor Jan-Emmanuel De Neve of Oxford University noted in his studies in Britain that once a person reaches a salary of £120,000, 'they would no longer detect a statistically significant relationship between further money and life satisfaction.'

To be fair, that income threshold for 'plateauing happiness' is getting higher, and out of reach for most, with inflation and as the cost of living goes up. The overarching take-away from studies on income and happiness is that income beyond a minimum level is important, but not the sole defining part of living a meaningful life. Yet we still focus exclusively on income in terms of defining 'success' (think of the *Sunday Times* Rich List, or our fixation on the world's richest individuals), instead of the multi-faceted components that lead to people leading meaningful lives.

For my seventeenth birthday, a close friend gave me a framed quote from Ralph Waldo Emerson that I still have in my bedroom: 'What is success? To laugh often and much; to win the respect of intelligent people and the affection of children; to earn the appreciation of honest critics and endure the betrayal of false friends; to appreciate beauty; to find the best in others; to leave the world a bit better, whether by a healthy child, a garden patch or a redeemed social condition; to know even one life has breathed easier because you have lived. This is to have succeeded!'

Wearing Flip-Flops to Buckingham Palace

My Nani rests on and off during the day, so to keep myself busy, I visit a local tourist attraction, Fort St George. While most of the fort buildings are now used for state government offices, including that of the Chief Minister of Tamil Nadu, a small museum is open to the public, sharing the history of Chennai (formerly Madras), particularly its ties to the British empire. A huge portrait of Queen Victoria, the Empress of India, looms over the room, with a small plaque on her life. She was born in 1819 and lived to eighty-one at a time when life expectancy for an average woman born that year was forty-one.

I get back to Nani's flat for dinner, remarking on Queen Victoria's long life, and she tells the story of meeting Queen Elizabeth II during a British state visit to India. Nana (my grandfather) worked in the Indian civil service, and Nani helped host the Queen. She shows me photos from their visit to the Taj Mahal.

I tell Nani the story of meeting the Queen and Prince Philip at Buckingham Palace during my first month abroad in Oxford in October 2003. Just a week into adjusting to life in England, my cohort of Rhodes Scholars were invited to a celebration of the Mandela–Rhodes collaboration. I wore my fanciest flip-flops bejewelled with rainbow-coloured plastic gems and a black mini-skirt, which I felt quite proud of. This was my nice 'Miami' event outfit. Our coach stopped on the motorway at a rest stop, and it was only in the bathroom when a British girl looked at me and sniggered, 'You're wearing that to meet the Queen!' that I realized perhaps my fashion efforts were lost in translation.

At the palace, we were expected to queue and meet the royals one at a time, before going on to meet Nelson Mandela. My friend Cyrus Habib, who is blind and was wearing sunglasses, asked if I would escort him on my elbow to meet the royals. As we approached, the Prince commented, 'You young lovebirds can't keep your hands off each other.' Before I could explain that Cyrus was blind, the meet-and-greet was over and then it was a few seconds with Mandela, who shook my hand and said, 'Cold hands, warm heart.' I've held on to that motto during the long winters in Scotland.

Queen Elizabeth II, the longest-serving monarch in British history, died on the 8th of September 2022 at Balmoral Castle. While there was global mourning about the death of a much-loved royal, there was also recognition of her long and illustrious life. She was born in 1926, when life expectancy for an average woman born that year was sixty-two. She outlived this by thirty-four years. Her death certificate lists cause of death as 'old age'. Old age is rarely given as the sole cause of death: it usually means there's not any clear identifiable disease or injury, but rather the slow decline into older age.

Queen Victoria's and Elizabeth II's long lives aren't unique for the royal family. A historian analysed the longevity of twenty-seven royals (six of the last British monarchs and their spouses and children) and found that on average they lived an additional thirty years compared to their subjects. If you want to learn how not to die too soon, a good place to look is in the royal quality of life.

In 2003, the daily routine of Prince Philip was published in the *Daily Mirror* after a reporter managed to get a job as a footman at Buckingham Palace. Each day started with breakfast at 8.30 a.m. in the Queen's private dining room overlooking the palace gardens. Breakfast was usually porridge oats or cereal alongside a cup of coffee. Each item had the same position each day, all brought by a palace footman following strict instructions on where breakfast items should be placed.

After breakfast, Prince Philip would then carry out royal duties such as solo visits or supporting the Queen at public appearances, as well as spending time playing polo (until his fifties) and, later in life, competitive carriage driving (racing horse-drawn carriages through the countryside). He spent much of his time at Wood Farm on the Sandringham estate, where he used to read, paint and host friends.

High tea was served at 5.00 p.m., followed by a relaxed dinner when the Queen and Prince Philip would change into comfortable clothes and enjoy a casual meal without guests or formality. His diet consisted of meat, fish, eggs, vegetables, fruit, nuts, seeds, high-fat dairy and healthy oils. He minimized consuming desserts or sugar, wheat, trans fats, and ultra-processed foods.

This strict diet meant that the Prince didn't carry much extra weight. His personal tailor John Kent said: 'He's got a fabulous physique. There's not an ounce of fat on him, which is why he wears his clothes so well. He's got fairly long legs, and doesn't carry much weight.' This was just before his ninety-sixth birthday, and he was rumoured to still be able to fit into the same naval uniform he wore on his wedding day.

In addition to his love of outdoor sports, Prince Philip followed a daily fitness routine created by the Royal Canadian Air Force in the 1950s called the 5BX. This is an eleven-minute workout involving five exercises: stretching (for two minutes), sit-ups (one minute), back extensions (one minute), push-ups (one minute) and running in place (six minutes). The result was that he had a high-quality and active life, including good posture and walking without a cane, until he died aged ninety-nine, months before his 100th birthday.

Most of us can only admire such a lifestyle from afar: a chef preparing home-cooked healthy meals, plenty of time for exercise with horse riding or strolls around the palace gardens, security that ensures safety against gun and knife violence, being driven in an SUV with motorcycle protection, the most exclusive health care with a dedicated team of royal personal physicians, and no stress about paying for any of it.

It's a life of privilege, full of time and money, where financial stress and poverty are just not a relevant concern. Wealth is indeed the best protection from an early and untimely death. It's the same reason that US presidents tend to live decades longer than the population they represent.

While I was writing this book, Catherine, Princess of Wales shared that she'd had cancer detected during abdominal surgery and was starting preventive chemotherapy. For someone aged forty-two with a healthy and active lifestyle, it felt like tragic bad luck. Fortunately, her cancer was detected early, and she doesn't need to wait in line for an NHS appointment. She will receive the best medical care, and hopefully early diagnosis and treatment means a good health outcome and Catherine continuing to live a long life.

There's no changing the birth lottery which determines who gets access to a royal lifestyle, and who ends up living in a slum in Nairobi or a rural village in Bangladesh. There's little point in wishing that one had the privileges of Prince Harry, Prince William or their children. What we can do is support governments that take steps to increase the life quality and expectancy of their populations – for everyone. The place to look is Finland.

The Happiest Place on Earth

Finland is one of the best places to live in the world, and the happiest according to the people who live there. That's probably why Santa Claus decided to base himself in Lapland. The Fragile States Index names it the most stable country in the world. It's one of the world's most equal societies, not only in terms of income but also gender, and its health outcomes are good too.

Life expectancy in Finland at 82.5 in 2023 is one of the highest in the world, and it even increased during the pandemic. The country reported the lowest rates of COVID cases and deaths among EU countries in 2020. In addition, 68 per cent of people reported being in good health, which is similar to the EU average. Mortality from treatable causes in Finland was lower than the EU average, which indicates a health system able to diagnose and treat conditions quickly and effectively. However, the country is struggling with the growing number of adolescents who are overweight or obese, which shows that diet is an ongoing challenge for almost all countries.

Coincidentally, while I was writing this chapter, my friend Jocelyn asked me where Lapland was. We Americans aren't taught much geography beyond the capitals and spelling of the fifty US states. I replied by talking about how great Finland is as a country, given its life expectancy, health status, management of the pandemic, and poverty reduction. She responded: 'Yeah, because it's a tiny country.' I said, 'What about Scotland? Finland has 5.5 million people, same as us here.' Her response: 'They've always been that way.'

Poor Jocelyn had to listen to me challenge that premise for the next half hour. Public health progress isn't about luck or culture, nor is it completely out of our control: it's down to the decision of one political leader or another, whether today or 250 years back.

Finland wasn't always the happy country its people say it is now. The government achieved this over the past century with explicit policy directives. For example, gender equality was an early objective and they achieved this through measures to improve the standing and protection of women in the labour force.

Finland was the first country in the world to grant equally to all men and women the right to not only vote but also stand for election. By 1917, Finnish women were provided with a month of maternity leave, which was extended to a year over the next few decades. In 2021, 47 per cent of MPs were women, and 58 per cent of ministers in government were women. Women and men are equally represented in the labour market, which is due to equal distribution of family leave (including paternity leave for fathers) and affordable good-quality childcare from a young age.

Finland also has good state provision of health and education for all. The health care system offers public health care services to everyone living in the country, funded by general taxation and social security payments. In 2023, the health care system in Finland ranked first in the world based on capacity to treat and cure diseases.

In addition, in the early 1970s the government decided to invest in a nationwide comprehensive state school education system of high quality, with the premise that basic education is free. This wasn't just how the 'Finnish were': in fact, post-Second World War, their educational system was made up of private, selective schools where wealthier children studied, and basic local schools. The result of the 1970s legislation was that incentives shifted away from fee-paying schools and towards attending the free state sector.

Private schools still exist in the country but they're a tiny percentage: only 2 per cent of all schools are private. As recounted by Melissa Benn in her book *Life Lessons*, 'Finland's politicians and educational figures recognized that a profoundly unequal education system did not simply reproduce inequality down the generations, but weakened the fabric of the nation itself.'

For those struggling and homeless, the government provides temporary housing for a certain period, help with job applications, and a universal basic income. This package helps people get back on their feet and back into the workforce. What do you get when you put a social scientist, a doctor, a politician and a bishop together? A report titled 'Nimi Ovessa' (Your Name on the Door), which starts from the premise that, 'You don't need to solve your problems before you get a home. Instead, a home should be the secure foundation that makes it easier to solve your problems.'

Since the start of the policy called Housing First in 2008, the number of long-term homeless people has fallen by more than 35 per cent, with rough sleeping basically eradicated in Finland. While it cost the government 250 million euros to create new homes and hire support workers, the savings in emergency health care, social services and legal costs are catching up, with roughly 15,000 euros a year saved per homeless person.

How do they manage to afford these policies? The Finnish government has improved tax compliance and stopped tax loopholes for corporations and super-wealthy individuals. For example, Finland taxes residents on their worldwide income. Non-dom status doesn't exist there as it does in Britain for wealthy individuals. If you want to live in Finland, you pay tax on your total income. You can't just live there and earn somewhere else to avoid paying tax locally. Estimates from Warwick University in 2022 predict that closing down non-dom status in Britain would raise an additional £3.2 billion per year for the government.

In addition, Finland has a high marginal tax rate, which means the more someone earns, the more they pay in tax. The result is quality health care for all, a world-class state education system, free university education and decent infrastructure. The country is built on the premise that everyone should have opportunities in life, regardless of their background, and pooling state money for health care and education benefits all. This approach increases equality and supports those who have had a more difficult start in life.

What to do seems simple: support women in concrete ways, provide health and education as core state services, ensure those who are struggling get support and help out of the pit they're in, and ensure those who should be paying tax – the super-wealthy – actually pay tax.

Compare this to the country you live in. For me as a British-American, the contrast is stark. In the US, the richest 400 families paid an 8.2 per cent average rate of tax from 2010 to 2018, in contrast to the average American who paid 13.3 per cent. The twenty-five richest Americans paid only 3.4 per cent tax, while seeing their net worth grow by $401 billion. This is because the rich figure out legal loopholes to pay a lower rate, or derive their income largely from investments. Unlike most Americans who pay their income tax from wages and working hard. It's nuts.

A similar story could be told in Britain: income gained from work (45 per cent top income tax rate) is taxed more than twice as much as income gained from profit made from selling shares (20 per cent capital gains tax). Robert Palmer, executive director at Tax Justice UK, says: 'At the moment someone who earns most of their money from their wealth – like the prime minister [at the time, Rishi Sunak] – pays a much lower tax rate than someone who relies on going out to work for their living. We need to fix this to make sure that income from wealth is taxed at the same rate as income from work.'

Income affects health: not just our ability to make choices over health behaviours such as diet and exercise, but also the level of chronic stress we feel about daily life. This is true at a community level too: even wealthier individuals do 'better' when there is less homelessness, less poverty and less class warfare.

How Much Money Is Enough Money?

Having a spectrum of wealth is part of the capitalist system, with capitalism well recognized as 'the worst economic system except for all the others'. But how broad that spectrum is, affects the health of the individuals within it. Societies that are more unequal tend to be unhealthier, while those that have managed to ensure a decent standard of living for the bottom 50 per cent, and a fair wealth distribution system, are generally healthier.

Implementing solutions like the kind put forward in Finland is largely a political choice made by a particular government that wanted to tackle inequality. Sadly, since the pandemic, in country after country, inequality is increasing. The charity Oxfam highlighted this issue in May 2022 when it released a brief, titled 'Profiting from Pain'.

Oxfam's research showed that the pandemic created a new billionaire every thirty hours. At the same time, 263 million people fell into extreme poverty, at a rate of a million every thirty-three hours. Billionaires' wealth rose more in the first twenty-four months of the COVID pandemic than in the previous twenty-three years combined. This was particularly true of food, energy and pharmaceutical billionaires. Oxfam estimates that two thirds of the wealth amassed since the pandemic has gone to the richest 1 per cent.

If we zoom out to 2025, rising fuel and food prices are causing problems across the globe. As executive director of Oxfam International Gabriela Bucher said: 'The extremely rich and powerful are profiting from pain and suffering. Some have grown rich by denying billions of people access to vaccines, others by exploiting rising food and energy prices. They are paying out massive bonuses and dividends while paying as little tax as possible.'

This rising inequality has consequences for health. As Bucher says: 'Millions are skipping meals, turning off heating, falling behind on bills and wondering what they can possibly do next to survive. Across East Africa, one person is likely dying every minute from hunger. This grotesque inequality is breaking the bonds that hold us together as humanity. This is inequality that literally kills.'

The increase in inequality is not because of the disease itself – it's because of the choices made by political leaders and governments during the pandemic. Blaming 'the pandemic' or lockdowns is a convenient scapegoat for populist leaders dealing with an increasingly angry and impoverished public. But it's not true. What happened was the use of a health crisis as an excuse to be greedy by certain elites.

In the UK, analysis of 1,200 government contracts worth nearly $22 billion during the pandemic found that almost half went to companies run by friends and associates of Conservative Party politicians, or those with no experience in the area. Jolyon Maugham, director of the Good Law Project, highlighted the 'vast financial rewards you could reap if you had a minister looking out for your interests'. His programme estimates that more than £4 in every £5 spent on PPE was wasted or 'lost'.

Even the super-rich are aware of how unfair this is, and are calling to be taxed more heavily. In a *Guardian* column in 2024, Abigail Disney, the grandniece of Walt Disney, who has a net worth of $120 million, wrote: 'The need to tax rich people like me has never been so dire. Extreme wealth concentration in the hands of a few oligarchs is a threat to democracy the world over.' She calls on governments to act and take the necessary steps to address inequality.

When looking at places with growing inequality, whether it's India, the US or Britain, the question in my mind is: when is enough wealth enough? Is it $100 million? Or $1 billion? How many houses mean that someone feels content? One or two or ten or fifteen? When do billionaires or even multimillionaires draw the line and say, 'I'm content with what I have'? Our society too often celebrates the accumulation of a huge fortune, or conflates success with wealth.

I often think of it in terms of being stuck on a tiny island with one person holding most of the land and food, four others doing okay, and five people going hungry with no shelter. Would this be considered fair and a good way of running the island? Probably not.

At a global and national level, we accept this distribution of wealth. The World Bank estimates that half the world's population lives under the poverty line of $6.85 per day, which is considered the basic floor for economic wellbeing. In Britain, food bank usage has increased 50 per cent since before the pandemic, with new demand from people who are in work such as health care staff and teachers. Poverty is too often seen as a choice, rather than a collective problem for government to address.

Many problems in Britain with NHS resources, education and housing are tied to this increased inequality. The richest 1 per cent are worth at least £3.6 million each, which means together they're wealthier than 70 per cent of the population combined. They often don't pay tax because of loopholes, or holding non-dom status. In fact, ex-Prime Minister Rishi Sunak's wife didn't pay tax on her foreign income until recently, using non-dom status as the legal justification. The richest 1 per cent in the UK are the most expensive top 1 per cent group in Europe, paying the lowest taxes of any such group in any large European country.

When people wonder why public health, medical care, trains, roads, housing and food in Britain or America aren't as good as in European countries, it's worth looking at what those countries invest in their public services, and how they generate resources to benefit the entire population. But instead of having these democratic conversations about a healthy, collective society, it's easier for governments to distract by pointing to external threats – and more often than not, immigration.

It's the classic distraction technique used to take pressure off politicians who know they're not delivering for their people. I often use this example with students: 'Twelve people on an island. Two have taken most of the food, shelter and resources. When the other ten ask them what's happening and why, the answer is: "Watch out! Those from the next island are coming to steal all that is yours. They're the real problem, not us."'

Sadly, if the media are willing to support this narrative of 'immigrants are the reason you don't have adequate housing, accessible health care, quality education or affordable food, and why your life feels hard', then people believe it. They elect populist politicians who spout this rhetoric and build this platform because it's an easy way to win votes, and simpler than trying to solve society's challenging problems.

More Action, Fewer Excuses

It might feel strange to hear an academic say, 'We don't need more research.' But I increasingly feel this way about most public health issues. We know what to do for a healthier society and world: from what to eat, to the air we breathe, to reducing income inequality. In this book, I've highlighted the clear knowledge we have. Scientifically we know how to create 'better' health individually and collectively: we have the knowledge and the tools. I've shown how different parts of the world are finding a way to make progress on these, and what can be learned. Here are some of my take-aways from looking across time and country:

First, progress is always possible. Anywhere in the world. We know what to do and it usually takes some kind of shock or trauma for governments to act and take the necessary policy steps. Cynical fatalism is the real issue. Just look at the contrast between Thailand and Sweden. Thailand's government believed that COVID suppression was possible and important, and they managed to keep pandemic deaths relatively low compared to Western counterparts like Sweden. Yet they seem to accept road traffic deaths as just part of life in the country, which means not enough has been done to take the necessary steps.

Sweden pioneered Vision Zero, the concept that there should be no deaths from road traffic accidents, and implemented the policy measures effectively. But they didn't think COVID suppression was possible, and their relatively high death toll, compared to their Scandinavian neighbours and East Asian countries, shows that this starting point became self-fulfilling.

In short, what leaders think is possible to change and make progress on, usually gets better. What they don't think is possible, because it's framed as too difficult, usually doesn't change. This is where vision from heads of state, ministers of health and other key political leaders is crucial. What usually drives them to act?

Grieving parents. In case study after case study, what emerges is how powerful a force parents can be, when they have a cause close to their heart. The loss of a child is devastating, especially so if their parents believe it was preventable. This drives certain parents to commit the rest of their life to ensuring no other children suffer the same fate from that cause. I think of Rosamund here, mum of Ella, the young girl who died due to air pollution in London. She said: 'It has been a long and truly painful journey. It has cost me everything, but I'd do it all again for the love of Ella. To be in a position that I'll end up saving millions of lives is a privilege.'

I think of the parents at Dunblane who drove gun legislation changes in Britain. Of the parents in the Netherlands who pushed for safer roads and cycling routes, especially for children. Of the parents in Jackson, Mississippi, whose children were out of school, and often sick, because of dirty water and who raised their voices for change. Of the senators in Washington DC, unhappy with how social media has been affecting the mental health of their own children and pushing for legislation to regulate it better. Of the young mum who died in Lagos leaving behind four children, resulting in her husband advocating for the end of medical detention. Never underestimate the power of a small group of angry parents to push for change. They usually get what they want, wherever it is in the world.

Second, when progress happens, it's usually when there's consensus across political parties that action is needed. I think here of the progress made against smoking in Britain: it wasn't seen as a Conservative, Labour or Green issue. It was seen as a public health issue that needed action. Same for reducing air pollution: a Labour London mayor brought in the first legislation to regulate emissions within the city in 2008, which was extended by the next Conservative mayor to an ultra-low emission zone, and the subsequent Labour mayor continued that push. Same for gun control: a Conservative prime minister took initial steps before a Labour prime minister pushed it even further.

This is just in Britain, but similar stories can be told about gun control in Colombia and Serbia, about safer roads in Japan, about mental health in France and about improved physical activity in the

Netherlands. Change is usually driven by a charismatic leader who decides to plant a flag, to leave a legacy, and to bring various factions along regardless of their underlying political beliefs.

Making a problem a partisan issue tied to a specific political party is an obstacle to change. I think here of gun control in the US, which breaks along Democratic and Republican party lines, and of former Prime Minister Rishi Sunak's efforts to frame reducing air pollution as an 'anti-car agenda' tied to Labour. Public health is political, in that it requires leadership, vision, priorities and decision-making, but improving the health of the public shouldn't be partisan.

Third, no country has it all figured out, and while the top ten health challenges are generally the same everywhere, the contribution of each to reducing life expectancy is different in various countries. In Thailand and Vietnam, road traffic injuries are a leading problem. In the US, it's gun violence and road traffic injuries. In Nigeria, it's lack of access to affordable health care. In Japan, it's poor mental health and suicides. In Britain, it's chronic diseases linked to unhealthy diet and sedentary behaviour with increasingly inaccessible health care. In India, it's dirty air and tobacco, while in Haiti, it's dirty water and violence. In the Netherlands, it's poor diet and smoking.

All countries can learn something from how other countries have approached an issue. In global public health, we look across countries at certain policy developments to understand the impact they are having on health outcomes, the cost–benefit calculation, and how exactly change happened.

The Japanese government has learned from Britain's approach to reducing smoking, and the UK government is learning from the Japanese approach to clean air. Shared learning takes a certain degree of humility on the part of governments, and the acceptance that progress is possible even if the cultural context seems radically different.

Imagine if the British government gave up looking at the Dutch approach to physical activity, or the Indian government didn't look at Britain's achievements to reduce smoking. Yes, Americans love their freedom to own guns; Australians also love their freedom, but were willing to curtail the freedom to own guns (with no restrictions) to protect the freedom of all to live without fear of being shot.

It seems ridiculous for 8 billion humans – who are largely the same, but organized within nation states which are just social and legal constructs – to think of ourselves as too different from each other because of skin colour, language or recent history. Most of the major changes in public health that have increased life expectancy have happened in the last century. Much of the 'bad luck' of being born into a country where gun ownership is rife or where there is no public health care provision stems from political choices made by leaders – either today or historically.

Fourth, risk factors seem to balance each other out in terms of their impact on health outcomes. For example, the Dutch are the most active people on the planet, but their diet is quite poor. The Japanese aren't very active compared to other populations, but their diet is very healthy. The consequence is that the Dutch and Japanese have roughly similar burdens of chronic disease, although the Japanese do stand out for longevity.

Most people do the best they can for their health in the circumstances they live under. The biggest two determinants are the country you live in (and the government's approach to the issue) and your disposable income and time. It's not because people are stupid, lazy, or don't know how to improve their health.

If you live in Britain, you just don't have to worry about the cost of health care or going bankrupt due to a medical accident. But you are stuck within a public system that has major backlogs, unless you have money that lets you override the system through accessing private care. If you live in the US, dying from gun violence is a major concern, even more so if you live in a deprived area, or come from a non-white background.

If you live in New Delhi, air pollution is a daily concern. It's reduced if you work indoors and can afford air purifiers, can buy bottled 'clean air' and move about in a car with an air-filtration device. If you live in Bangkok, getting hit by a car or truck is a massive problem, but it's reduced if you're able to be in a car yourself instead of on a motorbike or bicycle, or walking.

The point is that we're all in this together within a national context ... to a certain extent. Wealth protects against the major risk factors, and this is why getting to the heart of inequality is linked to improving health.

Fifth, the private sector is valuable, and while it's sometimes the solution, it's also sometimes part of the problem. I think of gun manufacturers who want to sell more guns and ammunition, because it makes them money. I think of cigarette manufacturers who push smoking in non-Western countries and vaping in high-income markets. I think of factories producing industrial emissions which dirty the air, and that have no incentive to worry about what happens next. I think of car manufacturers who want to sell more and larger cars, and for whom efforts to offer alternative modes of transport cut into their market.

I think of bottled water, bottled air, and air purification companies that thrive off a larger environmental problem by offering a product solution. I think of private health care providers who would prefer to charge whatever they want for health care, instead of being regulated by the state to ensure prices are reasonable and the care is of high quality. I think of major food companies that have massive profits tied to selling ultra-processed foods and ensuring these are part of school lunches and the staple diet of the population.

The problem here is that companies push a certain product to make money, but the health cost of these products is borne by individuals, the community, the health care system and the public sector. Gun manufacturers don't bear the cost of gun violence and the loss of life. The cost is borne by families losing loved ones and hospitals trying to save those dying. Factories producing harmful emissions don't bear the cost of dirty air: that's families losing loved ones and hospitals dealing with a rise in asthma admissions. The same goes for ultra-processed foods and the impact on childhood obesity, chronic disease in later life, and reduced life expectancy. This is why government regulation is essential: to ensure that those creating a certain problem also bear some of the cost of fixing it.

In fact, certain private industries benefit from the harm they inflict. Here's an example: gun sales go up in communities that have just experienced a mass shooting. Sales of large cars also increase in communities that have rising road traffic injuries and deaths. Why?

Because the solution is painted by these industries as: 'The problem would be reduced for you individually if you have this product.'

This is a major difference to those countries that have managed to link certain products to disability and death. The French government has linked larger cars and SUVs to increased road traffic deaths. The Serbian, Colombian, Australian, New Zealand and British governments have linked gun sales to increased deaths by guns. Somehow this logic seems to be backwards in the US.

When I pushed my friend Jocelyn on this, she said, 'Americans love their freedom.' I would say that freedom is also the freedom to not die too soon through preventable causes. For example, former Prime Minister Rishi Sunak tweeted in 2024: 'Only the @Conservatives will give people the freedom to travel how they want and when they want.' My response to that is: 'What about those who want freedom to travel with or without a car and want reliable public transport, safe cycling and freedom to breathe air that isn't polluted and causing damage to our lungs?'

Public health (and associated policies and legislation) has too often been framed as something that takes away, rather than taking steps to protect freedoms to help you live a long and healthy life.

The other framing is whether a health challenge is seen as an accident or bad luck, rather than something preventable by public policy. If it's seen as preventable, then progress is possible. Just look at road traffic injuries, water and sanitation systems, clean air, and universal access to health care. If it's seen as being in the wrong place at the wrong time, for example in a mass shooting, or living in Jackson during a water crisis or in Sri Lanka during a tsunami, then it's too easy for governments to say it's not their responsibility to do anything, and to push this onto individuals.

Who Wants to Be a Politician?

Much of this book has emphasized politics, especially leaders making decisive policy choices and finding a way to have these accepted within their political systems. But at a time when we need visionary and competent leadership prioritizing public health, we instead get heads of government who don't seem that interested. I think of Donald Trump, Ron DeSantis, Jair Bolsonaro, Rishi Sunak, Boris Johnson, and the list goes on. In New Zealand, Jacinda Ardern's efforts in public health are being undone by a replacement who is reversing some of her policies.

We see public cynicism around politicians, often voted one of the least trustworthy professions in public opinion polls, in the high abstention rate from voting and the underlying attitude of, 'Why bother voting, they're all the same.' It leads to the question of who wants to go into politics. What are the incentives to be a politician?

If you're going into politics to make a difference in people's lives, it's a hard road to walk. The growth of social media has brought constant death threats and public abuse. Even more so if you're a woman. Several women leaders have stepped down and pointed out the constant abuse taking its toll, including made-up online conspiracy theories. Think of Hillary Clinton running a paedophile ring from a pizza shop. The same day that former Scotland First Minister Nicola Sturgeon stepped down, a man was jailed for sending her an abusive email stating that she was going to 'face a hanging' for treason. Sturgeon reflected, 'Social media provides a vehicle for the most awful abuse of women, misogyny, sexism and threats of violence for women who put their heads above the parapet.' I'm just a scientist and I've faced it too – including doubts over my credentials, with people contacting Oxford and the Rhodes Trust to verify that I actually attended on a scholarship.

It's not just social media. Mainstream media puts politicians through a gruelling exercise. If billionaires have bought up the newspapers – in Britain, think of the *Daily Mail*, the *Sun*, the *Telegraph*, *The Times* – a certain narrative emerges trying to convince people to buy into a system that's failing them. For example, the COVID inquiry exposed how right-wing papers such as the *Daily Mail* were pushing the prime minister at the time, Boris Johnson, to lift restrictions against scientific advice in 2020 and to encourage people into offices when the risk of infection was high. This policy position suited billionaires protected in their country estates, who wanted their workers back being productive, even if the cost was their health or life.

Certain papers constantly run stories about how immigration is the reason why life is difficult – often portraying it as the main problem facing the country – rather than tackling the underlying choices made by a government to prioritize the 1 per cent elite over the 99 per cent of people who live here.

It means if you're a politician trying to address the substantive issues within a country, there's no easy way to get beyond this spin. Instead, you'll be hammered, day after day, with half-truths, so that you start to wonder, why bother at all? Space then opens for politicians who serve the interests of billionaires to get ahead. George Monbiot, a *Guardian* columnist, has referred to this as the oligarchy of Britain hiding behind the democratic front. It's the same story in the US and dozens of other countries.

I don't want to depress you. This book is supposed to be about hope and progress. For me, the core question for any society is whether we have the political will to make health a priority, and to invest in the necessary measures to improve life for all members of society. We are largely reliant on government to create the conditions within which we live.

Yes, if you're wealthy you can try to bubble yourself, but you're still part of a larger society. Voting for honest, visionary leaders is the best thing you can do for public health. The data and evidence are there. The policy experiments have been done. It's whether there's somebody willing to put in place policies for the good of all. This is the pathway, or the stumbling block, to better quality of life, and longer life.

What We Can Control

We can't predict what will happen in life, but let's not portray as bad luck or an accident – such as getting shot in a gun massacre in Kansas or falling sick while surfing on the English coast – what are clearly preventable health issues. While much is out of our control, there's a lot within our control too.

I hope you'll come away from this book inspired by how much progress we've made, energized by how much more we still need to do, and reflective on how politics and governments are the largest force shaping when and how we die. Getting to 100 is a collective endeavour for all of us, supported by our leaders. Everything is changeable. Everything is possible. It's down to the choices we make as a society. That's the politics of hope: we must imagine a healthier world and take the public policy steps towards it.

As someone who has studied global public health for over twenty years, I can say the one certainty is that life is getting better. In 1841, life expectancy at birth was roughly forty years old. I've just turned thirty-nine and still feel young. Back then, forty wasn't mid-life: it was life.

Epilogue

Anywhere you look, you'll find self-help lists with advice telling you, 'Here's how to age in a healthy way.' These lists generally focus on the same things, like not being overweight and sleeping enough, as if you have full control over your health and wellbeing. Many people do their best to follow these steps, within the constraints of time, financial resources and the environment and country they live in. I'm guessing since you're reading this book that you're one of these people too. Yes, we know from decades of public health research how to live healthy and long lives, and the policies underpinning this.

So if we have the knowledge to improve health and it's clear and simple, why don't governments implement these policies? And where does this leave you, the reader of this book, in terms of your own agency in effecting change and living longer?

Five Asks of Your Government

The current UK government could be doing more to improve your health, and that of your loved ones. And to be fair, there are areas in which previous UK governments – of various political stripes – have made significant progress, as I've talked about already: think of smoking regulation, the banning of handguns and reduction in firearm violence, and in Scotland, the public ownership of water and free provision of clean tap water in public spaces. Perhaps most internationally notable are the idea and values behind universal access to health care with the NHS. These gains can't be taken for granted. They're the result of decades of blood, sweat and tears to get leaders to act and implement certain policies. You are benefiting from that legacy each day, and living longer because of it.

But equally important is recognizing how much more could be

done. Here are five asks of the current UK government. Policies to advance health are not the preserve of a certain political party. As I've highlighted in the book, progress happens with collaboration across the political spectrum. None of them is about taking away freedoms: they're all about giving us an alternative possibility.

First, make fruit and vegetables cheaper and more accessible. I've laid out the evidence linking unhealthy diet to obesity and chronic disease. In 2022, more than 800,000 people were admitted to hospital in England and Wales with malnutrition: these were largely people with caloric-dense diets that lacked essential nutrients like protein, vitamins and minerals. In children these dietary deficiencies are reflected in height: 'The greater the deprivation, the shorter the child.'

Increasing fruit and vegetable consumption would be a direct way to tackle this, but it means looking at affordability. The UK imports 50 per cent of its vegetables and 84 per cent of its fruit. Since Brexit, food prices have increased overall by 6 per cent (in 2022 they increased by 19.1 per cent), with some perishable items like cucumbers increasing more than 50 per cent in price between 2022 and 2023. Overall, fruit and vegetable prices went up by 30 per cent, eggs by 37 per cent, milk by 33 per cent and chicken by 23 per cent. Buying fruit and vegetables is expensive in Britain, costing on average £11.79 per 1,000 kcal compared to £5.82 for 1,000 kcal of processed foods.

Food systems discussions can descend into complexity. Keep the ask simple: cheaper and more accessible fruit and vegetables, including in school meals. Again, there are examples of policy success in this area: take Wales. In 2022, the government guaranteed a large market, school meals, to courgette (zucchini) producers with the requirement that produce met certain quality standards. Farmers scaled up their production, knowing they could sell their vegetables, and wholesalers reduced the price since it was a bulk purchase for school meals in Cardiff. The evidence that innovative deals, like the Courgette Pilot, could lower the price of vegetables, support local producers and get more vegetables into school meals has led the Welsh government to fund an expanded scheme in 2023 to bring in more vegetables, wholesalers and producers.

Second, give us alternatives to cars, which means better public transport, accessible walking and cycling infrastructure, and affordable, publicly owned rail travel. This requires city officials looking at urban design and rethinking how people can get around using a network of buses, trams, trains, walking and cycling.

A huge issue in Britain are the railways: it makes no sense that flights from London to Edinburgh are cheaper than taking the train. This carries a health cost (given emissions from airplanes), an environmental cost (with climate change), and a time cost for those who have to get to airports hours early, especially as usually they are located outside of city centres, instead of trains which usually have hubs right in the middle of town and you can arrive mere minutes ahead of departure.

If we've learned anything recently, it's that getting people around the country cannot be left to the private sector. It requires public ownership of the railways and building a network of affordable travel that makes the safest, greenest and healthiest option also the cheapest one. Public transport should be exactly that: public. This is a win for physical activity, clean air and safer roads, as well as mental health.

Third, provide local access to lay therapists, which takes mental health provision out of medical clinics and into communities. The current model of mental health provision in Britain is that if you need help, you end up either on a long waitlist for a specialist, continually asking your GP for support, or going privately at high cost if you can afford it, or you end up in crisis, calling a charity helpline in distress. This approach isn't working.

Studies from India show how lay counsellors can reduce rates of depression and anxiety. Those providing support aren't medical professionals, or seeing people in hospitals. They're going out to communities to talk to people, listening to their worries, and escalating cases which they think require more specialized care. In the VISHRAM study I discussed earlier, roughly thirty counsellors provided care for some 100,000 people. This works out as one person responsible for 3,333 individuals, similar to how community health workers operate.

Some of the changes in Britain's mental health approach need to be drawn from innovations in low-income settings like rural India. In Britain (a population of roughly sixty-eight million people), this would require employing 20,000 counsellors in local areas to detect depression, provide listening and caring services, and refer onwards if specialized care is necessary. Given we already have an estimated 289,000 mental health professionals in the UK, this wouldn't be a huge addition or come at a major cost. But in contrast to our existing professionals, who largely work in clinical settings or private practice, lay therapists would be deployed in communities using an outreach model.

Sound expensive? It's actually cost-saving, reducing the workload on GPs who are currently responsible for mental health support on top of their other duties, as well as the number of patients reaching breaking point and requiring expensive hospital admission.

Fourth, bring all water companies in England and Wales into public ownership, like Scottish Water and Northern Ireland Water. Scottish Water is a public company accountable to Scottish ministers and the Scottish Parliament. While free at the point of use, it's collectively funded through council tax, with water and sanitation services included at a flat rate for all households.

In contrast, over 90 per cent of English water companies are owned by international investors, private equity and banks. These entities have enjoyed little accountability to the public in ensuring that water is provided affordably, and that untreated sewage is disposed of responsibly and not just dumped into local rivers and lakes. Efforts by the government to fine these companies for 'bad behaviour' or to bring officials in front of parliamentary committees haven't worked in improving water quality or affordability in England and Wales.

Water provision should be taken away from foreign profit-seeking corporations and put back at the core of what a government provides its citizens. Clean water is a human right and essential to staying alive.

Finally, invest more of the NHS budget into preventive and primary care. While we have worse overall health outcomes, the NHS spends more on hospital care compared with peer countries. But the UK spends far less on preventive and residential care. Budgeting for preventive and primary care would be cost-saving for the overall system, as spending in communities and local clinics means keeping people out of costly hospital care.

Yes, the NHS needs more money overall: the UK would need to

spend 21 per cent more to match the per-person spend in France, and 39 per cent more to match the spending in Germany, as I mentioned earlier. But it's also about how the health care budget is allocated and used. The offering shouldn't be, 'If you have a heart attack, we'll try our best to save you.' It should be, 'Let's help you stay healthy, identify early signs of heart disease, and keep you out of hospital.'

Don't Accept Lazy Excuses

When pushed as to why they don't act on those key asks, politicians often fall back on easy cop-outs such as, 'We don't know what to do,' 'It costs too much,' or 'It's impossible here in our culture.' I don't accept these lazy excuses. I've shown in this book that across the globe, regardless of culture or context, there are a multitude of concrete, tangible, real-life examples of what's possible when leaders want to act.

The 'blue zone' concept of looking at places with healthy ageing and people living past 100 is an important one. But let's turn it on its head. Instead of trying to pull out the habits of those living in these zones, or thinking we all need to move to one of these super-healthy communities, what about trying to transform more countries in the world into 'blue zones'?

Let's make more parts of the world healthier places to live. It won't take centuries. It's possible in the next ten to fifteen years, so hopefully within your lifetime. My hope is that by 2035, ten years after this book is published, fifty will be the new forty as the official mid-life. Hopefully living to 100 will include you too.

Acknowledgements

Just a few thank yous to all those who made this book possible. To my family and friends: you know who you are. I feel lucky to have so much love in my life. Especially Nani and Nana for teaching me what's important, and Amma and Appa for showing what's possible with hard work, an education and some luck. My research team and colleagues at Edinburgh University, particularly those who helped with research assistance: Genevie Fernandes, Lorna Thompson, Jay Patel, Bohee Lee, Ambele Judith Mwamelo, Shane Canning, Ines Hassan, Jonathan Grey and Maartje Kletter. Thank you, SS and DW, for reading early drafts and providing edits and feedback. I'm grateful to my university colleagues and those in research across the world who continue to do the scientific studies that I was able to draw on. This book wouldn't have been written without the vision of Connor Brown, who is the best editor a writer could ask for, the team at Viking/Penguin, as well as my agents Annabel Merullo and Andrew Gordon. And, finally, my thanks to all of you reading this book, for taking a chance on some 'radical' ideas on how not to die (too soon), and for spending your precious time going through this journey with me. I hope, if nothing else, you'll take away that progress is possible towards a happy, healthier world. So: dream big, keep moving and vote.

Bibliography

Web links are correct at the time of going to press.

1. Eternal Life

Abbott, E., 'Ten percent of all healthcare spending in the U.S. goes toward end-of-life care', WRVO Public Media, 2019 https://www.wrvo.org/health/2019-09-30/ten-percent-of-all-healthcare-spending-in-the-u-s-goes-toward-end-of-life-care

American Cancer Society, 'Key statistics for cervical cancer', 2024 https://www.cancer.net/cancer-types/cervical-cancer/statistics

The Annie E. Casey Foundation, 'Children in poverty in United States', 2024 https://datacenter.aecf.org/data/tables/43-children-in-poverty

Bawden, A., 'UK has some of worst cancer survival rates in developed world, report says', *Guardian*, 2024 https://www.theguardian.com/society/2024/jan/11/uk-cancer-survival-rates-developed-world-report

Chesson, H., Dunne, E., Hariri, S., et al., 'The estimated lifetime probability of acquiring human papillomavirus in the United States', *Sexually Transmitted Diseases*, 2014 https://www.ncbi.nlm.nih.gov/pmc/articles/PMC6745688/

Express News Service, 'In India, 5% own more than 60% of country's wealth: Oxfam report', 2023 https://indianexpress.com/article/business/economy/indias-richest-1-own-more-than-40-of-total-wealth-oxfam-8384156/

GAVI, 'Everything you need to know about the HPV vaccine', 2023 https://www.gavi.org/vaccineswork/everything-you-need-know-about-hpv-vaccine

GBD 2021 demographics collaborators, 'Global age-sex-specific mortality, life expectancy, and population estimates in 204 countries and territories and 811 subnational locations, 1950–2021, and the impact of the COVID-19 pandemic: a comprehensive demographic analysis for the Global Burden of Disease Study 2021', *Lancet*, 2024 https://www.thelancet.com/journals/lancet/article/PIIS0140-6736(24)00476-8/fulltext

Jolly, J., 'Number of billionaires in UK reached new record during Covid crisis', *Guardian*, 2021 https://www.theguardian.com/business/2021/may/21/number-of-billionaires-in-uk-reached-new-record-during-covid-pandemic

Napoletano, E., 'Here's how many billionaires and millionaires live in the U.S.', *Forbes Advisor*, 2023 https://www.forbes.com/advisor/retirement/how-many-billionaires-and-millionaires-live-in-the-u-s/

Oxfam, 'Pandemic creates new billionaire every 30 hours – now a million people could fall into extreme poverty at same rate in 2022', 2022 https://www.oxfam.org/en/press-releases/pandemic-creates-new-billionaire-every-30-hours-now-million-people-could-fall

Oxfam, 'Profiting from pain', 2022 https://www.oxfam.org/en/research/profiting-pain

Richardson, H., 'The Immortals: meet the billionaires forking out for eternal life', *Guardian*, 2023 https://www.theguardian.com/tv-and-radio/2023/sep/05/the-immortals-meet-the-billionaires-forking-out-for-eternal-life

Sridhar, D., 'We're all living longer. Instead of struggling to stay young, why not learn to age well?', *Guardian*, 2023 https://www.theguardian.com/commentisfree/2023/aug/14/living-longer-stay-young-age-millions-life

Sridhar, D., 'Yet again, we in Scotland have the lowest life expectancy in western Europe. Here's how to improve it', *Guardian*, 2024 https://www.theguardian.com/commentisfree/2024/apr/18/scotland-life-expectancy-western-europe-smoking-drinking-drugs-deprivation

World Health Organization, 'Cervical cancer', 2024 https://www.who.int/news-room/fact-sheets/detail/cervical-cancer

World Health Organization, 'Denmark', 2024 https://data.who.int/countries/208

World Health Organization, 'Japan', 2024 https://data.who.int/countries/392

2. Exercise: Just Do It

Abbas, W., 'UAE: "Children don't get bare minimum exercise", doctors suggest activities for kids', *Khaleej Times*, 2023 https://www.khaleejtimes.com/lifestyle/health/uae-children-dont-get-bare-minimum-exercise-doctors-suggest-activities-for-kids

Allen, L., Williams, J., Townsend, N., et al., 'Socioeconomic status and non-communicable disease behavioural risk factors in low-income and lower-middle-income countries: a systematic review', *Lancet Global Health*, 2017 https://www.ncbi.nlm.nih.gov/pmc/articles/PMC5673683/

Anjana, R. M., Pradeepa, R., Das, A. K., et al., 'Physical activity and inactivity patterns in India – results from the ICMR-INDIAB study (Phase-1) [ICMR-INDIAB-5]', *International Journal of Behavioral Nutrition and Physical Activity*, 2014 https://ijbnpa.biomedcentral.com/articles/10.1186/1479-5868-11-26

Chen, A., 'If BMI is the test of health, many pro athletes would flunk', NPR, 2016 https://www.npr.org/sections/health-shots/2016/02/04/465569465/if-bmi-is-the-test-of-health-many-pro-athletes-would-flunk

Dalibalta, S., Majdalawieh, A., Yousef, S., et al., 'Objectively quantified physical activity and sedentary behaviour in a young UAE population', *BMJ Open Sport & Exercise Medicine*, 2021 https://bmjopensem.bmj.com/content/7/1/e000957

Diaz, K., Howard, V., Hutto, B., et al., 'Patterns of sedentary behavior and mortality in U.S. middle-aged and older adults: a national cohort study', *Annals of Internal Medicine*, 2017 https://www.acpjournals.org/doi/10.7326/m17-0212

Doegah, P. T., Amoateng, A. Y., 'Understanding physical activity among young Ghanaians aged 15–34 years', *Cogent Medicine*, 2019 https://www.tandfonline.com/doi/full/10.1080/2331205X.2019.1617021

Erickson, K., Voss, M., Prakash, R. S., et al., 'Exercise training increases size of hippocampus and improves memory', *PNAS*, 2011 https://www.pnas.org/doi/abs/10.1073/pnas.1015950108

European Society of Cardiology, 'Sedentary lifestyle for 20 years linked to doubled mortality risk compared to being active', 2019 https://www.escardio.org/The-ESC/Press-Office/Press-releases/sedentary-lifestyle-for-20-years-linked-to-doubled-mortality-risk-compared-to-being-active

Express News Service, 'New research: physical activity sank during Covid-19 restrictions', 2021 https://indianexpress.com/article/explained/covid-lockdown-restrictions-physical-activity-mental-well-being-7333623/

Guthold, R., Stevens, G., Riley, L., et al., 'Global trends in insufficient physical activity among adolescents: a pooled analysis of 298 population-based surveys with 1.6 million participants', *Lancet Child & Adolescent Health*, 2020 https://www.thelancet.com/article/S2352-4642(19)30323-2/fulltext

Harvard Medical School, 'Big thighs may be wise', 2012 https://www.health.harvard.edu/staying-healthy/big-thighs-may-be-wise

Hernández-Morales, A., 'Don't lock me in my neighborhood! 15-minute city hysteria sweeps the UK', *Politico*, 2023 https://www.politico.eu/article/dont-lock-me-neighborhood-15-minute-city-hysteria-uk-oxford/

Hindustan Times, 'Children's physical activity dropped during Covid-19 lockdowns but didn't bounce back: UK research', 2022 https://www.hindustantimes.com/lifestyle/health/childrens-physical-activity-dropped-during-covid-19-lockdowns-but-didnt-bounce-back-uk-research-101652767418788.html

Horton, H., 'Why has the "15-minute city" taken off in Paris but become a controversial idea in the UK?', *Guardian*, 2024 https://www.theguardian.com/cities/2024/apr/06/why-has-15-minute-city-taken-off-paris-toxic-idea-uk-carlos-moreno

Ipsos, 'The Dutch are the most physically active nation, the Brazilians are the least', 2021 https://www.ipsos.com/en-nl/global-views-to-sports-2021

Ipsos Global Advisor, 'Global views on exercise and team sports', 2021 https://www.ipsos.com/sites/default/files/ct/news/documents/2021-08/Global%20views%20on%20exercise_v6__1.pdf

Kassa, M. D., Grace, J. M., 'Noncommunicable diseases prevention policies and their implementation in Africa: a systematic review', *Public Health Reviews*, 2022 https://www.ncbi.nlm.nih.gov/pmc/articles/PMC8865333/

Kodama, S., Saito, K., Tanaka, S., et al., 'Cardiorespiratory fitness as a quantitative predictor of all-cause mortality and cardiovascular events in healthy men and women: a meta-analysis', *JAMA*, 2009 https://pubmed.ncbi.nlm.nih.gov/19454641/

Landsverk, G., 'Khloe Kardashian promoted Flat Tummy shakes again, and influencers are warning they promote risky dieting habits', *Business Insider*, 2020 https://www.businessinsider.com/khloe-kardashian-vogue-williams-flat-belly-shakes-instagram-controversy-2020-1

Maghelal, P., Alawadi, K., Arlikatti, S., et al., 'Influence of the built environment on physical activity choices among Emirati male and female adolescents: an examination of parents' and students' perceptions', *Sustainability*, 2022 https://www.mdpi.com/2071-1050/14/1/444

Noetel, M., Sanders, T., Gallardo-Gómez, D., et al., 'Effect of exercise for depression: systematic review and network meta-analysis of randomised controlled trials', *British Medical Journal*, 2024 https://www.bmj.com/content/384/bmj-2023-075847

OECD, 'The Netherlands: Country Health Profile 2021', 2021 https://www.oecd.org/en/publications/netherlands-country-health-profile-2021_fd18ea00-en.html

Ramesh, R., 'Fatwa orders Indian tennis star to cover up', *Guardian*, 2005 https://www.theguardian.com/world/2005/sep/10/india.randeepramesh

Singh, B., Maher, C., Brinsley, J., 'Exercise is even more effective than counselling or medication for depression. But how much do you need?', *Guardian*, 2023 https://www.theguardian.com/lifeandstyle/2023/mar/02/exercise-is-even-more-effective-than-counselling-or-medication-for-depression-but-how-much-do-you-need

Singh, B., Olds, T., Curtis, R., et al., 'Effectiveness of physical activity interventions for improving depression, anxiety and distress: an overview of systematic reviews', *British Journal of Sports Medicine*, 2023 https://bjsm.bmj.com/content/57/18/1203

Sridhar, D., 'I'm an expert in public health. Which is why, aged 38, I've qualified as a personal trainer', *Guardian*, 2023 https://www.theguardian.com/commentisfree/2023/jan/01/public-health-personal-trainer-pandemic

Sridhar, D., 'The secret to why exercise is so good for mental health? "Hope molecules"', *Guardian*, 2023 https://www.theguardian.com/commentisfree/2023/may/04/exercise-mental-health-hope-molecules-mood-strength

Tarun, S., Arora, M., Rawal, T., et al., 'An evaluation of outdoor school environments to promote physical activity in Delhi, India', *BMC Public Health*, 2017 https://bmcpublichealth.biomedcentral.com/articles/10.1186/s12889-016-3987-8

Tullis, P., 'Has Paris become the healthiest city in the world?', *Town & Country*, 2022 https://www.townandcountrymag.com/leisure/travel-guide/a39715752/paris-bicycle-health-news/

Twenge, J., Campbell, W. K., 'Associations between screen time and lower psychological well-being among children and adolescents: Evidence from a population-based study', *Preventive Medicine Reports*, 2018 https://www.ncbi.nlm.nih.gov/pmc/articles/PMC6214874/

van der Zee, R., 'How Amsterdam became the bicycle capital of the world', *Guardian*, 2015 https://www.theguardian.com/cities/2015/may/05/amsterdam-bicycle-capital-world-transport-cycling-kindermoord

Verdot, C., Salanave, B., Aubert, S., et al., 'Prevalence of physical activity and sedentary behaviors in the French population: results and evolution between two cross-sectional population-based studies, 2006 and 2016', *International Journal of Environmental Research and Public Health*, 2022 https://www.ncbi.nlm.nih.gov/pmc/articles/PMC8871946/

Vitality, 'Walking 5,000 steps three times per week could save the NHS £15 billion', 2024 https://www.vitality.co.uk/media/5000-steps-three-times-a-week-could-save-the-nhs-15-billion/

World Health Organization, 'Physical activity', 2024 https://www.who.int/news-room/fact-sheets/detail/physical-activity

World Health Organization, 'Promoting cycling can save lives and advance health across Europe through improved air quality and increased physical activity', 2021 https://www.who.int/europe/news/item/03-06-2021-promoting-cycling-can-save-lives-and-advance-health-across-europe-through-improved-air-quality-and-increased-physical-activity

Yang, H. K., Kim, J.-Y., 'Effect of obesity in the recruiting market: the case of young Korean college graduates', *Korean Journal of Health Economics and Policy* (translated from Korean by Bohee Lee), 2015 https://www.kci.go.kr/kciportal/ci/sereArticleSearch/ciSereArtiView.kci?sereArticleSearchBean.artiId=ART002072607

Zakir, S. M. A., 'Dubai: hundreds of residents sweat it out on Day 1 of 30×30 fitness challenge', *Khaleej Times*, 2022 https://www.khaleejtimes.com/uae/dubai-fitness-challenge-kicks-off-hundreds-of-residents-sweat-it-out-on-day-1-of-30-day-workout-goa

3. What's a Balanced Diet?

Akinyemiju, T. F., Zhao, X., Sakhuja, S., et al., 'Life-course socio-economic status and adult BMI in Ghana; analysis of the WHO study on global ageing and adult health (SAGE)', *International Journal for Equity in Health*, 2016 https://www.ncbi.nlm.nih.gov/pmc/articles/PMC5111182/

Akowuah, P. K., Kobia-Acquah, E., 'Childhood obesity and overweight in Ghana: a systematic review and meta-analysis', *Journal of Nutrition and Metabolism*, 2020 https://pubmed.ncbi.nlm.nih.gov/32322414/

Basu, M., 'India, notorious for malnutrition, is now a land of obesity', CNN, 2017 https://www.cnn.com/interactive/2017/10/health/i-on-india-childhood-obesity/

BBC News, 'Boris Johnson hires personal trainer Harry Jameson', 2020 https://www.bbc.co.uk/news/uk-politics-53930665

BBC News, 'Lancet study: More than 100 million people in India diabetic', 2023 https://www.bbc.co.uk/news/world-asia-india-65852551

British Medical Journal, 'One in 10 UK adults could have diabetes by 2030, warns charity', 2021 https://www.bmj.com/content/375/bmj.n2453

Buettner, D., 'This Japanese 80% diet rule can help you live a longer life, says longevity researcher', CNBC, 2020 https://www.cnbc.com/2020/11/10/japanese-80-percent-diet-rule-can-help-you-live-longer-says-longevity-expert.html

Business Standard, 'One out of every three Indians "middle class"; to double by 2047: report', 2022 https://www.business-standard.com/article/current-affairs/every-one-in-three-indians-middle-class-to-double-by-2047-report-122110200522_1.html

Caleyachetty, R., Barber, T., Mohammed, N. I., et al., 'Ethnicity-specific BMI cutoffs for obesity based on type 2 diabetes risk in England: a population-based cohort study', *Lancet Diabetes & Endocrinology*, 2021 https://www.thelancet.com/journals/landia/article/PIIS2213-8587(21)00088-7/fulltext

Chatterjee, P., 'Action needed for child obesity in India', *Lancet Child & Adolescent Health*, 2023 https://www.thelancet.com/journals/lanchi/article/PIIS2352-4642(22)00309-1/abstract

Choi, W. H., Ahn, J., Jung, C. H., et al., 'Korean diet prevents obesity and ameliorates insulin resistance in mice fed a high-fat diet', *Journal of Ethnic Foods*, 2017 https://www.sciencedirect.com/science/article/pii/S2352618117300057

Chung, W., 'Economic impact of obesity in the Republic of Korea', ADBI Working Paper Series, 2017 https://www.adb.org/sites/default/files/publication/327566/adbi-wp755.pdf

Dash, K., 'McDonald's in India', Garvin School of International Management case study, 2005 http://www.dallariva.org/csumba/mba602/McDonald's%20in%20India.pdf

Dawson, L. J., 'What happened after an Appalachian town got shamed nationally', *Politico*, 2020 https://www.politico.com/news/magazine/2020/01/23/huntington-west-virginia-food-policy-101479

de-Graft Aikins, A., Addo, J., Ofei, F., et al., 'Ghana's burden of chronic non-communicable diseases: future directions in research, practice and policy', *Ghana Medical Journal*, 2012 https://www.ncbi.nlm.nih.gov/pmc/articles/PMC3645141/

Denmark National Board of Health, 'National action plan against obesity', 2003 https://www.sst.dk/~/media/681E3288F0A14C2EAA71ED9C4866D01F.ashx

Donnelly, L., 'Boris Johnson: "I was too fat"', *Telegraph*, 2020 https://www.telegraph.co.uk/news/2020/07/27/boris-johnson-obesity-weight-loss-coronavirus/

Erem, A. S., Appiah-Kubi, A., Konney, T. O., et al., 'Gynecologic oncology subspecialty training in Ghana: a model for sustainable impact on gynecologic cancer care in sub-Saharan Africa', *Frontiers in Public Health*, 2020 https://www.ncbi.nlm.nih.gov/pmc/articles/PMC7744480/

European Association for the Study of Obesity, 'Success in treatment against the odds: the Children's Obesity Clinic, Holbaek, Denmark', 2020 https://easo.org/success-in-treatment-against-the-odds-the-childrens-obesity-clinic-holbaek-denmark/

Falbe, J., Thompson, H., Becker, C., et al., 'Impact of the Berkeley excise tax on sugar-sweetened beverage consumption', *American Journal of Public Health*, 2016 https://www.ncbi.nlm.nih.gov/pmc/articles/PMC5024386/

Fields, D., 'Apple body shape linked to higher heart risk than pear-shape in diabetics', *News Medical & Life Sciences*, 2016 https://www.news-medical.net/news/20160404/Apple-body-shape-linked-to-higher-heart-risk-than-pear-shape-in-diabetics.aspx

Galaviz, K., Narayan, K. M. V., Lobelo, F., et al., 'Lifestyle and the prevention of type 2 diabetes: a status report', *American Journal of Lifestyle Medicine*, 2015 https://www.ncbi.nlm.nih.gov/pmc/articles/PMC6125024/

Gao, M., Piernas, C., Astbury, N., et al., 'Associations between body-mass index and COVID-19 severity in 6.9 million people in England: a prospective, community-based, cohort study', *Lancet Diabetes & Endocrinology*, 2021 https://www.thelancet.com/journals/landia/article/PIIS2213-8587(21)00089-9/fulltext

GBD 2021 diabetes collaborators, 'Global, regional, and national burden of diabetics from 1990 to 2021, with projections of prevalence to 2050: a systematic analysis for the Global Burden of Disease Study 2021', *Lancet*, 2023 https://www.thelancet.com/journals/lancet/article/PIIS0140-6736(23)01301-6/fulltext

Ghana Ministry of Health, 'National health policy', 2020 https://www.moh.gov.gh/wp-content/uploads/2020/07/NHP_12.07.2020.pdf-13072020-FINAL.pdf

Gregory, A., 'Ultra-processed foods need tobacco-style warnings, says scientist', *Guardian*, 2024 https://www.theguardian.com/global/article/2024/jun/27/ultra-processed-foods-need-tobacco-style-warnings-says-scientist

Guntupalli, A. M., 'Inquiry into the simultaneous existence of malnutrition and overweight in India', Working Paper, 2006 https://paa2006.populationassociation.org/papers/61837

Haas, B., '"Escape the corset": South Korean women rebel against strict beauty standards', *Guardian*, 2018 https://www.theguardian.com/world/2018/oct/26/escape-the-corset-south-korean-women-rebel-against-strict-beauty-standards

Han, S.-Y., Brewis, A. A., Sturtz Sreetharan, C., 'Employment and weight status: the extreme case of body concern in South Korea', *Economics & Human Biology*, 2018 https://www.sciencedirect.com/science/article/abs/pii/S1570677X17301892

Holden, S., Zlatevska, N., Dubelaar, C., 'Whether smaller plates reduce consumption depends on who's serving and who's looking: a meta-analysis', *Journal of the Association for Consumer Research*, 2016 https://www.journals.uchicago.edu/doi/abs/10.1086/684441

Hwang, J., Lee, E-.Y., Lee, C. G., 'Measuring socioeconomic inequalities in obesity among Korean adults, 1998–2015', *International Journal of Environmental Research and Public Health*, 2019 https://www.ncbi.nlm.nih.gov/pmc/articles/PMC6539011/

Katz, B., 'Kane Tanaka, world's oldest person, dies at 119', *Smithsonian Magazine*, 2022 https://www.smithsonianmag.com/smart-news/kane-tanaka-dies-119-oldest-person-180973930/

Kelly-Linden, J., 'Eating a healthy diet is too expensive for many Britons, research finds', *Telegraph*, 2020 https://www.telegraph.co.uk/global-health/climate-and-people/eating-healthy-diet-expensive-many-britons-research-finds/

Kingdon, C., 'The primary cause of Britain's childhood obesity emergency is clear: poverty', *Guardian*, 2023 https://www.theguardian.com/commentisfree/2023/apr/17/britain-childhood-obesity-emergency-is-poverty-type-2-diabetes

Kleinfield, N. R., 'Modern ways open India's doors to diabetes', *New York Times*, 2006 https://www.nytimes.com/2006/09/13/world/asia/13diabetes.html

Koehler, R., 'Skinny Koreans', *Seoul*, 2013 https://magazine.seoulselection.com/2013/04/12/skinny-koreans/

Korea Herald, 'Are Koreans really fat? Many of them think so, although they're actually not', *Straits Times*, 2023 https://www.straitstimes.com/asia/east-asia/are-koreans-really-fat-many-of-them-think-so-although-they-re-actually-not

Korean Ministry of Food and Drug Safety, 'Promoting healthy diets and safe food consumption', 2024 https://www.mfds.go.kr/eng/wpge/m_13/de011004l001.do

Lancet Regional Health Western Pacific, 'South Korea's population shift: challenges and opportunities', 2023 https://www.thelancet.com/journals/lanwpc/article/PIIS2666-6065(23)00183-9/fulltext

Lobo, V., Patil, A., Phatak, A., et al., 'Free radicals, antioxidants and functional foods: impact on human health', *Pharmacognosy Review*, 2010 https://www.ncbi.nlm.nih.gov/pmc/articles/PMC3249911/

Menon, S., 'Why has an Indian state imposed a "fat tax"?', BBC News, 2016 https://www.bbc.co.uk/news/world-asia-india-36771843

Misra, A., Pandey, R. M., Devi, J. R., et al., 'High prevalence of diabetes, obesity and dyslipidaemia in urban slum population in northern India', *International Journal of Obesity*, 2001 https://www.nature.com/articles/0801748

Mørk, T., Tsalis, G., Grunert, K. G., 'Campaigning for a healthier diet: evaluating the case of the Nordic "Keyhole" label 2014T: Trine Mørk', *European Journal of Public Health*, 2015 https://academic.oup.com/eurpub/article/25/suppl_3/ckv172.100/2578329

Nartey, J. N., Obilie-Mante, V., 'Evaluating the effects of sugary beverage consumption on child health in Ghana: trends, risks, and policy considerations', Working Paper, 2024 https://www.researchgate.net/publication/379221190_Evaluating_the_Effects_of_Sugary_Beverage_Consumption_on_Child_Health_in_Ghana_Trends_Risks_and_Policy_Considerations

National Academies of Science, Engineering and Medicine, 'Dietary reference intakes for energy', 2023, https://nap.nationalacademies.org/catalog/26818/dietary-reference-intakes-for-energy

NCD Alliance, 'Ghana launches national NCD policy and strategic plan at strategic roundtable on NCDs', 2022 https://ncdalliance.org/news-events/news/ghana-launches-national-ncd-policy-and-strategic-plan-at-strategic-roundtable-on-ncds

Nilson, E., Ferrari, G., Louzada M. L. C., et al., 'Premature deaths attributable to the consumption of ultraprocessed foods in Brazil', *American Journal of Preventive Medicine*, 2022 https://www.ajpmonline.org/article/S0749-3797(22)00429-9/abstract

Norden, 'The Keyhole: healthy choices made easy', 2010 https://norden.diva-portal.org/smash/get/diva2:700822/FULLTEXT01.pdf

Nyaaba, G. N., Stronks, K., Masana, L., et al., 'Implementing a national non-communicable disease policy in sub-Saharan Africa: experiences of key stakeholders in Ghana', *Health Policy OPEN*, 2020 https://www.ncbi.nlm.nih.gov/pmc/articles/PMC10297756/

OECD, 'Korea', 2024 https://www.oecd.org/en/countries/korea.html

Oh, K., Kim, Y., Kweon, S., et al., 'Korea National Health and Nutrition Examination Survey, 20th anniversary: accomplishments and future directions', *Epidemiology and Health*, 2021 https://www.ncbi.nlm.nih.gov/pmc/articles/PMC8289475/

Oh, S. W., 'Obesity and metabolic syndrome in Korea', *Diabetes & Metabolism Journal*, 2011 https://www.e-dmj.org/journal/view.php?number=73

Oxfam International, 'Ghana', 2024 https://www.oxfam.org/en/what-we-do/countries/ghana

Park, R., Myers, P., Langstein, H., 'Beliefs and trends of aesthetic surgery in South Korean young adults', *Archives of Plastic Surgery*, 2019 https://www.ncbi.nlm.nih.gov/pmc/articles/PMC6882691/

Popkin, B., Du, S., Green, W., et al., 'Individuals with obesity and COVID-19: a global perspective on the epidemiology and biological relationships', *Obesity Reviews*, 2020 https://onlinelibrary.wiley.com/doi/full/10.1111/obr.13128

Proulx, E., 'Taxes on sugar-sweetened drinks drive decline in consumption', *Berkeley Public Health*, 2024 https://publichealth.berkeley.edu/news-media/research-highlights/taxes-on-sugar-sweetened-drinks-drive-decline-in-consumption

Rauber, F., da Costa Louzada, M. L., Martínez Steele, E., et al., 'Ultra-processed food consumption and chronic non-communicable diseases-related dietary nutrient profile in the UK (2008–2014)', *Nutrients*, 2018 https://www.ncbi.nlm.nih.gov/pmc/articles/PMC5986467/

Sawadogo, W., Tsegaye, M., Gizaw, A., et al., 'Overweight and obesity as risk factors for COVID-19-associated hospitalisations and death: systematic review and meta-analysis', *BMJ Nutrition, Prevention & Health*, 2022 https://www.ncbi.nlm.nih.gov/pmc/articles/PMC8783972/

Searcey, D., Richtel, M., 'Obesity was rising as Ghana embraced fast food. Then came KFC', *New York Times*, 2017 https://www.nytimes.com/2017/10/02/health/ghana-kfc-obesity.html?_r=0&utm_content=buffer36267&utm_medium=social&utm_source=twitter.com&utm_campaign=buffer

Semley, J., ' "I miss eating": The truth behind the weight loss drug that makes food repulsive', *Guardian*, 2022 https://www.theguardian.com/food/2022/nov/09/i-miss-eating-weight-loss-drug-ozempic-food-repulsive

Simmonds, M., Llewellyn, A., Owen, C. G., et al., 'Predicting adult obesity from childhood obesity: a systematic review and meta-analysis', *Obesity Reviews*, 2016 https://pubmed.ncbi.nlm.nih.gov/26696565/

Sridhar, D., *The Battle Against Hunger: Choice, Circumstance, and the World Bank*, Oxford University Press, 2008

Sridhar, D., 'The Maharaja Mac: changing dietary patterns in India', in Unnithan-Kumar, M., Tremayne, S. (eds), *Fatness and the Maternal Body: Women's Experiences of Corporeality and the Shaping of Social Policy*, Berghahn Books, 2011

Sridhar, D., 'Why is cancer striking earlier? One answer could be a diet of ultra-processed foods', *Guardian*, 2023 https://www.theguardian.com/commentisfree/2023/jul/25/cancer-striking-earlier-ultra-processed-foods

Times of India, 'Why India is diabetes capital of the world', 2022 https://timesofindia.indiatimes.com/india/why-india-is-diabetes-capital-of-the-world/articlehow/95509990.cms

Timmins, G., O'Hare, R., 'Urgent action needed to reduce harm of ultra-processed foods to British children', *Imperial*, 2021 https://www.imperial.ac.uk/news/223573/urgent-action-needed-reduce-harm-ultra-processed/

Trust for America's Health, 'The state of obesity', 2019 https://www.tfah.org/wp-content/uploads/2019/09/2019ObesityReportFINAL-1.pdf

Trust for America's Health, 'U.S. obesity rates reach historic highs – racial, ethnic, gender and geographic disparities continue to persist', 2019 https://www.tfah.org/report-details/stateofobesity2019/

Ueno, H., Inoue, M., Ives, M., 'At 119, she was a symbol of how to live with wit and vitality', *Japan Times*, 2022 https://www.japantimes.co.jp/life/2022/05/02/lifestyle/kane-tanaka-japan-worlds-oldest-person/

UNICEF, '2018 Global Nutrition Report reveals malnutrition is unacceptably high and affects every country in the world, but there is also an unprecedented opportunity to end it', 2018 https://www.unicef.org/rosa/press-releases/2018-global-nutrition-report-reveals-malnutrition-unacceptably-high-and-affects

US Centers for Disease Control and Prevention, 'National diabetes statistics report', 2024 https://www.cdc.gov/diabetes/php/data-research/index.html

US Department of Agriculture, 'What is MyPlate?', 2024 https://www.myplate.gov/eat-healthy/what-is-myplate

US Food and Drug Administration, 'The Nutrition Facts label', 2024 https://www.fda.gov/food/nutrition-education-resources-materials/nutrition-facts-label

Vallgårda, S., Holm, L., Jensen, J. D., 'The Danish tax on saturated fat: why it did not survive', *European Journal of Clinical Nutrition*, 2014 https://www.nature.com/articles/ejcn2014224

van Tulleken, C., *Ultra-Processed People: Why Do We All Eat Stuff That Isn't Food... and Why Can't We Stop?*, Penguin, 2023

The White House, 'Remarks by the First Lady at food icon announcement', 2011 https://obamawhitehouse.archives.gov/the-press-office/2011/06/02/remarks-first-lady-food-icon-announcement

Whiting, K., 'Want to live a long, healthy life? 6 secrets from Japan's oldest people', World Economic Forum, 2021 https://www.weforum.org/agenda/2021/09/japan-okinawa-secret-to-longevity-good-health/

Willcox, B., Willcox, D. C., Suzuki, M., 'Demographic, phenotypic, and genetic characteristics of centenarians in Okinawa and Japan: part 1 – centenarians in Okinawa', *Mechanisms of Ageing and Development*, 2017 https://pubmed.ncbi.nlm.nih.gov/27845177/

World Health Organization, 'Denmark, trans fat ban pioneer: lessons for other countries', 2018 https://www.who.int/news-room/feature-stories/detail/denmark-trans-fat-ban-pioneer-lessons-for-other-countries

4. Don't Smoke

Almond, S., 'Brother, can you spare a Marlboro?', *Miami New Times*, 1992 https://www.miaminewtimes.com/news/brother-can-you-spare-a-marlboro-6362343

American Lung Association, '10 health effects caused by smoking you didn't know about', 2024 https://www.lung.org/research/sotc/by-the-numbers/10-health-effects-caused-by-smoking

Ash, 'Use of vapes (e-cigarettes) among young people in Great Britain', 2024 https://ash.org.uk/uploads/Use-of-vapes-among-young-people-in-Great-Britain-2024.pdf

Bhatia, G., 'Tobacco endgame: can India share the dream?', *Indian Journal of Psychological Medicine*, 2022 https://www.ncbi.nlm.nih.gov/pmc/articles/PMC10011840/

Bulletin of the World Health Organization, 'China wrestles with tobacco control', 2010 https://www.ncbi.nlm.nih.gov/pmc/articles/PMC2855607/

Caini, Y., 'In Shanghai, tobacco use goes up in smoke, hits record low', *Sixth Tone*, 2023 https://www.sixthtone.com/news/1012385

Di Cicco, M. E., Ragazzo, V., Jacinto, T., 'Mortality in relation to smoking: the British Doctors Study', *Breathe*, 2016 https://www.ncbi.nlm.nih.gov/pmc/articles/PMC5298160/

Dingding, X., 'Smoke-free list extends to healthcare facilities', *China Daily*, 2009 https://www.chinadaily.com.cn/life/2009-12/11/content_9161633.htm

Domachowski, L., 'Tragedy of Roy Castle as he died of lung cancer without ever smoking a cigarette', *Mirror*, 2020 https://www.mirror.co.uk/3am/celebrity-news/tragedy-roy-castle-died-lung-22618117

Doward, J., 'Britain is quitting smoking. Can our success inspire the rest of the world?', *Guardian*, 2015 https://www.theguardian.com/society/2015/apr/05/smoking-lost-cool-west-globally-growing-habit-tobacco-ban

Global Action to End Smoking, 'State of smoking and health in India', 2024 https://globalactiontoendsmoking.org/research/tobacco-around-the-world/india/

Goodchild, M., Zheng, R., 'Tobacco control and Healthy China 2030', *Tobacco Control*, 2019 https://tobaccocontrol.bmj.com/content/28/4/409

Griffin, N., 'Thank you for vaping: how tobacco companies are attracting a new generation', *Irish Examiner*, 2022 https://www.irishexaminer.com/news/spotlight/arid-40913324.html

Jeffreys, B., Rohrer, F., 'Who, what, why: what's behind the idea of banning 10-packs of cigarettes?', BBC News, 2013 https://www.bbc.co.uk/news/magazine-24441618

Joshi, M., 'India may soon ban sale of loose cigarettes, smoking zones at airports may go', WION, 2022 https://www.wionews.com/india-news/india-may-soon-ban-sale-of-loose-cigarettes-542479

Kilgore, E., Mandel-Ricci, J., Johns, M., et al., 'Making it harder to smoke and easier to quit: the effect of 10 years of tobacco control in New York City', *American Journal of Public Health*, 2014 https://www.ncbi.nlm.nih.gov/pmc/articles/PMC4061988/

Kohrman, M., 'Smoking among doctors: governmentality, embodiment, and the diversion of blame in contemporary China', *Medical Anthropology*, 2008 https://www.tandfonline.com/doi/full/10.1080/01459740701831401

Levy, D., Currie, L., Clancy, L., 'Tobacco control policy in the UK: blueprint for the rest of Europe?', *European Journal of Public Health*, 2013 https://academic.oup.com/eurpub/article/23/2/201/682561

Rani, M., Bonu, S., Jha, P., et al., 'Tobacco use in India: prevalence and predictors of smoking and chewing in a national cross sectional household survey', *Tobacco Control*, 2003 https://tobaccocontrol.bmj.com/content/12/4/e4

Schreiber, H., 'Students petition for mascot to use vape instead of pipe to represent "the diverse and ever-changing student body"', *yahoo!life*, 2018 https://www.yahoo.com/lifestyle/students-petition-mascot-use-vape-instead-pipe-represent-diverse-ever-changing-student-body-004423006.html

Tannen, J. N., 'Working to curb a dangerous trend', *University of Miami News*, 2019 https://news.miami.edu/stories/2019/11/working-to-curb-a-dangerous-trend.html

Tansley, J., 'The Evening Read: I'll always be proud of everything that Roy achieved', *Liverpool Echo*, 2014 https://www.liverpoolecho.co.uk/news/liverpool-news/fiona-castyle-wife-roy-castle-7639474

Truth Initiative, '4 marketing tactics e-cigarette companies use to target youth', 2018 https://truthinitiative.org/research-resources/tobacco-industry-marketing/4-marketing-tactics-e-cigarette-companies-use-target

Tsugawa, Y., Hashimoto, K., Tabuchi, T., et al., 'What can Japan learn from tobacco control in the UK?', *Lancet*, 2017 https://www.thelancet.com/journals/lancet/article/PIIS0140-6736(17)32169-4/fulltext

UK Department of Health and Social Care, 'Smokers urged to swap cigarettes for vapes in world first scheme', 2023 https://www.gov.uk/government/news/smokers-urged-to-swap-cigarettes-for-vapes-in-world-first-scheme

World Health Organization, 'WHO framework convention on tobacco control', 2024 https://fctc.who.int

Wynder, E., Graham, E., Croninger, A., 'Experimental production of carcinoma with cigarette tar', *Cancer Research*, 1953 https://aacrjournals.org/cancerres/article/13/12/855/467062/Experimental-Production-of-Carcinoma-with

5. Struggling to Cope

AP news wire, 'France offers state-funded therapy, tackles mental health', *Independent*, 2021 https://www.independent.co.uk/news/emmanuel-macron-france-paris-germany-britain-b1928628.html

Armson, S., 'The Rev Chad Varah', *Guardian*, 2007 https://www.theguardian.com/news/2007/nov/10/guardianobituaries.obituaries

Bonadiman, C. S. C., Naghavi, M., Melo, A. P. S., 'The burden of suicide in Brazil: findings from the Global Burden of Disease Study 2019', *Revista da*

Sociedade Brasileira de Medicina Tropical, 2022 https://www.ncbi.nlm.nih.gov/pmc/articles/PMC9009430/

Cho, Y., Inagaki, M., 'The general principles of suicide prevention policy from the perspective of clinical psychiatry', *Psychiatria et Neurologia Japonica*, 2014 https://journal.jspn.or.jp/Disp?style=abst&vol=116&year=2014&mag=0&number=8&start=683&lang=EN

Donovan, R., Anwar-McHenry, J., 'Act-Belong-Commit', *American Journal of Lifestyle Medicine*, 2014 https://www.ncbi.nlm.nih.gov/pmc/articles/PMC6124955/

Donovan, R., Koushede, V. J., Drane, C. F., et al., 'Twenty-one reasons for implementing the Act-Belong-Commit – "ABCs of Mental Health" campaign', *International Journal of Environmental Research and Public Health*, 2021 https://www.ncbi.nlm.nih.gov/pmc/articles/PMC8583649/

Eddleston, M., Sheriff, M. H. R., Hawton, K., 'Deliberate self harm in Sri Lanka: an overlooked tragedy in the developing world', *British Medical Journal*, 1998 https://www.ncbi.nlm.nih.gov/pmc/articles/PMC1113497/

European Commission, 'Final report summary – GO4HEALTH (Formulating new goals for global health, and proposing new governance for global health that will allow the achievement of these goals)', 2024 https://cordis.europa.eu/project/id/305240/reporting

Frontline, 'Vidarbha shows the way to check suicides', 2017 https://frontline.thehindu.com/science-and-technology/vidarbha-shows-the-way-to-check-suicides/article9559744.ece

Gibson, O., '*Sun* on the ropes over "Bonkers Bruno" story', *Guardian*, 2003 https://www.theguardian.com/media/2003/sep/23/pressandpublishing.mentalhealth

Grasdalsmoen, M., Eriksen, H. R., Lønning, K. J., et al., 'Physical exercise, mental health problems, and suicide attempts in university students', *BMC Psychiatry*, 2020 https://bmcpsychiatry.biomedcentral.com/articles/10.1186/s12888-020-02583-3

Guddal, M. H., Stensland, S. Ø., Småstuen, M. C., et al., 'Physical activity and sport participation among adolescents: associations with mental health in different age groups. Results from the Young-HUNT study: a cross-sectional survey', *BMJ Open*, 2019 https://www.ncbi.nlm.nih.gov/pmc/articles/PMC6731817/

Harvard University Center on the Developing Child, 'Epigenetics and child development: how children's experiences affect their genes', 2024 https://developingchild.harvard.edu/resources/what-is-epigenetics-and-how-does-it-relate-to-child-development/

Heissel, A., Heinen, D., Brokmeier, L. L., et al., 'Exercise as medicine for depressive symptoms? A systematic review and meta-analysis with meta-regression', *British Journal of Sports Medicine*, 2023 https://bjsm.bmj.com/content/57/16/1049

Kannuri, N. K., Jadhav, S., 'Cultivating distress: cotton, caste and farmer suicides in India', *Anthropology & Medicine*, 2021 https://www.ncbi.nlm.nih.gov/pmc/articles/PMC8734467/

Lambert, J., Barnstable, G., Minter, E., et al., 'Taking a one-week break from social media improves well-being, depression, and anxiety: a randomized controlled trial', *Cyberpsychology, Behavior, and Social Networking*, 2022 https://www.liebertpub.com/doi/10.1089/cyber.2021.0324

Lancet, 'Commission: Ending stigma and discrimination in mental health', 2022 https://www.thelancet.com/commission/stigma-and-discrimination-in-mental-health

OECD, 'The future of health systems', 2024 https://www.oecd.org/en/topics/policy-issues/the-future-of-health-systems.html

Patel, V., Saxena, S., Lund, C., et al., 'The *Lancet* Commission on global mental health and sustainable development', *Lancet*, 2018 https://www.thelancet.com/journals/lancet/article/PIIS0140-6736(18)31612-X/abstract

Patel, V., Weobong, B., Weiss, H., et al., 'The Healthy Activity Program (HAP), a lay counsellor-delivered brief psychological treatment for severe depression, in primary care in India: a randomised controlled trial', *Lancet*, 2016 https://www.thelancet.com/journals/lancet/article/PIIS0140-6736(16)31589-6/fulltext

Pettersson, E., Lichtenstein, P., Larsson, H., et al., 'Genetic influences on eight psychiatric disorders based on family data of 4 408 646 full and half-siblings, and genetic data of 333 748 cases and controls', *Psychological Medicine*, 2019 https://www.ncbi.nlm.nih.gov/pmc/articles/PMC6421104/

Rachiotis, G., Stuckler, D., McKee, M., et al., 'What has happened to suicides during the Greek economic crisis? Findings from an ecological study of suicides and their determinants (2003–2012)', *BMJ Open*, 2015 https://pubmed.ncbi.nlm.nih.gov/25807950/

Royal College of Psychiatrists, 'Thousands of people with a mental disorder sent to prison when they need treatment', 2021 https://www.rcpsych.ac.uk/news-and-features/latest-news/detail/2021/06/07/thousands-of-people-with-a-mental-disorder-sent-to-prison-when-they-need-treatment

Saint Onge, J. M., Krueger, P. M., Rogers, R. G., 'The relationship between major depression and nonsuicide mortality for U.S. adults: the importance of health behaviors', *Journals of Gerontology. Series B, Psychological Sciences and Social Sciences*, 2014 https://www.ncbi.nlm.nih.gov/pmc/articles/PMC4049146/

Samaritans, 'Our history', 2024 https://www.samaritans.org/about-samaritans/our-history/

Santé publique France, 'CoviPrev: une enquête pour suivre l'évolution des comportements et de la santé mentale pendant l'épidémie de COVID-19', 2023 https://www.santepubliquefrance.fr/etudes-et-enquetes/coviprev-une-enquete-pour-suivre-l-evolution-des-comportements-et-de-la-sante-mentale-pendant-l-epidemie-de-covid-19

Saraceno, B., van Ommeren, M., Batniji, R., et al., 'Barriers to improvement of mental health services in low-income and middle-income countries', *Lancet*, 2007 https://pubmed.ncbi.nlm.nih.gov/17804061/

Scheper-Hughes, N., *Death Without Weeping: The Violence of Everyday Life in Brazil*, University of California Press, 1993

Science Museum, 'Telephones save lives: the history of the Samaritans', 2018 https://www.sciencemuseum.org.uk/objects-and-stories/telephones-save-lives-history-samaritans

Siva, N., 'Sri Lanka struggles with mental health burden', *Lancet*, 2010 https://www.thelancet.com/journals/lancet/article/PIIS0140-6736(10)60370-4/fulltext

Sri Lankan Mental Health Directorate, 'The mental health policy of Sri Lanka, 2005–2015', 2005 https://extranet.who.int/countryplanningcycles/sites/default/files/planning_cycle_repository/sri_lanka/nmhp_sri_lanka.pdf

Sridhar, D., 'Making the SDGs useful: a Herculean task', *Lancet*, 2016 https://www.thelancet.com/journals/lancet/article/PIIS0140-6736(16)31635-X/fulltext

Sridhar, D., 'Social media could be as harmful to children as smoking or gambling – why is this allowed?', *Guardian*, 2023 https://www.theguardian.com/commentisfree/2023/jul/04/smoking-gambling-children-social-media-apps-snapchat-health-regulation

Thomson, W., 'Lifting the shroud on depression and premature mortality: a 49-year follow-up study', *Journal of Affective Disorders*, 2011 https://www.sciencedirect.com/science/article/abs/pii/S0165032710006099

Trautmann, S., Rehm, J., Wittchen, H.-U., 'The economic costs of mental disorders', *EMBO Reports*, 2016 https://www.ncbi.nlm.nih.gov/pmc/articles/PMC5007565/

US Department of Health and Human Services, 'Surgeon General issues new advisory about effects social media use has on youth mental health', 2023 https://www.hhs.gov/about/news/2023/05/23/surgeon-general-issues-new-advisory-about-effects-social-media-use-has-youth-mental-health.html

Wang, S., Wright, R., Wakatsuki, Y., 'In Japan, more people died from suicide last month than from Covid in all of 2020. And women have been impacted most', CNN, 2020 https://www.cnn.com/2020/11/28/asia/japan-suicide-women-covid-dst-intl-hnk/index.html

Wellcome Trust, 'Leading psychiatrist calls for roll-out of lay counselling to tackle massive burden of harmful drinking and depression in India', 2016 https://wellcome.org/press-release/leading-psychiatrist-calls-roll-out-lay-counselling-tackle-massive-burden-harmful

World Economic Forum, 'Therapy sessions will soon be free for French citizens. Here's why', 2021 https://www.weforum.org/agenda/2021/10/therapy-sessions-mental-health-france/

World Health Organization, 'Mental health', 2022 https://www.who.int/news-room/fact-sheets/detail/mental-health-strengthening-our-response

World Health Organization, 'One-third of people in prison in Europe suffer from mental health disorders', 2023 https://www.who.int/europe/news/item/15-02-2023-one-third-of-people-in-prison-in-europe-suffer-from-mental-health-disorders

6. Guns, Guns, Guns

Addley, E., 'Judy Murray on the Dunblane massacre: "I just left the car and ran"', *Guardian*, 2014 https://www.theguardian.com/sport/2014/jun/17/judy-murray-dunblane-massacre-just-left-car-and-ran

Barbash, F., 'Britain votes to ban handguns', *Washington Post*, 1997 https://www.washingtonpost.com/archive/politics/1997/06/12/britain-votes-to-ban-handguns/928b2c18-67de-4082-ade8-39f1aa6060de/

Barry, E., 'These countries restricted assault weapons after just one mass shooting', *Time*, 2022 https://time.com/6182186/countries-banned-guns-mass-shooting/

BBC News, 'Parkland shooting: how the attack unfolded', 2022 https://www.bbc.co.uk/news/world-us-canada-43071281

Brodzinsky, S., 'Colombia guerrilla-turned-mayor bans guns from the streets of Bogotá', *Guardian*, 2012 https://www.theguardian.com/world/2012/jan/31/colombia-bogota-mayor-bans-guns

Collie, J., 'Andy Murray on surviving the Dunblane massacre: I had no idea at the time how tough it was . . . I hope I've given my town something to be proud of', *Standard*, 2019 https://www.standard.co.uk/sport/tennis/andy-murray-on-surviving-the-dunblane-massacre-i-had-no-idea-at-the-time-how-tough-it-was-i-hope-i-ve-given-my-town-something-to-be-proud-of-a4036216.html

Face the Nation, 'Transcript: Parkland student activists on "Face the Nation," March 25, 2018', CBS News, 2018 https://www.cbsnews.com/news/transcript-parkland-students-jaclyn-corin-ryan-deitsch-delaney-tarr-cameron-kasky-emma-gonzalez-on-face-the-nation-march-25-2018/

Gammon, K., 'Laws that keep kids away from guns reduce deaths, whereas others lead to more shootings', *Science*, 2023 https://www.science.org/content/article/u-s-gun-research-report-child-access-prevention-laws-cut-firearm-deaths

Goldstick, J., Cunningham, R., Carter, P., 'Current causes of death in children and adolescents in the United States', *New England Journal of Medicine*, 2022 https://www.nejm.org/doi/full/10.1056/NEJMc2201761

Henley, J., 'Boy, 13, kills eight children and security guard in Belgrade school shooting', *Guardian*, 2023 https://www.theguardian.com/world/2023/may/03/pupil-arrested-after-nine-killed-in-belgrade-school-shooting

Jacobs, B., '"It can change": Obama demands gun control action after Oregon shooting', *Guardian*, 2015 https://www.theguardian.com/us-news/2015/oct/01/obama-gun-control-laws-oregon-umpqua-community-college-shooting

Janetsky, M., 'Colombian leader's promise of "total peace" may prove too ambitious', *Guardian*, 2022 https://www.theguardian.com/world/2022/sep/22/colombia-gustavo-petro-total-peace

Mansoor, S., 'The "good guys with guns" keep failing to stop mass shootings', *Time*, 2022 https://time.com/6182970/good-guys-guns-mass-shootings-uvalde/

Modan, N., 'Will school shootings in 2023 outpace last year's record high?', K-12 Dive, 2023 https://www.k12dive.com/news/will-school-shootings-in-2023-outpace-last-years-record-high/646765/

Moyes, J., 'Are you going to ban cricket bats?', *Independent*, 1996 https://www.independent.co.uk/news/are-you-going-to-ban-cricket-bats-1315164.html

Never Again, 'Gun Control', 2024 https://www.neveragain.com/gun-control/

Obama, B., 'Obama's Newtown speech – full text', *Guardian*, 2012 https://www.theguardian.com/world/2012/dec/17/obama-speech-newtown-school-shooting

Patel, J., Leach-Kemon, K., Curry, G., et al., 'Firearm injury – a preventable public health issue', *Lancet Public Health*, 2022 https://www.thelancet.com/journals/lanpub/article/PIIS2468-2667(22)00233-X/fulltext

Reuters, 'Australia marks 25 years since worst mass shooting', 2021 https://www.reuters.com/world/asia-pacific/australia-marks-25-years-since-worst-mass-shooting-2021-04-28/

Shoichet, C., 'Former rebel, now mayor, vows to ban weapons on the streets of Bogotá', CNN, 2012 https://www.cnn.com/2012/01/02/world/americas/colombia-rebel-turned-mayor/index.html

Smith, D., 'Trump's solution to school shootings: arm teachers with guns', *Guardian*, 2018 https://www.theguardian.com/us-news/2018/feb/21/donald-trump-solution-to-school-shootings-arm-teachers-with-guns

Solly, M., 'How the 1996 Dunblane massacre pushed the U.K. to enact stricter gun laws', *Smithsonian Magazine*, 2021 https://www.smithsonianmag.com/history/how-1996-dunblane-massacre-pushed-uk-enact-stricter-gun-laws-180977221/

Stuff, 'Australia took action with its gun laws. Why didn't New Zealand?', 2019 https://www.stuff.co.nz/national/christchurch-shooting/111394340/australia-took-action-against-gun-laws-why-didnt-new-zealand

US Supreme Court, 'District of Columbia v. Heller, 554 U.S. 570 (2008)', 2008 https://supreme.justia.com/cases/federal/us/554/570/

Vecino-Ortiz, A. I., Guzman-Tordecilla, D. N., 'Gun-carrying restrictions and gun-related mortality, Colombia: a difference-in-difference design with fixed effects', *Bulletin of the World Health Organization*, 2020 https://www.ncbi.nlm.nih.gov/pmc/articles/PMC7047021/

Vinall, F., 'Serbians hand in thousands of guns after two mass killings', *Washington Post*, 2023 https://www.washingtonpost.com/world/2023/05/12/serbia-gun-laws-mass-shooting/

Wahlquist, C., 'It took one massacre: how Australia embraced gun control after Port Arthur', *Guardian*, 2016 https://www.theguardian.com/world/2016/mar/15/it-took-one-massacre-how-australia-made-gun-control-happen-after-port-arthur

The White House, 'Remarks by President Biden marking one year since the school shooting in Uvalde, Texas', 2023 https://www.whitehouse.gov/briefing-room/speeches-remarks/2023/05/24/remarks-by-president-biden-marking-one-year-since-the-school-shooting-in-uvalde-texas/

World Health Organization, 'Guns, knives, and pesticides: reducing access to lethal means', 2009 https://iris.who.int/handle/10665/44060

Yuhas, A., 'The right to bear arms: what does the second amendment really mean?', *Guardian*, 2017 https://www.theguardian.com/us-news/2017/oct/05/second-amendment-right-to-bear-arms-meaning-history

Zhou, L., Narea, N., Millhiser, I., et al., 'America's unique, enduring gun problem, explained', Vox, 2024 https://www.vox.com/23142734/apalachee-georgia-school-shooting-gun-violence

7. Vision Zero

Bailey, A., 'Tackling a neglected mass killer: road deaths', *Financial Times*, 2023 https://www.ft.com/content/536332c8-6ad4-4dc2-9781-f93912f73840

Beech, H., 'Thailand's roads are deadly. Especially if you're poor', *New York Times*, 2019 https://www.nytimes.com/2019/08/19/world/asia/thailand-inequality-road-fatalities.html

Buddi, M., 'Time-bound travel rule at Tirumala reduces accidents', *Times of India*, 2013 https://timesofindia.indiatimes.com/city/hyderabad/time-bound-travel-rule-at-tirumala-reduces-accidents/articleshow/20928652.cms

Edwards, M., Leonard, D., 'Effects of large vehicles on pedestrian and pedalcyclist injury severity', *Journal of Safety Research*, 2022 https://www.sciencedirect.com/science/article/abs/pii/S0022437522000810

Euronews, 'How Sweden became the EU's road safety champion', 2018 https://www.euronews.com/2018/02/20/how-sweden-became-the-eu-s-road-safety-champion

European Commission, 'National road safety profile – Sweden', 2023 https://road-safety.transport.ec.europa.eu/system/files/2023-02/erso-country-overview-2023-sweden_0.pdf

Global Road Safety Facility, 'Kenya's road safety country profile', 2024 https://www.roadsafetyfacility.org/country/kenya

Haas, T., Sander, H., 'The European car lobby: a critical analysis of the impact of the automotive industry', Working Paper, 2019 https://www.researchgate.net/profile/Tobias-Haas-8/publication/335145100_The_European_Car_Lobby_A_

Critical_Analaysis_of_the_Impact_of_the_Automotive_Industry/links/5d52af8c45 85153040709c60/The-European-Car-Lobby-A-Critical-Analaysis-of-the-Impact-of-the-Automotive-Industry.pdf

Hendrie, D., Lyle, G., Cameron, M., 'Lives saved in low- and middle-income countries by road safety initiatives funded by Bloomberg Philanthropies and implemented by their partners between 2007–2018', *International Journal of Environmental Research and Public Health*, 2021 https://www.ncbi.nlm.nih.gov/pmc/articles/PMC8583449/

Karoney, C., 'Kenyan marathon world record holder Kelvin Kiptum dies in road accident', BBC News, 2024 https://www.bbc.co.uk/news/world-africa-68270866

Kristianssen, A.-C., Andersson, R., Belin, M.-A., et al., 'Swedish Vision Zero policies for safety – a comparative policy content analysis', *Safety Science*, 2018 https://www.sciencedirect.com/science/article/pii/S0925753517309013

Laville, S., 'Exclusive: carmakers among key opponents of climate action', *Guardian*, 2019 https://www.theguardian.com/environment/2019/oct/10/exclusive-carmakers-opponents-climate-action-us-europe-emissions

Nation Africa, 'Children, teenagers make up a fifth of road deaths this year', 2021 https://nation.africa/kenya/newsplex/children-teenagers-make-up-a-fifth-of-road-deaths-this-year-477934

Philanthropy News Digest, 'Public-private partnership launched to reduce road deaths in Kenya', 2022 https://philanthropynewsdigest.org/news/public-private-partnership-launched-to-reduce-road-deaths-in-kenya

Robbins, S., 'Thailand's killer roads', Sky News, 2020 https://news.sky.com/story/killer-roads-why-thailand-has-one-of-the-worst-death-rates-from-driving-in-the-world-12051841

Sridhar, D., 'The rows over "anti-motorist" Ulez and LTNs lose sight of the truth: they save lives', *Guardian*, 2023 https://www.theguardian.com/commentisfree/2023/aug/04/uk-must-follow-europe-lead-prioritising-walking-cycling-public-transport

Swedish Transport Administration, 'Vision Zero – no one should be killed or severely injured in road traffic', 2020 https://bransch.trafikverket.se/contentassets/63f0b8caf88045a2a32dffb37ff26ccb/infoblad_nollvisionen_eng_korr2.pdf

Vecino-Ortiz, A. I., Nagarajan, M., Elaraby, S., et al., 'Saving lives through road safety risk factor interventions: global and national estimates', *Lancet*, 2022 https://www.sciencedirect.com/science/article/abs/pii/S0140673622009187

Watkins, K., Sridhar, D., 'Road traffic injuries: the hidden development crisis', Make Roads Safe, 2009 https://www.globalfueleconomy.org/media/44127/road-traffic-injuries-kevin-watkins-2009.pdf

Willsher, K., 'Paris to charge SUV drivers higher parking fees to tackle "autobesity"', *Guardian*, 2023 https://www.theguardian.com/world/2023/jul/11/paris-charge-suv-drivers-higher-parking-fees-tackle-auto-besity

World Bank Group, 'Mortality caused by road traffic injury (per 100,000 population) – Kenya', 2024 https://liveprod.worldbank.org/en/indicator/sh-sta-traf-p5

World Health Organization, 'A New Year's resolution "for life"', 2023 https://www.who.int/thailand/news/detail/03-01-2023-a-new-year-s-resolution--for-life

World Health Organization, 'Road traffic injuries', 2023 https://www.who.int/news-room/fact-sheets/detail/road-traffic-injuries

World Health Organization, 'Save lives: a road safety technical package', 2017 https://www.who.int/publications/i/item/save-lives-a-road-safety-technical-package

Zipper, D., 'How Japan won its "Traffic War"', 2022 https://www.bloomberg.com/news/articles/2022-09-06/what-drove-japan-s-remarkable-traffic-safety-turnaround

8. The Water Fountain

Anthony, A., 'Feargal Sharkey's mission to save our chalk streams', *Observer*, 2018 https://www.theguardian.com/music/2018/dec/01/feargal-sharkey-mission-save-our-chalk-streams-water-environment

Bagcchi, S., 'Dilip Mahalanabis', *Lancet Infectious Diseases*, 2023 https://www.thelancet.com/journals/laninf/article/PIIS1473-3099(22)00818-0/fulltext

Begum, F., 'Mapping disease: John Snow and cholera', Royal College of Surgeons of England, 2016 https://www.rcseng.ac.uk/library-and-publications/library/blog/mapping-disease-john-snow-and-cholera/

Black, D. A. K., McCance, R. A., Young, W. F., 'A study of dehydration by means of balance experiments', *Journal of Physiology*, 1944 https://www.ncbi.nlm.nih.gov/pmc/articles/PMC1393454

Bouhlel, Z., Köpke, J., Mina, M., et al., 'Global bottled water industry: a review of impacts and trends', United Nations University, 2023 https://collections.unu.edu/view/UNU:9106

Bouhlel, Z., Smakhtin, V., 'How the bottled water industry is masking the global water crisis', United Nations University, 2023 https://unu.edu/article/how-bottled-water-industry-masking-global-water-crisis

Busby, M., 'Swimmers avoiding the water over fears of raw sewage on UK beaches', *Guardian*, 2023 https://www.theguardian.com/environment/2023/jul/31/swimmers-avoiding-the-water-over-fears-of-raw-sewage-on-uk-beaches

CBS News, 'Could a 100-million-ton iceberg alleviate S. Africa's water woes?', 2018 https://www.cbsnews.com/news/south-africa-cape-town-water-crisis-plan-drag-iceberg-from-antarctica/

Chin, C.-S., Sorenson, J., Harris, J. B., et al., 'The origin of the Haitian cholera outbreak strain', *New England Journal of Medicine*, 2011 https://pubmed.ncbi.nlm.nih.gov/21142692/

Clinton, C., Sridhar, D., 'The lurking threat to child survival', CNN Opinion, 2015 https://www.cnn.com/2015/09/01/opinions/clinton-sridhar-ebola-public-health/index.html

Danopoulous, E., Twiddy, M., West, R., et al., 'A rapid review and meta-regression analyses of the toxicological impacts of microplastic exposure in human cells', *Journal of Hazardous Materials*, 2022 https://www.sciencedirect.com/science/article/abs/pii/S0304389421028302?dgcid=author

Dickie, G., 'Rising bottled water consumption signals safe drinking water goal is under threat, says U.N. think tank', Reuters, 2023 https://www.reuters.com/business/environment/rising-bottled-water-consumption-signals-safe-drinking-water-goal-is-under-2023-03-16/

Gates, M., *The Moment of Lift: How Empowering Women Changes the World*, Flatiron Books, 2019

Grazia Pakistan, 'Professor Devi Sridhar – breaking stereotypes', 2022 https://www.grazia.pk/professor-devi-sridhar-breaking-steriotypes/

Helgertz, J., Önnerfors, M., 'Public water and sewerage investments and the urban mortality decline in Sweden 1875–1930', *The History of the Family*, 2019 https://www.tandfonline.com/doi/full/10.1080/1081602X.2018.1558411

Kane, I., Clare, M. A., Miramontes, E., et al., 'Seafloor microplastic hotspots controlled by deep-sea circulation', *Science*, 2020 https://www.science.org/doi/10.1126/science.aba5899

Landry, S., 'Exotic animals on the loose in Dade', *Tampa Bay Times*, 2005 https://www.tampabay.com/archive/1992/10/29/exotic-animals-on-the-loose-in-dade/

Laville, S., 'England's privatised water firms paid £57bn in dividends since 1991', *Guardian*, 2020 https://www.theguardian.com/environment/2020/jul/01/england-privatised-water-firms-dividends-shareholders

Laville, S., 'Raw sewage discharged into English rivers 375,000 times by water firms', *Guardian*, 2022 https://www.theguardian.com/environment/2022/mar/31/sewage-released-into-english-rivers-for-27m-hours-last-year-by-water-firms

Mahr, K., 'How Cape Town was saved from running out of water', *Guardian*, 2018 https://www.theguardian.com/world/2018/may/04/back-from-the-brink-how-cape-town-cracked-its-water-crisis

Makuta, I., O'Hare, B., 'Quality of governance, public spending on health and health status in Sub Saharan Africa: a panel data regression analysis', *BMC Public Health*, 2015 https://www.ncbi.nlm.nih.gov/pmc/articles/PMC4578603/

Pandey, M., 'Prime drink: How KSI and Logan Paul made it so popular', BBC News, 2023 https://www.bbc.co.uk/news/newsbeat-64145389

Rayasam, R., 'In Jackson, the water is back, but the crisis remains', *KFF Health News*, 2022 https://kffhealthnews.org/news/article/jackson-mississippi-bottled-water-crisis/

Rios, E., 'Jackson water crisis heaps more disruption on city's schoolchildren', *Guardian*, 2022 https://www.theguardian.com/us-news/2022/aug/31/jackson-water-crisis-schools-mississippi

Scottish Water, 'Your water your life', 2024 https://www.scottishwater.co.uk/your-home/campaigns/your-water-your-life

Serageldin, I., 'Water wars? A talk with Ismail Serageldin', *World Policy Journal*, 2009/10 https://www.jstor.org/stable/40468735

Stein, F., 'Health in Haiti', University of Edinburgh lecture, 2019 https://www.ed.ac.uk/usher/news-events/events/cghr-lecture-health-in-haiti

Sweney, M., 'Coca-Cola's Ronaldo fiasco highlights risk to brands in social media age', *Guardian*, 2021 https://www.theguardian.com/media/2021/jun/18/coca-colas-ronaldo-fiasco-highlights-risk-to-brands-in-social-media-age

Tulchinsky, T., 'John Snow, cholera, the Broad Street pump; waterborne diseases then and now', *Case Studies in Public Health*, 2018 https://www.ncbi.nlm.nih.gov/pmc/articles/PMC7150208/

UK Department of Health and Social Care, 'Sewage in water: a growing public health problem', 2022 https://www.gov.uk/government/news/sewage-in-water-a-growing-public-health-problem

UN Water, 'WHO/UNICEF Joint Monitoring Program for Water Supply, Sanitation and Hygiene (JMP) – progress on household drinking water, sanitation and hygiene 2000–2022: special focus on gender', 2023 https://www.unwater.org/publications/who/unicef-joint-monitoring-program-update-report-2023

Ungoed-Thomas, J., Jenz, M., 'Fifty-seven swimmers fall sick and get diarrhoea at world triathlon championship in Sunderland', *Observer*, 2023 https://www.theguardian.com/environment/2023/aug/05/investigation-after-57-world-triathlon-championship-swimmers-fall-sick-and-get-diarrhoea-in-sunderland-race

UNICEF, 'Diarrhoea', 2024 https://data.unicef.org/topic/child-health/diarrhoeal-disease/

UNICEF, 'Moving with the times: 1980–1988', 2018 https://www.unicef.org/stories/learning-experience-19801988

Wiesinger, H., Wang, Z., Hellweg, S., 'Deep dive into plastic monomers, additives, and processing aids', *Sustainable Systems*, 2021 https://pubs.acs.org/doi/full/10.1021/acs.est.1c00976

Wood, J., 'Rising bottled water use signals threat to UN water goal, and other environment stories you need to read this week', World Economic Forum, 2023 https://www.weforum.org/agenda/2023/03/climate-crisis-water-environment-floods-stories/

World Health Organization, 'Cholera – Haiti', 2022 https://www.who.int/emergencies/disease-outbreak-news/item/2022-DON427

9. Just Breathe

Bawden, T., 'Ella Kissi-Debrah: government urged to set tougher UK air pollution limits after death of girl, 9, from asthma', *iNews*, 2021 https://inews.co.uk/news/environment/ella-kissi-debra-death-asthma-government-uk-air-pollution-limits-966182

Cape Town City Health Department, 'Air quality management plan for the city of Cape Town', 2005 https://resource.capetown.gov.za/documentcentre/Documents/City%20strategies,%20plans%20and%20frameworks/AnnexD_Air_Quality_Management_Plan.pdf

Clarke-Ezzidio, H., 'Rosamund Kissi-Debrah: "Without Ulez expansion, more children are going to die"', *New Statesman*, 2023 https://www.newstatesman.com/spotlight/healthcare/2023/08/rosamund-kissi-debrah-air-pollution-ulez-expansion

Dockery, D., Pope, C. A., Xu, X., et al., 'An association between air pollution and mortality in six U.S. cities', *New England Journal of Medicine*, 1993 https://www.nejm.org/doi/full/10.1056/NEJM199312093292401

European Research Council, 'Pre-natal exposure to urban AIR pollution and pre- and post-natal brain development', 2023 https://cordis.europa.eu/project/id/785994/reporting

Fuller, G., 'UK study adds to evidence of air pollution link to long-term illness', *Guardian*, 2022 https://www.theguardian.com/environment/2022/dec/30/uk-study-adds-to-evidence-of-air-pollution-link-to-long-term-illness

Fuller, G., Friedman, S., Mudway, I., 'Impacts of air pollution across the life course – evidence highlight note', Imperial College London, 2023 https://www.london.gov.uk/sites/default/files/2023-04/Imperial%20College%20London%20Projects%20-%20impacts%20of%20air%20pollution%20across%20the%20life%20course%20-%20evidence%20highlight%20note.pdf

Goldstein, M. R., Lewin, R. K., Allen, J. J. B., 'Improvements in well-being and cardiac metrics of stress following a yogic breathing workshop: randomized controlled trial with active comparison', *Journal of American College Health*, 2022 https://www.tandfonline.com/doi/full/10.1080/07448481.2020.1781867

Hindustan Times, '"Delhi worse than hell": Supreme Court rebukes Centre, states on air pollution', 2019 https://www.hindustantimes.com/india-news/get-15-explosives-kill-people-at-one-go-sc-rebukes-centre-states-on-pollution/story-zv7hFJDndV2rlrfwvXz3rK.html

Hornyak, T., 'Reading the air: Tokyo still has work to do on air pollution', *Japan Times*, 2019 https://www.japantimes.co.jp/life/2019/05/11/environment/reading-air-tokyo-still-work-air-pollution/

Howard, R., Beevers, S., Dajnak, D., 'Up in the air: how to solve London's air quality crisis: part 2', Policy Exchange, 2016 https://policyexchange.org.uk/wp-content/uploads/2016/03/up-in-the-air-part-2.pdf

Khan, S., *Breathe: Tackling the Climate Emergency*, Penguin, 2023

Komariah, M., Ibrahim, K., Pahria, T., et al., 'Effect of mindfulness breathing meditation on depression, anxiety, and stress: a randomized controlled trial among university students', *Healthcare (Basel)*, 2022 https://www.ncbi.nlm.nih.gov/pmc/articles/PMC9819153/

Mataranyika, M., '11 out of Africa's 15 most polluted cities are all in South Africa – report', News 24, 2021 https://www.news24.com/fin24/economy/11-out-of-africas-15-most-polluted-cities-are-all-in-south-africa-report-20211124

Mayor of London, 'Mayor confirms world's first Ultra Low Emission Zone', 2015 https://www.london.gov.uk/press-releases/mayoral/ultra-low-emission-zone

Moshakis, A., 'Fresh air for sale', *Guardian*, 2018 https://www.theguardian.com/global/2018/jan/21/fresh-air-for-sale

Rai, A., 'Supreme Court declares Delhi smog an emergency and recommends immediate shutdown of city', *Independent*, 2021 https://www.independent.co.uk/asia/india/delhi-air-pollution-supreme-court-b1957056.html

Safi, M., 'Pollution stops play at Delhi Test match as bowlers struggle to breathe', *Guardian*, 2017 https://www.theguardian.com/world/2017/dec/03/pollution-stops-play-at-delhi-test-match-as-bowlers-struggle-to-breathe

Seppälä, E., Bradley, C., Moeller, J., et al., 'Promoting mental health and psychological thriving in university students: a randomized controlled trial of three well-being interventions', *Frontiers in Psychiatry*, 2020 https://www.frontiersin.org/journals/psychiatry/articles/10.3389/fpsyt.2020.00590/full

Singh, A., 'The alarming rise of India's pay-to-breathe industry', *Wired*, 2023 https://www.wired.com/story/breathing-is-a-luxury-in-indias-air-crisis/

Stack, M., 'Raising kids in Delhi's worsening air', *New Yorker*, 2018 https://www.newyorker.com/culture/personal-history/raising-kids-in-delhis-worsening-air

Tokyo City, 'Zero emission Tokyo strategy', 2020 https://www.kankyo.metro.tokyo.lg.jp/documents/d/kankyo/outline-of-zero-emission-tokyo-strategy

Walker, P., 'Sunak "backs drivers" with curbs on 20mph limits and bus lanes', *Guardian*, 2023 https://www.theguardian.com/politics/2023/sep/29/rishi-sunak-plan-for-motorists-would-limit-travel-choices-campaigners-say

10. I Need a Doctor

African Union, '77th session of the United Nations General Assembly address by H. E. Macky Sall, President of the Republic of Senegal, current Chairman of the African Union', 2022 https://au.int/en/pressreleases/20220920/77th-session-united-nations-general-assembly-address-he-macky-sall

Bryce, E., Udobang, W., 'Nigerian hospitals are locking up women unable to pay their childbirth bills', *Vice*, 2019 https://www.vice.com/en/article/nigeria-hospital-detention-folake-oduyoye/

Delamothe, T., 'Founding principles', *British Medical Journal*, 2008 https://www.ncbi.nlm.nih.gov/pmc/articles/PMC2405823/

Emanuel, E. J., 'Cancer patients shouldn't be responsible for out-of-pocket costs', *STAT News*, 2023 https://www.statnews.com/2023/05/23/financial-toxicity-cancer-costs-cost-sharing/

Frenk, J., González-Pier, E., Gómez-Dantés, O., et al., 'Comprehensive reform to improve health system performance in Mexico', *Lancet*, 2006 https://www.thelancet.com/journals/lancet/article/PIIS0140-6736(06)69564-0/abstract

Kliff, S., '"Am I a bad person?" Why one mom didn't take her kid to the ER – even after poison control said to', Vox, 2019 https://www.vox.com/health-care/2019/5/10/18526696/health-care-costs-er-emergency-room

Kottasová, I., 'Britain's health service is part of its national psyche. It's also on life support', CNN, 2020 https://edition.cnn.com/2020/04/18/uk/nhs-love-affair-uk-intl-gbr/index.html

Lancet, 'Press Release: Mexico achieves universal health coverage in less than a decade', 2012 https://www.eurekalert.org/news-releases/567242

Leonhardt, M., 'Uninsured Americans could be facing nearly $75,000 in medical bills if hospitalized for coronavirus', CNBC, 2020 https://www.cnbc.com/2020/04/01/covid-19-hospital-bills-could-cost-uninsured-americans-up-to-75000.html

Levey, N., 'She was already battling cancer. Then she had to fight the bill collectors', NPR, 2022 https://www.npr.org/sections/health-shots/2022/07/09/1110370391/cost-cancer-treatment-medical-debt

McDonald, T., Touchton, M., Knaul, F. M., et al., 'The rise and fall of Seguro Popular: Mexico's health care odyssey', *Think Global Health*, 2023 https://www.thinkglobalhealth.org/article/rise-and-fall-seguro-popular-mexicos-health-care-odyssey

Peterson-KFF Health System Tracker, 'Access and coverage', 2024 https://www.healthsystemtracker.org

Richards, M. A., 'The size of the prize for earlier diagnosis of cancer in England', *British Journal of Cancer*, 2009 https://www.ncbi.nlm.nih.gov/pmc/articles/PMC2790715/

Sahara Reporters, 'Community protests government hospital, after death of detained patient', 2015 https://saharareporters.com/2015/02/03/community-protests-government-hospital-after-death-detained-patient

Sen, A., 'More than 100 million women are missing', *New York Review of Books*, 1990 https://www.nybooks.com/articles/1990/12/20/more-than-100-million-women-are-missing/

Sridhar, D., 'A healthy workforce means a healthy economy. Britain can't afford to be so ill', *Guardian*, 2022 https://www.theguardian.com/commentisfree/2022/oct/18/healthy-workforce-economy-britain-liz-truss-ill

Sridhar, D., 'Hundreds of British people are needlessly going blind. Why?', *Guardian*, 2023 https://www.theguardian.com/commentisfree/2023/apr/19/british-people-going-blind-doctors-tory-cuts

Sumriddetchkajorn, K., Shimazaki, K., Ono, T., et al., 'Universal health coverage and primary care, Thailand', *Bulletin of the World Health Organization*, 2019 https://www.ncbi.nlm.nih.gov/pmc/articles/PMC6560367/

Tichenor, M., 'The power of data: global malaria governance and the Senegalese data retention strike', in Adams, V. (ed.), *Metrics: What Counts in Global Health*, Duke University Press, 2016

Tichenor, M., Sridhar, D., 'Universal health coverage, health systems strengthening, and the World Bank', *British Medical Journal*, 2017 https://www.bmj.com/content/358/bmj.j3347

UHC 2030, 'Act with ambition: UHC Day event', 2016 https://www.uhc2030.org/news-and-events/news/act-with-ambition-uhc-day-event-375420/

World Health Organization Senegal, 'President Macky Sall of Senegal urges African leaders to prioritise investment in health: Regional Committee for Africa gets underway in Dakar, Senegal', 2018 https://www.afro.who.int/news/president-macky-sall-senegal-urges-african-leaders-prioritise-investment-health-regional

11. How to Live

BBC Radio 4, 'How much money do you need to be happy?', 2023 https://www.bbc.co.uk/programmes/articles/1yxp6zSJHfjQh9TMxoj8LPL/how-much-money-do-you-need-to-be-happy

Benn, M., 'The only way to end the class divide: the case for abolishing private schools', *Guardian*, 2018 https://www.theguardian.com/news/2018/aug/24/the-only-way-to-end-the-class-divide-the-case-for-abolishing-private-schools

Brown, F., 'Sunak paid half a million pounds in tax last year, according to his tax returns', Sky News, 2024 https://news.sky.com/story/rishi-sunaks-tax-return-shows-he-paid-more-than-half-a-million-pounds-in-tax-last-year-13067577

Connor, L., 'The secrets to the Duke of Edinburgh's long life', *Independent*, 2021 https://www.independent.co.uk/life-style/health-and-families/philip-guards-polo-club-british-buckingham-palace-studies-b1829067.html

Disney, A., 'World leaders have a chance to raise taxes for rich people like me. I'm begging them to take it', *Guardian*, 2024 https://www.theguardian.

com/commentisfree/2024/apr/18/world-leaders-raise-taxes-rich-people-inequality-abigail-disney

Finland Toolbox, 'Finland – society committed to gender equality', 2024 https://toolbox.finland.fi/life-society/finland-society-committed-to-gender-equality/

Henley, J., '"It's a miracle": Helsinki's radical solution to homelessness', *Guardian*, 2019 https://www.theguardian.com/cities/2019/jun/03/its-a-miracle-helsinkis-radical-solution-to-homelessness

Kahneman, D., Deaton, A., 'High income improves evaluation of life but not emotional well-being', *PNAS*, 2010 https://www.pnas.org/doi/10.1073/pnas.1011492107

Kangas, O., Kalliomaa-Puha, L., 'National strategies to fight homelessness and housing exclusion: Finland', European Commission, 2019 https://ec.europa.eu/social/BlobServlet?docId=21600&langId=en

Leiserson, G., Yagan, D., 'What is the average federal individual income tax rate on the wealthiest Americans?', The White House, 2021 https://www.whitehouse.gov/cea/written-materials/2021/09/23/what-is-the-average-federal-individual-income-tax-rate-on-the-wealthiest-americans/

Olshansky, S. J., 'Long live the monarchy! British royals tend to survive a full three decades longer than their subjects', *The Conversation*, 2021 https://theconversation.com/long-live-the-monarchy-british-royals-tend-to-survive-a-full-three-decades-longer-than-their-subjects-158766

Sinmaz, E., '"It could be your next-door neighbour": how female MPs cope with misogynistic abuse', *Guardian*, 2023 https://www.theguardian.com/politics/2023/feb/17/how-female-mps-cope-with-misogynistic-abuse

Sridhar, D., 'With my nani in Chennai I was loved just for being me. Isn't that the essence of Christmas?', *Guardian*, 2023 https://www.theguardian.com/commentisfree/2023/dec/25/nani-chennai-india-love-family-christmas

Statista, 'Ranking of health care systems of countries worldwide in 2023, by score', 2023 https://www.statista.com/statistics/1376344/care-systems-ranking-of-countries-worldwide/

Sutin, A., Stephan, Y., Luchetti, M., et al., 'Loneliness and risk of dementia', *Journals of Gerontology. Series B, Psychological Sciences and Social Sciences*, 2020 https://www.ncbi.nlm.nih.gov/pmc/articles/PMC7424267/

Weale, S., 'Top of the class: Labour seeks to emulate Finland's school system', *Guardian*, 2019 https://www.theguardian.com/education/2019/sep/27/top-class-finland-schools-envy-world-ofsted-education

World Happiness Report, 'World Happiness Report 2024', 2024 https://worldhappiness.report

Epilogue

Food Cardiff, 'Courgette Pilot: agroecological Welsh veg for primary schools in Wales', 2023 https://www.foodsensewales.org.uk/app/uploads/2023/01/CourgetteReport_Eng.pdf

Sridhar, D., 'Are the British and Irish really world-beating fruit and veg eaters? I doubt it', *Guardian*, 2024 https://www.theguardian.com/commentisfree/2024/jan/17/british-irish-world-beating-fruit-and-veg-eaters

Index

abdominal muscles, 17
Abe, Shinzo, 92
Abu Dhabi, United Arab Emirates, 39, 242
abuse, 106–7, 263
Accra, Ghana, 41, 42
Act-Belong-Commit, 126
addiction, 112, 201
adolescence, 109
Adoo-Kissi-Debrah, Ella, 214, 215, 216, 220, 258
Afghanistan, 25
African Union, 238
Agarwal, Anurag, 80
ageing, 5–6, 27
   metabolism and, 57–8
air pollution, 12, 13, 40, 202–21, 258, 259, 260
   air purifiers, 204–5, 220
   bottled air, 209–10, 220
   causes, 211
   health effects, 205–9
   public policy and, 212–21
Akiode, Abiola, 229
Allen, Pat, 142
Alpers, Philip, 142
American football, 53
Amnesty International, 125
Amsterdam, Netherlands, 32–4, 43
antidepressant medication, 108
anti-obesity drugs, 58
anti-vaxx movement, 106
anxiety, 107, 111, 115, 200
Ardern, Jacinda, 143–4, 263

Artibonite River, 191
asthma, 204, 206–7, 208, 212, 214, 227, 261
Auerbach, John, 69
Australia
   air quality in, 211
   gun violence in, 140–42, 150, 154, 259, 262
   mental health in, 114, 126
   obesity in, 61
   smoking in, 93
   water in, 187

Bahrain, 211
Bangladesh, 114, 211, 221
Battle Against Hunger, The (Sridhar), 75, 179
Bawumia, Mahamudu, 42
'beach body', 17, 19
Beigel, Scott, 132
Beijing, China, 97, 210, 213
Belgium, 10, 188
Belgrade, Serbia, 146–7
Belliard, David, 36
Benn, Melissa, 252
Berkeley, California, 71
Beveridge, William, 232
Bezos, Jeff, 5
Biden, Joseph, 150, 192
Big Short, The (2015 film), 121
Bill & Melinda Gates Foundation, 179
von Bismarck, Otto, 233
Blair, Tony, 136
Blantyre, Malawi, 178–9

blindness, 54, 85, 226–8
blood pressure, 20, 21, 22, 26, 54, 107, 108, 200, 206–7, 245
blood transfusions, 5
Bloomberg, Michael, 158
blue zones, 11–12, 46–7, 57
body fat percentage, 17–18, 20
body image, 17–18, 62–3, 83
body mass index (BMI), 9, 20, 28, 47, 50, 52–3, 55, 67–8
Bogotá, Colombia, 144–5
Bolsonaro, Jair, 263
bottled air, 209–10, 220
bottled water, 186–8, 199
Boxing Day tsunami (2004), 124, 262
Bradford Hill, Tony, 86, 89
Brazil, 3, 50, 94, 116, 139, 144
Breathe (Khan), 214
breathing, 200–202, 219
Bridgeways Family Resource Centre, 103
Brin, Sergey, 5
British American Tobacco, 101, 102
British Journal of Sports Medicine, 108
Bruno, Frank, 117
Brussels, Belgium, 188
Bucher, Gabriela, 254
Buckingham Palace, London, 247–50
Buettner, Dan, 11
Burkina Faso, 211
Burundi, 185

Calico, 5
calories, 47, 50, 51, 52, 56–8, 59, 83
Cameroon, 42
Canada, 61, 151, 210
cancer, 1–4, 46, 73, 222–3
 cervical cancer, 1–4
 colorectal cancer, 86
 diet and, 50, 73
 early diagnosis, 1–4, 222–3
 lung cancer, 84, 85, 86

Cape Town, South Africa, 196–7, 217–19
cardio exercises, 22
cardiovascular disease, 18, 21, 26, 37, 53, 54, 60, 65, 246
cars, *see* driving
Castillo, Alex, 101
Castle, Roy, 87–8, 89
Catherine, Princess of Wales, 250
centenarians, 45–6
cervical cancer, 1–4
Chad, 211
Chandrachud, Dhananjaya Yeshwant, 203
Chang, Kiara, 50
Cheeseman, Hazel, 90
Chennai, Tamil Nadu, 16, 53, 77, 157, 202, 245, 247–8
Chertorivski, Salomón, 238–9
Child Survival and Development Revolution, 180–81
children; childhood
 diet and, 57, 66–8, 80–81, 82–3, 261
 poverty and, 8, 83, 115
 road traffic accidents and, 157–8, 160, 169–72, 175
 trauma and, 118, 120–21
 water and, 178–82, 199
China, 88, 97–9, 210, 221, 240
Chitta Vritti, 201
cholera, 182–4, 190–91, 194, 199
cholesterol, 22, 46, 65, 74
Christchurch massacre (2019), 143–4
chronic diseases, 6, 11, 20, 260, 261
 diet and, 51, 71–4, 259
 sedentary behaviour and, 29, 30, 37, 38, 41, 259
chronic pain, 3, 22, 23, 112
chronic stress, 200–201

cities
    air pollution in, 212–19
    exercise and, 29, 30–8, 43–4
    fifteen-minute cities, 36–8, 44
Clark, Lindsay, 224–5
climate change, 35, 37, 196, 219, 269
Clinton, Bill, 105
Clinton, Chelsea, 181
Clinton, Hillary, 263
Coca-Cola, 76, 197–8
Coles, Stephen, 46
Colombia, 139, 144–6, 151, 154, 258, 262
colorectal cancer, 86
Comprehensive Mental Health Action Plan (2013), 113
Cooray, Sherva, 125
core exercises, 23
corruption, 173–4, 189
cortisol, 200
COVID-19 pandemic (2019–23), 9, 14, 15, 105
    children and, 181
    conspiracy theories, 106, 182–3
    Finnish response, 250
    healthcare systems and, 225, 241
    inequality and, 254–5
    media and, 263
    mental health and, 109, 125, 127
    obesity and, 55–6
    sedentary behaviour and, 40–41
    Swedish response, 165, 257
    Thai response, 173–4, 257
    vaccines, 106, 243
Croninger, Adele, 86
cycling, 32–8, 43, 160, 161, 162, 164, 169, 170, 175, 176

Daily Mail, 263
Danone, 186
De Neve, Jan-Emmanuel, 246
De Silva, Mary, 123

Deaton, Angus, 246
Delhi, India, 7, 8, 40, 157–8, 199, 202–5, 260
dementia, 27, 246
Democratic Republic of the Congo, 113, 185
den Uyl, Joop, 33
Denmark, 9, 10, 18, 51, 63–6, 67, 82
depression, 27, 108, 111, 112, 115–30
    'be happy' campaigns, 126–7
    causes, 118, 120–22
    stigma and, 117, 125, 129–30
    suicide, 112, 120, 121–5, 127–9, 148, 153, 259
    therapy, 109, 120, 125–6
DeSantis, Ron, 263
'developing world', 28, 118
    see also low-income countries
diabetes, 49, 53–5, 74, 77, 80, 85, 245
diarrhoeal diseases, 178, 180–84, 190–91
Diaz, Keith, 26
diet; eating habits, 11, 44, 45–52, 56–83, 260, 268
    anti-obesity drugs, 58–9
    calories, 47, 50, 51, 52, 56–8, 59, 83
    cancer and, 50
    childhood and, 57, 66, 80–81, 82
    emotional eating, 48
    fast foods, 29, 76–7, 79–81
    metabolism and, 57–8
    obesity and, 49–50, 51, 59–83
    over-eating, 47–8, 57
    public policy and, 60–83
    socioeconomic status and, 52, 58–9, 63, 72, 74–81, 82, 268
    ultra-processed foods, *see* ultra-processed foods
Disney, Abigail, 255
Djokovic, Novak, 134
DNA, 86, 121
Doll, Richard, 86, 89

Dominican Republic, 165, 168–9
dopamine, 27, 108
Dramamine, 224–5
drinking and driving, 162, 165, 171, 172–4, 175
driving; roads, 12, 32–8, 156–76, 257, 259, 261–2
  air pollution and, 212, 219, 220
  children and, 157–8, 160, 162, 169–72, 175
  cyclists and, 160, 161, 162, 164, 169, 170, 175, 176
  death statistics, 159–60
  drinking and driving, 162, 165, 171, 172–4, 175
  helmet laws, 160, 162, 172, 173, 175
  infrastructure and, 162, 164
  law enforcement and, 162, 172–3, 175
  leadership and, 161, 162
  parking, 167, 168
  pedestrian crossings, 162, 164, 171, 175
  post-crash survival, 162
  public transport alternatives, 162, 166–7, 175, 176, 213, 215, 218, 268–9
  seatbelts, 160, 162, 175
  size of cars, 167–8, 175
  socioeconomic status and, 168, 173
  speed management, 162, 164, 169, 171, 175
  vehicle safety standards, 162
Dubai, United Arab Emirates, 38–40
Duke University, 151
Dunblane massacre (1996), 134–8, 153, 258

E. coli, 194
Eastwood, Greg, 11
eating habits, *see* diet
Ebola, 181–2
e-cigarettes, 101–5

Edinburgh, Scotland, 37, 44, 108, 131, 176, 187–8, 220
education, 179, 251–2
Egypt, 186
El Salvador, 139
Elder, Jack, 143
Elizabeth II, Queen, 247–8
Ella Roberta Foundation, 214, 215, 216, 220, 258
Emerson, Ralph Waldo, 247
epigenetics, 121
erectile dysfunction, 85
Estonia, 211
European Air Quality Index, 208
European Union, 44, 165
Everglades, Florida, 177–8
Evian, 186, 187
exercise, 11, 13, 15–44
  barriers to, 23–4, 29–30
  calorie burning, 56
  cardio training, 22
  COVID-19 pandemic and, 40–41
  ethnicity and, 16, 24–5
  fitness campaigns, 38–41
  genetics and, 42–4
  mental health and, 27, 30, 107–9, 111, 112
  public policy and, 66
  resistance training, 22–3
  social media and, 17–20, 40–41, 43
  socioeconomic status and, 28, 29, 41–2, 43, 58
  triangle workout, 22, 24
  urbanization and, 29, 30–38, 43–4
  women and, 16–20, 24–5

Facebook, 110
family, 246
farmer suicides, 122–4
Farron, Tim, 196
fast foods, 29, 76–7, 79–81

fat taxes, 65, 81
fatalism, 96, 220, 257
Feis, Aaron, 132
fermentation, 62
FIA Foundation, 159
fifteen-minute cities, 36–8
Finland, 211, 213, 250–53
Fischer Boel, Mariann, 65
Flat Tummy Co., 19
Fletcher, Nick, 37
Florida, United States, 5, 84, 131–4, 177–8
Flyn, Cal, 232
food, *see* diet
Food and Drug Administration (FDA), 69, 70
Food Foundation, 59
Formula One, 159
Fort St George, Chennai, 247–8
Foster, Yolanda, 125
Fragile States Index, 250
Framework Convention on Tobacco Control (2005), 94–5, 98
France, 34–7, 43, 61, 125, 168, 188, 233, 262, 271
free radicals, 47
freedom
   COVID-19 pandemic and, 165
   gun control and, 140–44, 259, 262
   road safety and, 165, 262
Frenk, Julio, 105, 238, 240, 241
friendships, 246

gang violence, 145–6, 148, 153, 190, 218
Garrett, Laurie, 115
Gates, Melinda, 179
gender, 16–20
genetics, 121
Germany, 61, 102, 185, 233, 271
Gerontology Research Group, 46
Ghana, 41, 51, 71–4, 82

girls' education, 179
Global Ministerial Conference on Road Safety, 157, 159
Goa, India, 80, 95, 123
GOBI, 180–81
Godefrooij, Tom, 34
González Posso, Camilo, 146
Good Law Project, 255
Goody, Jade, 1, 3
Google, 5
Grazia, 19–20, 179
Greece, 11, 121, 210
green space, 13, 30
Grenada, 211
grief, 121, 258
Groningen, Netherlands, 34
Guam, 211
Guatemala, 114, 139, 144, 158
gun violence, 12, 13, 131–55, 258, 259, 261–2
   'freedom' and, 140–44
   mental health and, 133, 153
   stable countries and, 138–40
   suicide, 148, 153
Guterres, António, 190

Habib, Cyrus, 248
Haiti, 188–91, 199, 259
happiness, 246–7, 250–51
hara hachi bu, 47
Harvard University, 7, 50
HDL cholesterol, 54, 65
healthcare, 222–44, 259
   Beveridge model, 232
   Bismarck model, 233
   demography and, 242
   early diagnosis, 1–4, 222–3
   out-of-pocket model, 223–5, 228–31, 233, 259
   private, 226–8, 233, 243
   universal provision, 231–44, 262

heart disease, 18, 21, 53, 54, 246
Helm, Dieter, 195
Henman, Tim, 134
Hidalgo, Anne, 35–6, 37
high blood pressure, 21
Highendsmoke, 102
Hinduism, 156
hippocampus, 27
Hippocrates, 182
HIV, 13–14
homelessness, 252, 254
hope molecules, 27, 108
housing, 252
Howard, John, 141–2
HPV, 1–4
Hugo, Victor, 111
Human Development Index, 71
Huntington, West Virginia, 69
Hurricane Andrew (1992), 177–8
hydration, 11
hypertension, 20, 21, 22, 26, 54, 107, 108, 200, 206–7, 245

Iceland, 151, 211
Ikaria, Greece, 11
ikigai, 7
illiteracy, 77, 96–7
immigration, 256
Imperial College London, 49
income, 246, 252, 253–7
India, 3, 7, 16, 51, 74–81, 82
  air pollution in, 202–5, 209, 210, 211, 221, 260
  diabetes in, 53, 54–5, 74, 77, 80, 245
  farmer suicides, 122–4
  fitness campaigns in, 40
  gun violence in, 154
  healthcare in, 229–31, 240
  inequality in, 8, 74–81
  mental health in, 122–4, 269
  obesity in, 74–81, 82

Pakistan War (1971), 180
  road safety in, 156–8
  sedentary behaviour in, 28
  smoking in, 88, 94, 259
  undernutrition in, 74, 75, 115, 179
  water in, 198, 199
Indian Ocean tsunami (2004), 124, 262
individualism, 12, 14
inequality, 7–8, 23–4, 173, 254
InfluenceMap, 35–6
Initiative for Global Road Safety, 158
Instagram, 17, 19, 20, 38, 43, 102, 104, 109, 110
IQAir, 211
Iran, 210
Iraq, 211
Ireland, 103
Irvine, Ross, 138
Islam, 24–5
Italy, 10, 51, 185, 188

Jackson, Mississippi, 191–3, 199, 258, 262
Jameson, Harry, 56
Japan
  air pollution in, 212–13, 259
  COVID-19 pandemic in, 10
  diet in, 45–7, 57, 60, 82, 260
  gun violence in, 136, 149
  healthcare in, 233
  life expectancy in, 9, 12, 46–7, 57, 260
  road safety in, 158, 163, 165–8, 258
  smoking in, 91–2
  suicide in, 127–9, 259
  water in, 185
Johnson, Boris, 56, 215, 263
Johnson, Bryan, 5
Jones, Erica, 192
Journal of Safety Research, 167
Juul, 101, 102

Kahneman, Daniel, 246
Kardashian, Khloé, 19
Kaufman, Elinore, 148
Kearney, Grace, 103
Kent, John, 249
Kenya, 169–72, 185
Kerala, India, 81
Keyhole labels, 64–5
Khan, Amir, 106
Khan, Sadiq, 214–15
Kibogong, Duncan, 171
kimchi, 62
Kiptum, Kelvin, 171
knife crime, 139
Kodakkal, Revathy, 204
Krafft, Maria, 163
Krähenmann, Moritz, 209
KSI, 198
Kuwait, 211

Lakmal, Suranga, 202
Lam, Moses, 210
Lancet
 diabetes research, 74
 exercise research, 29
 gun violence research, 139
 healthcare research, 240–41
 mental health research, 113, 114, 116–17, 118, 122, 123
 road traffic research, 174
 water pollution research, 180
Langenhoff, Simone, 32–3
Lapland, Finland, 250, 251
LDL cholesterol, 65
life expectancy, 8–14, 31, 60, 115, 250, 265, 271
 air pollution and, 204, 208
 blue zones, 11–12, 46–7, 271
 diet and, 46–7, 60
 mental health and, 112
 smoking and, 93

Life Lessons (Benn), 252
Lipa, Dua, 187
lipoproteins, 22
literacy, 77, 96–7
Livingstone, Ken, 215
locomotor activity, 27
London School of Economics, 26
London, England
 air pollution in, 214–16, 258
 Broad Street cholera outbreak (1854), 182–4
loneliness, 246
López Obrador, Andrés Manuel, 241
Loughton, Carolyn, 142
low-income countries
 diet and, 71
 exercise and, 28, 29
 healthcare and, 233–4
 mental health and, 118
 road safety and, 159, 168, 169
 water and, 180, 184–5, 186, 198–9
Lund University, 184
lung cancer, 84, 85, 86, 87–8

M-19 guerrilla group, 144
Macron, Emmanuel, 125
Mahalanabis, Dilip, 180
Maharashtra, India, 74
Major, John, 136
al-Maktoum, Hamdan bin Mohammed, 38
Malawi, 178–9
malnutrition, *see* undernutrition
Mandela, Nelson, 248
March for Our Lives (2018), 133
Marshall-Andrews, Robert, 136
maternal mortality, 115
maternity leave, 251
Maugham, Jolyon, 255
McDonald's, 76, 79–81
McKinnon, Brett, 138

Medellín, Colombia, 145–6
Mejía, Carolina, 169
memory, 27
menstruation, 17
mental health, 27, 30, 106–30, 259, 269–70
  'be happy' campaigns, 126–7
  causes, 118, 120–22
  'development' and, 118
  exercise and, 27, 30, 107–9, 111, 112
  gun violence and, 133, 153
  individual-level intervention, 118
  prisoners and, 119
  rights-based approach, 118
  social media and, 109–11
  spectrum, 118
  stigma and, 117, 125, 129–30
  suicide, 112, 120, 121–5, 127–9, 148, 259
  therapy, 109, 120, 125–6
metabolic syndrome, 54
metabolism, 57–8
Mexico, 139, 140, 144, 210, 238–41
Miami, Florida, 84, 131, 177
miasma, 182
microbiome, 50–51
Millennium Development Goals, 73, 114
Millett, Christopher, 49
mindfulness, 111, 200
Mirza, Sania, 24
Mishra, Arun, 203
Mizelle, Richard, 193
Moholdt, Trine, 26
Moïse, Jovenel, 190
Moment of Lift, The (Gates), 179
Monaco, 169
Monbiot, George, 264
monkey brain, 201
Monteiro, Carlos, 51
Moreno, Carlos, 36

Moscow Ministerial (2009), 157, 159
Mount, Simon, 143
Mozambique, 185
MPOWER, 94–5, 99
Murray, Andy, 134, 138
Murthy, Vivek, 109, 111
muscles
  body fat and, 17–18
  cardio training and, 22
  resistance training and, 22
  strength training and, 23
mutuelles, 236–7
myokines, 27, 108
MyPlate, 70

National Cancer Institute, 223
National Football League (NFL), 53
National Health Service (NHS), 1–4, 226–8, 232, 243–4, 256, 267, 270
  cervical cancer screening, 1–4
  e-cigarette figures, 102
  elective care, 226
  mental health support, 108
  smoking cessation support, 90
  waiting lists, 222, 226, 250, 260
National Institute of Mental Health, 121
National Rifle Association (NRA), 133, 151
Neira, Maria, 209
Nepal, 190
Nestlé, 186, 199
Netherlands
  air pollution in, 212, 213
  diet in, 260
  exercise in, 30–34, 43, 259
  healthcare in, 233
  life expectancy in, 10
  road safety in, 30–34, 154, 163, 212, 258
  smoking in, 94
neurotransmitters, 27, 108

Never Again MSD, 132
New York City, New York, 92–4, 100
New Zealand, 61, 94, 100, 142–4, 150, 154, 211, 262, 263
newspapers, 263–4
Nigeria, 113, 223, 224, 228–9, 258, 259
Nishimura, Takao, 212
nitrogen dioxide, 208
noradrenaline, 27, 108
Nordic countries, 63
North, Mick, 135
North, Sophie, 138
Norway, 25–6, 109, 154, 212, 213
Novo Nordisk, 58
Nyaaba, Gertrude Nsorma, 73

Obama, Barack, 149–50, 224
Obama, Michelle, 70
obesity, 9, 12, 20, 52–4, 59–83
    anti-obesity drugs, 58–9
    childhood obesity, 66–8, 80–81, 82–3
    COVID-19 and, 55–6
    diet and, 49–50, 51, 52–4, 59–83
    sedentary behaviour and, 24, 28
    socioeconomic status and, 52, 58–9, 63, 72, 77, 115
    stigma, 62–3, 83
Oduyoye, Folake, 228–9, 258
Ogino, Shuji, 50
O'Hare, Bernie, 178
Okinawa, Japan, 46–7, 57, 246
oligarchy, 264
Omaswa, Francis, 115
oral rehydration salts (ORS), 180
O'Regan, Whitney Platzer, 104
over-eating, 47–8
Oxfam, 254
Oxford University, 195
Oxford, Oxfordshire, 37
Ozempic, 58–9

Page, Larry, 5
Pakistan, 180, 211, 221
Palmer, Robert, 253
pandemics, 8–9
Paquette, Troy, 210
Paris, France, 34–7, 43, 168, 188
Parkland school shootings (2018), 131–4
passive smoking, 87–8
Patel, Jay, 138–9
Paul, Logan, 198
periodontitis, 86
personal fitness trainers, 17, 21, 24
pesticides, 124, 139, 153
Petro, Gustavo, 144, 146
Philip, Duke of Edinburgh, 137, 247–50
Philip Morris, 101–2
Pilates, 23
Pitt, Brad, 121
plastic pollution, 187, 199
plateauing happiness, 246
Policy Exchange, 215
Poliscanova, Julia, 36
pollution
    air pollution, 12, 13, 40, 202–21
    plastic pollution, 187, 199
    water contamination, 178, 182–4, 190–91, 193–6
Ponce de León, Juan, 5
populism, 61, 255, 256
Port Arthur massacre (1996), 140–42
Port-au-Prince, Haiti, 188, 199
Pothas, Nic, 202
Poulain, Michel, 11
poverty, *see* socioeconomic status
pranayama, 201
pregnancy, 85
Preventable (Sridhar), 165, 225
Prime Hydration, 198
prisons, 119
psychotherapy, 108
public abuse, 106–7, 263

public policy
  air pollution and, 212–21
  diet and, 60–83
  guns and, 134–55
  healthcare, 231–44
  road safety and, 160–76
  smoking and, 87–105
public transport, 162, 166–7, 175, 176, 213, 215, 218, 268–9
Puerto Rico, 211

Raducanu, Emma, 187
Ramana, Nuthalapati Venkata, 203
relationships, 246
resistance training, 22–3
Resneck Jr, Jack, 110
Rivera, Grant, 149
roads, *see* driving
role models, 25
Rome, Italy, 188
Ronaldo, Cristiano, 197–8
Rooney, Coleen, 48
rotavirus, 180
Routh, John, 85
Royal Canadian Air Force, 249
Royal College of Paediatrics, 83, 103
Royal College of Psychiatrists, 119
Rubio, Marco, 133

Sakolsatayadorn, Piyasakol, 236
Sall, Macky, 236, 237–8
Samaritans, 120, 122, 128
Sandringham estate, Norfolk, 248
Sandy Hook massacre (2012), 149
Santo Domingo, Dominican Republic, 168
Sardinia, 11
Saudi Arabia, 29
Save LIVES, 160–63, 169, 174
Scalia, Antonin, 152
Schatz, Brian, 110

Scheper-Hughes, Nancy, 116
schizophrenia, 112
Scotland, 15, 16, 131
  air quality in, 220
  COVID-19 in, 9–10
  Dunblane massacre (1996), 134–8, 153, 258
  road safety in, 176
  water in, 187–8
Scott, Rick, 133
Scottish Water, 188, 195
Sebastien (mascot), 84–5, 101, 104–5
secondary smoking, 87–8
sedentary behaviour, 25–44, 259
  COVID-19 pandemic and, 40–41
  fitness campaigns, 38–41
  genetics and, 42–4
  mental health and, 27, 30
  socioeconomic status and, 28, 29, 41–2, 43
  urbanization and, 29, 30–38, 43–4
Seguro Popular, 239–41
semaglutide, 58–9
Sen, Amartya, 230–31
Senegal, 236–8
Serageldin, Ismail, 196
Serbia, 146–7, 151, 154, 258, 262
serotonin, 27, 108
Severn Trent, 195
sewage, 188–9, 192, 193–6, 199
Shanghai, China, 99
Sharapova, Maria, 187
Sharkey, Feargal, 193–4, 199
Siddiqui, Haseeb-ul-hasan, 24
SimSmoke, 91
Singapore, 187
Singh, Ben, 27
Siripanich, Tairjing, 173–4
skin colour, 16
Skinner, Frank, 17
Smakhtin, Vladimir, 186

Smith, Angela, 136
smoking, 13, 24, 41, 84–105, 259, 261
    advertising, 89, 93, 94, 95, 98, 102, 104
    age restrictions, 89, 90, 93–4, 100
    bans on, 88–92, 96, 97, 98
    cessation support, 90, 100
    children and, 89, 90, 93–4, 96, 100
    DNA, effects on, 86
    e-cigarettes, 101–5
    lung cancer and, 84, 85, 87–8
    MPOWER, 94–5, 99
    public policy and, 87–105
    secondary/passive, 87–8
    taxes on, 96, 98, 100
Snapchat, 104
Snow, John, 182–4
Snowdrop Campaign, 135
social media
    abuse on, 106, 263
    body image on, 17–18, 109
    diet and food on, 72, 78
    e-cigarette marketing on, 102, 104
    fitness on, 17–18, 19, 38–41, 43, 109, 201–2
    mental health and, 109–11, 258
    relationships on, 246
    thigh gap trend, 17–18
socioeconomic status, 7–8, 23–4
    diet and, 52, 58–9, 63, 72, 74–81, 82, 115, 268
    driving and, 168, 173
    exercise and, 28, 29, 41–2, 43, 58
    healthcare and, 223–4, 243
    mental health and, 121
    water and, 191–3, 198
South Africa, 30, 196–7, 217–19
South Korea, 53, 60–63, 66–7, 82, 210
Spain, 10
Squires, Peter, 135
Sri Lanka, 124–5, 262

Stack, Megan, 205
Stairmaster, 22
Stein, Felix, 189–90
strength training, 23
stress, 106, 200–201
strokes, 21, 54, 62, 246
Sturgeon, Nicola, 263
substance abuse, 112, 201
sugar taxes, 65
sugary drink tax, 71
suicide, 112, 120, 121–5, 127–9, 148, 153, 259
sulphur dioxide, 208
Sun, 263
Sunak, Rishi, 216, 253, 256, 259, 262, 263
superfoods, 11
Sustainable Development Goals, 114, 118, 174
SUVs, 167–8, 175
Swanson, Jeffrey, 151
Sweden, 158, 160, 163–5, 169, 213, 257
Switzerland, 100, 210, 211, 213

Taliban, 25
Tamil Nadu, India, 16, 53, 77, 124, 157, 202, 245, 247–8
Tanaka, Kane, 45–6
Tanzania, 3, 113
taxation, 252–7
    on food, 65, 71, 81
    on smoking, 96, 98, 100
Taylor, Anna, 59
Taylor, Pamela, 119
Telegraph, 263
television, 78
Thailand, 165, 172–4, 234–6, 243, 257, 259, 260
Thatcher, Margaret, 195
thighs, 17–18
'thinspiration', 18

Thorp Report (1997), 142, 143
Tiafoe, Frances, 187
TikTok, 104, 110
Times, The, 263
Tirupati temple, Andhra Pradesh, 156
toes, ability to touch, 21, 23
Tokyo, Japan
   air quality in, 212–13
   Olympic Games (2020), 91, 212
   public transport in, 166
Top Up Tap, 188
trans-saturated fat ban, 65
triangle workout, 22, 24
Trump, Donald, 132, 263
Trust for America's Health, 68–9
Turkey, 29, 240
Twitter, 110
type-2 diabetes, 49, 53–5, 74, 77, 80, 85, 245

Ueda, Michiko, 128
Uganda, 114, 115, 185
Ultra-Low Emission Zone, 215
ultra-processed foods, 49–52, 56, 57, 72, 77, 261
   public policy and, 65, 67, 74, 81–3
undernutrition, 72, 74, 75, 115, 179
unemployment, 121–2
United Arab Emirates, 38–40, 68, 242
United Kingdom, 7–8
   air pollution in, 207, 214–16, 220, 258, 259, 262
   COVID-19 in, 9–10, 15, 55–6, 173–4, 255, 263–4
   diabetes in, 54
   diet in, 49–50, 51, 52, 59–60, 82, 83, 268
   fifteen-minute cities in, 37
   gun violence in, 134–8, 149, 150, 153, 155, 258
   healthcare in, 1–4, 222, 224, 226–8, 232, 243–4, 260, 267, 270–71
   inequality in, 7–8, 255–6
   life expectancy in, 9–10
   mental health in, 269–70
   obesity in, 28, 49–50, 55–6, 59, 83
   road safety in, 158, 176, 268–9
   royal family, 247–50
   sedentary behaviour in, 28, 30
   smoking in, 87–91, 100, 102, 103–4, 259
   taxation in, 252, 253
   water in, 185, 188, 193–6, 199, 270
United Nations
   Children's Fund (UNICEF), 75, 180–81, 185
   Comprehensive Mental Health Action Plan (2013), 113
   Firearms Protocol, 139
   Framework Convention on Tobacco Control (2005), 94–5, 98
   Millennium Development Goals, 73, 114
   Save LIVES, 160–63, 169, 174
   Sustainable Development Goals, 114, 118, 174
United States, 7–8
   air pollution in, 207
   COVID-19 in, 225
   diabetes in, 54
   diet in, 51, 59–60, 82
   gun violence in, 131–4, 139, 148–53, 259
   healthcare in, 224–5, 230, 243
   inequality in, 7–8
   life expectancy in, 10
   obesity in, 61, 68–71
   road safety in, 167, 175–6
   sedentary behaviour in, 26, 28, 30
   smoking in, 92–4
   taxation in, 253
   water in, 185, 191–3, 199, 258, 262

United Utilities, 195
universal basic income, 252
University of Bath, 110
University of Brighton, 135
University of Houston, 193
University of Miami, 84, 101, 104–5
University of Pennsylvania, 148
University of São Paulo, 51
urbanization, 29, 30–38, 43–4, 211
Uvalde shooting (2022), 150

van Putten, Maartje, 33
vaping, 101–5
Varah, Chad, 120
Venezuela, 139, 144
Véran, Olivier, 126
Victoria, Queen, 247
Victoria's Secret, 17–18
Vidarbha Stress and Health Program (VISHRAM), 122–3, 269
Vietnam, 210, 259
Vision Zero, 160, 163–5, 169, 257
Vitality Air, 210
Vitality Health, 26
VPZ, 102
Vučić, Aleksandar, 147

Wade, Abdoulaye, 238
Waghmore, Suryakant, 204
Wake Forest University, 151
Wang, Chen, 97
Wang, Peter, 132
Warwick University, 252–3
WASH, 182
water, 177–99, 258, 259, 262
　bottled water, 186–8, 199
　contamination of, 178, 182–4, 188–91, 193–6, 199
　diseases and, 178, 180–84, 190–91
　sanitation and, 182–5
　shortages, 196–7, 199

Watkins, Kevin, 157
wealth, 246, 254–7
Wellcome Trust, 123, 189
Whitty, Chris, 196
Williams, Robin, 117
Williams, Steve, 69
women
　body image and, 17–18, 62–3, 109
　education and, 179
　exercise and, 16–20, 24–5
　healthcare and, 230–31
　public abuse of, 263
　smoking and, 96
Wood Farm, Sandringham estate, 248
World Air Quality Report (2020), 218
World Bank, 113, 190, 196, 256
World Economic Forum, 242
World Health Organization (WHO), 28, 38, 51, 63, 74, 103
　air pollution and, 204, 206, 208, 211, 218
　gun violence and, 139
　healthcare and, 231
　mental health and, 113, 116, 119, 125
　road safety and, 160–63
　smoking and, 94–5, 98
　water and, 180, 185

Xi Jinping, 98

Yach, Derek, 89
Yamane, David, 151
Yang Gonghuan, 99
yoga, 23, 200, 201
Your Water Your Life, 188
YouTube, 40–41, 102, 198

Zambia, 3
zero-emission vehicles, 212
Zurich, Switzerland, 213